Preface

Welcome to the 4th edition of *Vocabulary for the College-Bound Student*!

Continuing a tradition dating back to its first edition in1964,*VCB* strives to help high school students build the superior vocabulary so esssential for success not only in college work but also in professional life.

To that end, *VCB* focuses on showing students how they can develop vocabulary-acquisition skills that will ensure lifelong vocabulary growth. These skills include deriving the meaning of unknown words from their contexts or from their elements (such as prefixes and roots drawn from other languages).

In addition, *VCB* provides students with abundant, varied opportunities to practice their new words, often through exercises serving a range of objectives common in the English classroom. For example, in addition to reinforcing the students' command of new vocabulary, one exercise teaches concise expression, and another teaches close reading. Still another exercise, asking students to write "minicompositions" of no more than three sentences, teaches an important composition skill, such as stating an opinion and supporting it with reasons or examples.

The ample word stock of *VCB*'s 3rd edition, drawing on the contributions to English vocabulary from Greek, Latin, Anglo-Saxon, French, Italian, and Spanish, has been enriched by some 10% (as the revised and expanded word list shows). In particular, Chapter 10's selection of Spanish loanwords contributed to English has been increased by a third.

To the 3rd edition's variety and abundance of exercises, we have added in the longer chapters four additional types of exercises. "Similar and Contrary" offers concise review of synonyms and antonyms. "Matchmaking," "Sentence Completion," and "Fill and Match" offer challenging contexts relevant to preparation for pre-college vocabulary tests.

The vocabulary-building procedures of *VCB*'s 3rd edition have been retained.

Learning New Words From the Context (Chapter 2) is an adventure in critical thinking. It presents eighty short passages in which possibly unfamiliar words can be defined with help from clues in the context. By teaching students how to interpret such clues, this chapter provides them with a lifelong tool for vocabulary growth, *and at the same time, it makes them better readers*.

Building Vocabulary Through Central Ideas (Chapter 3) involves students in studying twenty-five groups of related words. In the FLATTERY group, they will learn *adulation, cajole, obsequious,* etc.—and in the REASONING group, *analogy, axiomatic, specious,* etc.

Words Derived From Greek (Chapter 4) teaches derivatives from twenty-five Ancient Greek word elements. For example, from EU, meaning "good," we get *euphemism, euphoria, euthanasia,* etc.—and from DYS, meaning "bad," *dysfunction, dyspepsia, dystrophy,* etc.

Words Derived From Latin (Chapter 5), the largest source of English words, teaches derivatives from thirty Latin prefixes and roots. The root VOR, for example, meaning "eat," gives us *carnivorous, frugivorous, voracious,* etc.—and the root FRACT, meaning "break," yields *fractious, infraction, refractory,* etc.

Words From Classical Mythology and History (Chapter 6) teaches not only derivatives from the myths of the Ancient Greeks and Romans—*amazon, hector, narcissistic,* etc. It also teaches derivatives from classical history—*Draconian, Lucullan, marathon,* etc.

Anglo-Saxon Vocabulary (Chapter 7) teaches derivatives from prefixes like WITH, meaning "back": *withdraw, withhold,* etc.—and suffixes like LING, meaning "little": *sapling, stripling,* etc. It also pairs some Anglo-Saxon words with nearly synonymous Latin-derived words—for example, *flay* with *excoriate*—to help students enrich their vocabularies.

French Words in English (Chapter 8) teaches about one hundred fifty loanwords integrated into English from French—*clairvoyant, canard, concierge, martinet, nonpareil,* etc.

Italian Words in English (Chapter 9) teaches loanwords from Italian—*alfresco, crescendo, diva, imbroglio, impresario,* etc.

Spanish Words in English (Chapter 10) teaches loanwords from Spanish—*aficionado, bonanza, incommunicado, peccadillo,* etc.

Expanding Vocabulary Through Derivatives (Chapter 11) offers additional instruction in forming derivatives, so that when students learn *plausible,* for example, they may convert it, when necessary, to *implausible, plausibly, implausibly, plausibility,* or *implausibility.* The chapter also reviews some pertinent spelling guidelines.

Vocabulary Questions on Pre-College Tests (Chapter 12) discusses The Analogy Question (SAT I), The Sentence-Completion Question (SAT I), and The As-Used-In Question (SAT I and ACT Reading Test). Each of these three questions is briefly analyzed and then followed by a list of *VCB*'s exercises that students may find useful for practice. In addition, relevant examples from other Amsco publications are included.

The Dictionary of Words Taught in This Text is appended for ease of reference and review.

Students should be encouraged to use their newly learned words whenever appropriate in their writing and classroom discussions. Only through actual use will they be able to incorporate such words into their vocabularies. They should also be encouraged to own a good dictionary and to develop the dictionary habit.

—The Authors

VOCABULARY
for the College-Bound Student

FOURTH EDITION

HAROLD LEVINE

Chairman Emeritus of English,
Benjamin Cardozo High School, New York

NORMAN LEVINE

Associate Professor of English,
City College of the City University of New York

ROBERT T. LEVINE

Professor of English,
North Carolina A&T State University

Amsco School Publications, Inc.,
a division of Perfection Learning®

Text and Cover Design: One Dot Inc.
Composition: Brad Walrod/High Text Graphics, Inc.

Please visit our Web sites at: *www.amscopub.com* and *www.perfectionlearning.com*

When ordering this book, please specify:
Either **13441** *or*
VOCABULARY FOR THE COLLEGE-BOUND STUDENT

ISBN: 978-1-56765-104-1

Vocabulary books by the authors

A Scholarship Vocabulary Program, Books I–III

Vocabulary and Composition Through Pleasurable Reading, Books I–V

Vocabulary for Enjoyment, Books I–III

Vocabulary for the High School Student, Books A, B

Vocabulary for the High School Student

Vocabulary for the College-Bound Student

The Joy of Vocabulary

Contents

Chapter 3 Building Vocabulary Through Central Ideas 46

Chapter 4 Words Derived From Greek 107

Chapter 5 Words Derived From Latin 146

Chapter 6 **Words From Classical Mythology and History**   203

Chapter 12 Vocabulary Questions on Pre-College Tests   305

Dictionary of Words Taught in This Text   317

Chapter

1

The Importance of Vocabulary to You

Vocabulary and thinking

Words stand for ideas. Words are the tools of thought. If your word power is limited, your ability to think will also be limited, since you can neither receive ideas nor communicate with others except within the confines of an inadequate vocabulary. But if you broaden your vocabulary, you will find it easier to do the thinking that success in life often demands.

Vocabulary and college admission

College admissions officers will be interested in the extent of your vocabulary, for a good vocabulary will suggest that you are likely to do well in college. It will suggest, too, that you have done wide reading, since reading is the principal way of developing a good vocabulary. In the college-entrance and scholarship tests you are likely to take, you will find vocabulary a major ingredient.

Vocabulary growth through reading

People who read widely gradually build up extensive vocabularies, especially if they have a curiosity about words. This curiosity, motivating them to regard an unfamiliar word as a breakdown in communication between author and reader, sends them thumbing through the dictionary. As you, too, develop such word curiosity, you will be assuring yourself a lifetime of vocabulary growth.

Though reading is the basic means of vocabulary growth, it is a relatively slow means. For the college-bound student who has not yet achieved a superior vocabulary, reading needs to be supplemented by a direct attack that will yield comparatively rapid growth—and that is the purpose of this book.

Vocabulary growth through this book

This book will involve you in a five-pronged attack on vocabulary.

Attack #1: Learning New Words From the Context

Often, you can discover the meaning of an unfamiliar word from its context–the other words with which it is used. Note, for example, how you can determine the meaning of *parsimonious* in the following sentence:

> People vary in their tipping habits from the very generous to the very *parsimonious*.

As you can see from the above context, *parsimonious* is the opposite of *generous,* so *parsimonious* means "stingy."

Chapter 2 will teach you the various clues for learning the meaning of a possibly unfamiliar word, like *parsimonious*, from its context. As you learn to use these clues, you will be broadening your vocabulary and—what is even more important—becoming a more skillful reader.

Attack #2: Learning Vocabulary in Groups of Related Words

Vocabulary growth that evolves from a day's reading has one serious disadvantage: it is poorly organized. The new words you encounter as you read usually bear little relationship to one another. This, of course, does not mean that you should think any the less of reading as a means of vocabulary building. It does, however, suggest that you may achieve relatively rapid vocabulary growth by studying *groups of related words.*

In Chapter 3, you will find twenty-five groups of words related by "central ideas." Each group presents words revolving about one idea—joy, sadness, flattery, age, relatives, reasoning, etc. The new words are further explained in hundreds of illustrative sentences having one feature in common: they present new vocabulary in contexts that make the meaning easy to see and remember.

Attack #3: Learning Vocabulary Derived From Greek and Latin

The principle of the lever has enabled humans, using relatively little effort, to do a great amount of work. You can apply the same principle to learning vocabulary. If you study the important Greek and Latin prefixes and roots in Chapters 4–5, you can gain word leverage. Each prefix or root will help you learn the meanings of many of its numerous English offspring.

Rounding out the attack based on Greek and Latin word elements are two briefer chapters. Chapter 6 will teach you useful English words derived from classical (Latin and Greek) mythology and history. Chapter 7, dealing with Anglo-Saxon and its interplay with Latin, will contribute further to your word hoard.

Attack #4: Learning Vocabulary Borrowed From French, Italian, and Spanish

Because English has borrowed heavily from the Romance languages French, Italian, and Spanish, you are sure to encounter Romance-language loanwords in books, newspapers, magazines, and other media. A vital as well as substantial part of English, these words are often keys to the passages in which they occur. Chapters 8–10 present hundreds of such loanwords, and you will be seeing that to learn them is to acquire a valuable vocabulary asset.

Attack #5: Learning to Form Derivatives

Suppose you have just learned a new word—*fallible*, meaning "liable to be mistaken." If you know how to form derivatives, you really have learned not merely one new word—*fallible*—but several new words: *fallible* and *infallible*, *fallibly* and *infallibly, fallibility* and *infallibility*, etc.

Focusing on how to form and spell derivatives, Chapter 11 gives you the opportunity to gain another word-leveraging skill, one enabling you to add many new words to your vocabulary whenever you learn one new word.

"Exercising" new vocabulary

Muscular exercise is essential, especially during your years of physical growth. Vocabulary exercise, too, is essential in your periods of word growth.

To learn new words effectively, you must put them to use right from the start—and often. The challenging drills and tests in this book offer you abundant opportunities for varied vocabulary exercise. But please make sure to do even more on your own!

Thus, in your reading and listening experiences, be conscious of vocabulary. In your speaking and writing, take the initiative on suitable occasions to use new vocabulary. Such follow-up is a must if you are to make new words securely yours.

Chapter

2.

Learning New Words
From the Context

What is the context?

Most of the time, a word is used not by itself but with other words. These other words are its *context*. The meaning of a word is often found in its context—the other words with which it is used.

Suppose, for example, we were asked for the meaning of *strike*. We would not be able to give a definite answer because *strike,* as presented to us, is all by itself; it has no context.

But if we were asked to define *strike* in one of the following sentences, we would have no trouble telling its meaning from its *context*—the other words with which it is used.

1. *Strike* three! You're out!
   (*Strike* means "a ball pitched over the plate between a batter's knees and armpits.")

2. There were no milk deliveries because of a *strike.*
   (*Strike* means "a work stoppage because of a labor dispute.")

3. He made a fist as if to *strike* me.
   (*Strike* means "hit.")

How can the context help you expand your vocabulary?

Here is an amazing fact: the context can often give you the meaning not only of common words like *strike*, **but also of unfamiliar words, including words you have never before seen or heard!**

"What," asks a friend, "is *xenophobic?*"
"How should I know?" you say. "I never heard of it."
"It's in today's paper," says the friend. "Here it is."

You take the newspaper and read the sentence with the strange word: "The new ruler is *xenophobic;* he has ordered all foreigners to leave the country."

"Aha!" you say. "Now I know: *xenophobic* means *'afraid or distrustful of foreigners.'* The context gives us the meaning."

Of course, you are right.

What can this chapter do for you?

This chapter will teach you how to use the context to get the meaning of unfamiliar words. Once you learn this skill, it will serve you for the rest of your life in two important ways: (1) it will keep enlarging your vocabulary; and (2) it will make you an even better reader.

Contexts With Contrasting Words

Pretest 1

Each passage below contains a word in italics. If you read the passage carefully, you will find a clue to the meaning of this word in an opposite word **(antonym)** or a contrasting idea.

Below each passage, write *(a)* the clue that led you to the meaning, and *(b)* the meaning itself. The answers for the first two passages have been filled in for you as examples.

1. "That you, Joe?" he asked . . .
"Who else could it be?" I *retorted.*—WILLIAM R. SCOTT

    a. CLUE: *Retorted* is the opposite of "asked."

    b. MEANING: *Retorted* means "answered."

2. Some substances that cause cancer were once regarded as *noncarcinogenic.*

    a. CLUE: *Noncarcinogenic* is in contrast with "that cause cancer."

    b. MEANING: *Noncarcinogenic* means "not cancer-causing."

3. At this stage we cannot tell whether the new regulations will be to our advantage or *detriment.*

    a. CLUE: _____

    b. MEANING: _____

4. If his health *ameliorates,* he will stay on the job; if it becomes worse, he will have to resign.

    a. CLUE: _____

    b. MEANING: _____

5. In this firm the industrious are promoted, and the *indolent* are encouraged to leave.

   a. CLUE: _____

   b. MEANING: _____

6. Parents, I suppose, were as much a problem *formerly* as they are today.—GRETCHEN FINLETTER

   a. CLUE: _____

   b. MEANING: _____

7. If you are going to get up before dawn tomorrow, you had better *retire* by 11 P.M.

   a. CLUE: _____

   b. MEANING: _____

8. Evidence presented at the trials of the two public officials showed that they had *subverted* the laws they were supposed to uphold.

   a. CLUE: _____

   b. MEANING: _____

9. Many who used to waste fuel are *conserving* it now that it has become so much more expensive.

   a. CLUE: _____

   b. MEANING: _____

10. Only one lower wing and the landing gear had been completely demolished. The rest of the machine was virtually *intact*.—EDWIN WAY TEALE

    a. CLUE: _____

    b. MEANING: _____

11. Those who volunteered to help turned out to be more of an *impediment* than an aid.

    a. CLUE: _____

    b. MEANING: _____

12. The Sullivan home, which used to stand on this corner, was erected in 1929 and *razed* in 2002.

    a. CLUE: _____

    b. MEANING: _____

13. Time has proved that Seward's purchase of Alaska from Russia in 1867 for $7,200,000 was wisdom, not *folly.*

    a. CLUE: _____

    b. MEANING: _____

14. When millions face starvation, we cannot be *parsimonious* in doling out aid; we must be generous.

    a. CLUE: _____

    b. MEANING: _____

15. . . . A wave of rebelliousness ran through the countryside. Bulls which had always been *tractable* suddenly turned savage, sheep broke down hedges and devoured clover, cows kicked the pail over . . . —GEORGE ORWELL

    a. CLUE: _____

    b. MEANING: _____

16. Children will tell how old they are, but older people are inclined to be *reticent* about their age.

    a. CLUE: _____

    b. MEANING: _____

17. The organization is trying to put on a show of *harmony* though there is deep conflict within its ranks.

    a. CLUE: _____

    b. MEANING: _____

18. Those who heeded our advice did well; those who *ignored* it did not.

    a. CLUE: _____

    b. MEANING: _____

19. Her learner's permit is still in effect, but mine is *invalid.*

    a. CLUE: _____

    b. MEANING: _____

20. There once was a society in Hawaii for the special purpose of introducing *exotic* birds. Today when you go to the islands, you see, instead of the exquisite native birds that greeted Captain Cook, mynas from India, cardinals from the United States or Brazil, doves from Asia . . . —RACHEL CARSON

    a. CLUE: _____

    b. MEANING: _____

Study Your New Words, **Group 1**

You have just defined twenty new words simply by contrasting them with other words or expressions in the context. Now, to reinforce your grasp of these words and make them a part of your active vocabulary, study the following. (For the meaning of the pronunciation symbols, see the list on the inside back cover.)

WORD	MEANING	TYPICAL USE
ameliorate (*v.*) ə-'mēl-yə-ˌrāt	become better; make better; improve; enhance (*ant.* **worsen**)	We expected business conditions to *ameliorate,* but they grew worse.
*amelioration (*n.*) ə-ˌmēl-yə-'rā-shən	improvement (*ant.* **degradation**)	
conserve (*v.*) kən-'sərv	keep from waste, loss, or decay; save (*ant.* **waste**)	One way to *conserve* water is to repair leaking faucets.
conservation (*n.*) ˌkän-sər-'vā-shən	preservation from loss, injury, or waste	
conservationist (*n.*) ˌkän-sər-'vā-shə-nəst	one who advocates the conservation of natural resources	
detriment (*n.*) 'de-trə-mənt	injury, damage, or something that causes it; disadvantage (*ant.* **advantage**)	Skipping meals can be a *detriment to* your health.
detrimental (*adj.*) ˌde-trə-'men-tᵊl	harmful; damaging	
exotic (*adj.*) ig-'zä-tik	1. introduced from another country; foreign (*ant.* **native; indigenous**)	The chrysanthemum, an exotic plant, was brought from the Orient.
	2. strikingly unusual; strange	This wallpaper has an *exotic* charm.
folly (*n.*) 'fä-lē	lack of good sense; foolish action or undertaking (*ant.* **wisdom**)	It is *folly* to go on a long drive with a nearly empty gas tank.
formerly (*adv.*) 'fȯr-mər-lē	in an earlier period; previously (*ant.* **now**)	Our physics instructor was *formerly* an engineer.
former (*adj.*) 'fȯr-mər	preceding; previous (*ant.* **latter**)	
harmony (*n.*) 'här-mə-nē	peaceable or friendly relations; accord; agreement; tranquillity; concord (*ant.* **conflict; disharmony**)	A boundary dispute is making it impossible for the neighbors to live in *harmony.*
harmonious (*adj.*) här-'mō-nē-əs	friendly; amicable	

*Note that *amelioration* is a bonus word—you can understand it instantly if you know *ameliorate.* Useful bonus words, like *amelioration,* will be introduced from now on.

ignore (*v.*)
ig-'nȯr

refuse to take notice of; disregard (*ant.* **heed**)

You may get into a serious accident if you *ignore* a Stop sign.

  ignoramus (*n.*)
  ,ig-nə-'rā-məs

ignorant, stupid person; dunce; dolt; dullard; nincompoop

impediment (*n.*)
im-'pe-də-mənt

something that hinders or obstructs; hindrance; obstacle (*ant.* **aid**)

A person's lack of education is often an *impediment* to advancement.

  impede (*v.*)
  im-'pēd

interfere with or slow the progress of; hinder; obstruct

indolent (*adj.*)
'in-də-lənt

disposed to avoid exertion; lazy; idle; lethargic (*ant.* **industrious**)

I was so comfortable in the reclining chair that I became *indolent* and did not feel like studying.

  indolence (*n.*)
  'in-də-ləns

idleness; laziness

intact (*adj.*)
in-'takt

untouched by anything that damages or diminishes; left complete or entire; uninjured (*ant.* **imperfect**)

The tornado demolished the barn but left the farmhouse *intact*.

invalid (*adj.*)
in-'va-ləd

not binding in law; having no force or effect; void; nugatory (*ant.* **valid**)

The courts have ruled that a forced confession is *invalid* and cannot be introduced as evidence.

  invalidate (*v.*)
  in-'va-lə-,dāt

abolish; annul

  invalid (*n.*)
  'in-və-ləd

sickly or disabled person

noncarcinogenic (*adj.*)
,nän-,kär-sᵊn-ō-'je-nik

not producing, or tending to produce, cancer (*ant.* **carcinogenic**)

Cancer-causing ingredients must be replaced by others that are *noncarcinogenic*.

parsimonious (*adj.*)
,pär-sə-'mō-nē-əs

unduly sparing in the spending of money; stingy; miserly; tightfisted (*ant.* **generous**)

Are we too generous in funding road improvement but too *parsimonious* in financing education?

  parsimony (*n.*)
  'pär-sə-,mō-nē

stinginess; parsimoniousness (ant. **generosity; liberality**)

raze (*v.*)
'rāz

destroy utterly by tearing down; demolish; level (ant. **erect**)

The building was so badly damaged in the fire that it had to be *razed*.

reticent (*adj.*)
're-tə-sənt

inclined to be silent or secretive; uncommunicative; reserved (ant. **frank**)

Have you noticed that people who boast about their successes are *reticent* about their failures?

  reticence (*n.*)
  're-tə-səns

restraint in communicating (ant. **frankness**)

retire (*v.*) ri-'tīr	1. withdraw from active duty or business	Does your grandfather plan to retire at 65 or continue to work?
	2. go to bed (*ant.* **rise**)	Please do not phone after 10 P.M. because my folks retire early.
retort (*v.*) ri-'tȯrt	answer; reply sharply or angrily (*ant.* **ask**)	"Giving up?" she asked. "Absolutely not!" I *retorted*.
retort (*n.*) ri-'tȯrt	quick, witty, or sharp reply; answer	
subvert (*v.*) səb-'vərt	overturn or overthrow from the foundation; undermine (*ant.* **uphold**)	We are *subverting* our fuel-conservation efforts when we heat rooms that are not occupied.
subversion (*n.*) səb-'vər-zhən	sabotage; undermining	
tractable (*adj.*) 'trak-tə-bəl	easily led, taught, or controlled; yielding; docile; amenable (*ant.* **unruly; intractable**)	A child who misbehaves may be more *tractable* in a small group than in a large one.
tractability (*n.*) ,trak-tə-'bi-lə-tē	obedience	

Apply What You Have Learned

EXERCISE 2.1: SENTENCE COMPLETION

Which choice, A or B, makes the sentence correct? Write the *letter* of your answer in the space provided.

1. When I heard the noise, I ignored it. I went _____.
   (A) on with my work   (B) to investigate

2. The more we conserve heat, the _____ fuel we have for future use.
   (A) more   (B) less

3. It is folly if you _____.
   (A) speed on an icy road   (B) reduce your speed in a heavy rainstorm

4. The reticent witness provided _____ details.
   (A) few   (B) abundant

5. I like _____ food, but I also have a craving for exotic dishes.
   (A) foreign   (B) American

6. You would not expect parsimonious persons to _____.
   (A) collect bits of string   (B) spend freely

7. Because of _____, the company is doing its utmost to ameliorate service.

    (A) a shortage of raw materials   (B) customer complaints

8. The stolen jewels were found intact; _____ was missing.

    (A) nothing   (B) a diamond ring

9. Most of the listeners were tractable; they _____ the speaker's instructions.

    (A) readily followed   (B) totally disregarded

10. Carcinogenic materials _____ to our health.

    (A) are a threat   (B) pose no danger

EXERCISE 2.2: CONCISE WRITING

Express the thought of each sentence below in no more than four words. The first two sentences have been rewritten as examples.

1. "Wait outside!" he replied in a sharp and angry tone of voice.

    "Wait outside!" he retorted.

2. We are opposed to the waste, mismanagement, and destruction of our natural resources.

    We are conservationists.

3. The advice that they have been giving is doing more harm than good.

4. His inclination to exert himself as little as possible is self-defeating.

5. Is there a possibility that friendly relations can be restored?

6. The house that they lived in was leveled.

7. All the things that belonged to her arrived with nothing missing or damaged.

8. At an earlier period of time, land could be bought for very little money.

9. Wills that have not been signed are not binding in law.

_____

10. What time was it when you went to bed for the night?

_____

EXERCISE 2.3: CLOSE READING

Carefully read the statements below and answer the questions.

STATEMENTS

A fallen tree was blocking traffic on Bainbridge Road.

The Z Company had a disastrous year but decided to stay in business.

Russ has said very little about what had happened.

Angela's motto was "Take it easy." She could have done much more if she had wanted, but she kept saying, "Why kill myself?"

Our new storm door has reduced heat loss.

The ABC Company's employees had never gone on strike.

Billy refused to remain in his seat, despite the pleas of his parents and the usher.

While the rest of us were trying to sell tickets, one member of the cast was privately telling people that the play was not worth seeing.

Despite her large income, Alicia bought only the barest necessities.

The hurricane destroyed the lakeside dining area and the flower gardens, but the inn itself suffered no damage.

QUESTIONS

1. What was impeding something? _____

2. Who was intractable? _____

3. Who seemed indolent? _____

4. Who was reticent? _____

5. Who appeared to be parsimonious? _____

6. What was helping to conserve something? _____

7. Who probably expected some amelioration? _____

8. Who was subversive? _____

9. Who seemed to be enjoying harmony? _____

10. What was left intact? _____

EXERCISE 2.4: ANTONYMS

Complete the sentence by inserting the antonym of the italicized word. Select your antonyms from group 1.

1. Truly, I do not care whether you *heed* my suggestion or _____ it.

2. Now that the *conflict* is over, _____ may soon be restored.

3. As an officer of the club, you should *uphold* the constitution, not _____ it.

4. I cannot see the *wisdom* of your actions; they are pure _____.

5. Usually I *rise* at 6:45 A.M. and _____ by 11 P.M.

6. The newcomer, *unruly* at first, is becoming more _____.

7. Not all the trees on the school grounds are *native* to our soil. Some are _____.

8. An early start turned out to be not to our *advantage,* but to our _____.

9. _____, she worked as a bookkeeper. *Now* she is studying for a law degree.

10. Did the medicine _____ your condition or *worsen* it?

EXERCISE 2.5: COMPOSITION

Answer in a sentence or two.

1. What is one way to conserve energy that many people ignore?

_____

_____

_____

2. Is it always folly to raze a structurally sound building? Explain.

_____

_____

_____

3. Why do conservationists want to prevent even the most exotic plants and animals from disappearing from the face of the earth?

_____

_____

_____

4. Give an example of how a reticent witness can subvert the process of justice.

_____

_____

_____

5. Would you rather have a parsimonious friend or an indolent one? Why?

_____

_____

_____

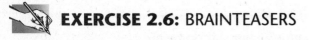

EXERCISE 2.6: BRAINTEASERS

Fill in the missing letters, as in the following sample:

He knows math, but in art and literature he is a(n) <u>i g n o</u> r a m <u>u s</u>.

1. Skipping breakfast may be __ __ __ __ __ **m e n** __ __ __ to your health.

2. Please step aside. You are **i m p** __ __ __ __ __ __ our progress.

3. Turn off that noise. Let's have some peace and __ __ __ __ __ __ **i l l** __ __ __.

4. When its own crops fail, a nation must buy food from __ __ __ **t i c** sources.

5. A license that expired yesterday is no longer __ __ **l i d**.

6. __ __ __ __ __ __ __ **v a t** __ __ __ can help prevent future shortages.

7. Though formerly enemies, they are now on __ **a r m** __ __ __ __ __ __ __ terms.

8. Our sugar is __ __ **d i g** __ __ __ __ __, but our tea is imported.

9. Did he tell you anything, or is he still __ __ __ __ __ __ __ __ __ **c a t** __ __ __?

10. __ __ **d u s t** __ __ __ __ __ workers deserve higher pay than indolent ones.

Part
2

Contexts With Similar Words

Often you can learn the meaning of an unfamiliar word from a *similar* word or expression in the context. Do you know what *castigated* means? If not, you should be able to find out from the following:

> The candidate denounced his opponent for her views on foreign policy, and she *castigated* him for his attitude toward education.

Here, the meaning of *castigated is* given to us by a similar word in the context, *denounced.*

Do you know what *remote* means? If not, you can learn it from the following passage:

> There lay a young man, fast asleep—sleeping so soundly, so deeply, that he was far, far away from them both. Oh, so *remote* . . .
> —KATHERINE MANSFIELD

The context teaches us that *remote* means "far."
Let's try one more. Find the meaning of *reluctantly* in the next passage.

> My mother scolded me for my thoughtlessness and bade me say good-bye to them. *Reluctantly* I obeyed her, wishing that I did not have to do so.
> —RICHARD WRIGHT

The clue here is in the words *wishing that I did not have to do so.* They suggest that *reluctantly* means "unwillingly."

Pretest 2

Write the meaning of the italicized word. (Hint: Look for a *similar* word or expression in the context.)

1. Mr. Smith had already become acquainted with British *cinemas* in small towns. Also, he was a Southern Californian and had that familiarity with movies that belongs to all Southern Californians.—ERIC KNIGHT

cinemas means _____

2. Burke tossed the circular into the wastebasket without *perusing* it. He never reads junk mail.

perusing means _____

3. The dealer asked for $1200. He *spurned* my offer of $1100, and when I went to $1150, he refused that too.

spurned means _____

4. Your whistling *galls* me. In fact, your entire behavior irritates me.

   galls means _____

5. I said the water was *tepid*. She didn't believe me. She tested it herself to see if it was lukewarm.

   tepid means _____

6. Eileen and I hated the book [*Bird Life for Children*], so we were quite prepared to *despise* birds when we started off that morning on our first bird walk.—Ruth McKenney

   despise means _____

7. Everyone brimmed with enthusiasm. Carl was particularly *ebullient*.

   ebullient means _____

8. She is eager to bet me she will win the match, but I told her I do not *wager*.

   wager means _____

9. A fight started between two of the opposing athletes. Several of their teammates joined in. It was quite a *scuffle*.

   scuffle means _____

10. ... the picture changed and sport began to *wane*. A good many factors contributed to the decline of sport.—E. B. White

    wane means _____

11. Later I realized I had made some *inane* remarks, and I was ashamed of myself for having been so silly.

    inane means _____

12. She was supposed to be *indemnified*—the repair bill came to $680—but she has not yet been repaid.

    indemnified means _____

13. Dorene is quite *finicky* about her penmanship. I am much less fussy.

    finicky means _____

14. The fact is, we have all been a good deal puzzled because the affair is so simple, and yet *baffles* us altogether.—Edgar Allan Poe

    baffles means _____

15. Though the starting salary is only $500 a week, Roberta has been promised an early promotion and a higher *stipend*.

    stipend means _____

16. They *exhorted* us to join them for dinner, but we resisted their urging and thanked them very much.

exhorted means _____

17. When an Englishman has anything surprising to tell he never *exaggerates* it, never overstates it . . .—STEPHEN B. LEACOCK

exaggerates means _____

18. I know how to change a tire, but tuning an engine is beyond my *expertise*.

expertise means _____

19. Asians who have never been to the *Occident* learn much about Western culture from films and television.

Occident means _____

20. Gerald suspected we were being watched. "Really?" I asked. "What makes you think we are under *surveillance*?"

surveillance means _____

Study Your New Words, Group 2

You have just tried to define twenty new words with the help of similar words or expressions in the context. To strengthen your grasp of these new words, study the following:

WORD	MEANING	TYPICAL USE
baffle (*v.*) 'ba-fəl	bewilder; perplex; fill with confusion; puzzle; frustrate	At last, we have found a solution to a problem that has been *baffling* us.
baffling (*adj.*) 'ba-fliŋ	frustrating; bewildering	
cinema (*n.*) 'si-nə-mə	movies; motion-picture industry	Which do you like better, TV or the *cinema*?
cinematography (*n.*) ˌsi-nə-mə-'tä-grə-fē	art of making motion pictures	
despise (*v.*) di-'spīz	look down on with contempt or disgust; loathe; regard as inferior (*ant.* **admire**)	The world *admires* heroes and *despises* cowards.
despicable (*adj.*) 'di-spi-kə-bəl	worthy of contempt; contemptible (*ant.* **laudable**)	
ebullient (*adj.*) i-'bul-yənt	overflowing with enthusiasm; exuberant; effervescent; high-spirited; vivacious	Thousands of *ebullient* fans thronged the airport to greet the new champions.

ebullience (*n.*)
i-'bùl-yəns

exuberance

exaggerate (*v.*)
ig-'za-jə-,rāt

overstate; go beyond the limits of the actual truth; magnify (*ant.* **minimize**)

You *exaggerated* when you called me an excellent cook. I can't make anything except instant pudding.

   exaggeration (*n.*)
ig-,za-jə-'rā-shən

overstatement (*ant.* **understatement**)

exhort (*v.*)
ig-'zȯrt

arouse by words; advise strongly; urge

The newscaster *exhorted* drivers to leave their cars at home because of the slippery roads.

   exhortation (*n.*)
,ek-,sȯr-'tā-shən

urgent recommendation or advice

expertise (*n.*)
,ek-spər-'tēz

specialized skill or technical knowledge; know-how; expertness

The Waldos lack the *expertise* to prepare their tax return, so they hire an accountant to do it.

finicky (*adj.*)
'fi-ni-kē

excessively concerned with trifles or details; hard to please; fussy; particular; fastidious; persnickety

Abe showed me I had forgotten to dot one of my i's. He is very *finicky* about such matters.

gall (*v.*)
'gȯl

make sore; irritate mentally; annoy; vex

Our two-term senator's absenteeism *galls* the voters—so polls show.

   gall (*n.*)
'gȯl

brazen boldness; nerve (*ant.* **meekness**)

inane (*adj.*)
i-'nān

lacking significance or sense; pointless; silly; insipid; jejune; vapid (*ant.* **deep; profound**)

I asked him how the water was, and he said "wet." Now isn't that *inane*?

   inanity (*n.*)
i-'na-nə-tē

foolishness; shallowness

indemnify (*v.*)
in-'dem-nə-,fī

compensate for loss, damage, or injury; reimburse; repay

Some of the tenants were not *indemnified* for their losses in the fire, as they carried no insurance.

Occident (*n.*)
'äk-sə-dənt

west; countries of America and Europe (*ant.* **Orient**)

The plane that landed in Shanghai brought tourists from the United States, Canada, Brazil, Italy, and other countries in the *Occident*.

   occidental (*adj.*)
,äk-sə-'den-t^əl

western (*ant.* **oriental**)

peruse (*v.*)
pə-'rüz

read; look at fairly attentively; study

Before signing a contract, you should *peruse* its contents and discuss any questions you may have with your attorney.

   perusal (*n.*)
pə-'rü-zəl

reading; study

scuffle (*v.*) ˈskə-fəl	struggle at close quarters in a rough and confused manner; wrestle; grapple	The players who *scuffled* with the umpires were suspended and heavily fined.
scuffle (*n.*)	brawl; fight	
spurn (*v.*) ˈspərn	thrust aside with disdain or contempt; reject (*ant.* **accept**)	We wanted to assist, but they *spurned* all offers of aid.
stipend (*n.*) ˈstī-ˌpend	fixed pay for services; salary; regular allowance awarded a scholarship winner	Maria's scholarship will pay her an annual *stipend* of $5000 for four years.
surveillance (*n.*) sər-ˈvā-ləns	close watch over a person, group, or area; supervision	The police kept the suspect under continuous *surveillance*.
tepid (*adj.*) ˈte-pəd	moderately warm; lukewarm	The soup was served hot, but I didn't get to it for about five minutes, and by then it was *tepid*.
tepidly (*adv.*) ˈte-pəd-lē	unenthusiastically; lukewarmly	
wager (*v.*)	risk (something) on the outcome of a contest or uncertain event; gamble; bet	Those who had *wagered* we would win are out of some money; we lost the game.
wager (*n.*) ˈwā-jər	bet	
wane (*v.*) ˈwān	decrease in power or size; dwindle; decline; sink (*ant.* **wax**)	The show's *waning* popularity has cut advertising revenues.

Apply What You Have Learned

 **EXERCISE 2.7:** SENTENCE COMPLETION

Which choice, A or B, makes the sentence correct? Write the *letter* of your answer in the space provided.

1. They spurned my suggestion and did as _____.

(A) they pleased   (B) I advised

2. To send someone a birthday card _____ her or his birthday is absolutely inane.

(A) six months after   (B) three days before

3. The Independents have just _____ two more seats; their influence is waning.

(A) won   (B) lost

4. After four years of service in the American embassy in _____, Williams is longing to return to the Occident.

   (A) Tokyo   (B) Madrid

5. Our guests are not finicky; they are _____ to please.

   (A) hard   (B) easy

6. Asked if she were coming to Class Night, an ebullient senior answered: _____

   (A) "Maybe."   (B) "Sure!"

7. The _____ provides live entertainment.

   (A) theater   (B) cinema

8. He is just under five eleven, and when he gives his height, he says: _____. He does not exaggerate.

   (A) "six feet"   (B) "five ten"

9. We are keeping _____ the suspects; they are under surveillance.

   (A) a lookout for   (B) an eye on

10. Surely you would not want to _____ someone you despise.

    (A) ignore   (B) associate with

 **EXERCISE 2.8:** CONCISE WRITING

Express the thought of each sentence below in no more than four words.

1. Stephanie sometimes makes a statement that goes beyond the limits of the actual truth.

   _____

2. We were greeted in a manner that was lacking in enthusiasm.

   _____

3. Those who hold insurance policies will be compensated for their losses.

   _____

4. A close watch is being kept over our comings and goings.

   _____

5. We pay no attention to remarks that have no sense or significance.

   _____

6. He does not have the specialized skills that she has.

   _____

7. Don't be so overly concerned with trifles and minor details,

   _____

8. They were seen struggling at close quarters in a rough and confused manner.

_____

9. Michael looks down with contempt on people who are inclined to avoid exertion.

_____

10. People from the United States visit the countries of Asia.

_____

EXERCISE 2.9: CLOSE READING

Carefully read the statements below and answer the questions.

STATEMENTS

A closed-circuit TV screen enabled the security guard to watch the three visitors as they rode up in the elevator.

Joyce was dissatisfied with the way George had set the table because some of the spoons and forks were not exactly parallel.

It took five minutes for Armand to replace the washer of the leaking faucet.

Dan's insurance company paid in full for the damage to Barbara's car.

Roger urged the audience to contribute generously for the relief of the earthquake victims.

The producer said the play had opened to a full house, but Emily, who attended the performance, recalls seeing a number of vacant seats.

Susan protested that Denny's conclusions made no sense at all.

Many residents enthusiastically supported the mayor's program.

The pushing and shoving began when a latecomer tried to get in at the head of the line. Two people were hurt.

Before the match, both rivals had agreed that the loser would pay for the refreshments.

QUESTIONS

1. Who detected an exaggeration? _____

2. Who was finicky? _____

3. Who made a wager? _____

4. Who indemnified someone? _____

5. Who started a scuffle? _____

6. Who was under surveillance? _____

7. Who was ebullient? _____

8. Who was exhorted? _____

9. Who demonstrated mechanical expertise? _____

10. Who stated that something was inane? _____

EXERCISE 2.10: SYNONYMS AND ANTONYMS

A. In the blank space, insert a SYNONYM from group 2 for the italicized word.

_____   1. These bills *annoy* me.

_____   2. Charlie Chaplin was a star of the silent *movies*.

_____   3. The crowd was *exuberant*.

_____   4. The water was *lukewarm*.

_____   5. You are acquiring *know-how* in carpentry.

B. In the blank space, insert an ANTONYM from group 2 for the italicized word.

_____   6. Do not *minimize* your achievements.

_____   7. The freighter is bound for the *Orient*.

_____   8. Their behavior was *admirable*.

_____   9. She said something very *profound*.

_____   10. The winner will probably *accept* the award.

EXERCISE 2.11: COMPOSITION

Answer in a sentence or two.

1. What is one thing that might baffle a visitor from the Orient? Why?

_____

_____

_____

2. Why should a bank maintain surveillance over an employee with an excessive fondness for wagering?

_____

_____

_____

3. What would you say to someone who exaggerates the damage you did to his or her property and asks to be indemnified?

_____

_____

_____

4. If you are hurt in an accident, why would it be inane to minimize your injury?

_____

_____

_____

5. Does a married employee deserve a higher stipend than an unmarried one with the same expertise? Explain.

_____

_____

_____

 **EXERCISE 2.12:** BRAINTEASERS

Fill in the missing letters.

1. Infants learning to walk need continuous __ __ __ **v e i l** __ __ __ __ __.

2. The problem baffles us. We are bewildered and __ **r u s t** __ __ __ __ __.

3. I noticed the article, but I had no time to __ __ __ **u s e** it.

4. Marco Polo's travels led to trade between China and the __ __ __ __ **d e n** __.

5. If the offer had been reasonable, it would not have been __ __ **u r n** __ __.

6. We cannot praise what you have done because it is not __ __ __ __ **a b l e**.

7. The unemployed watched their savings __ **w i n** __ __ __.

8. Making a movie requires some __ __ **p e r** __ __ __ __ in cinematography.

9. Many remained in their homes, despite repeated __ __ __ __ __ **t a t** __ __ __ s that they leave for higher ground.

10. Stop fussing over petty details. Don't be so __ **a r t** __ __ __ __ __ __.

"Commonsense" Contexts

Do you know what *reel* means in the following sentence?

> It weighs a ton, and strong porters *reel* under its weight.
> —W. SOMERSET MAUGHAM

Note that the context contains neither a contrasting nor a similar word to help with the meaning of *reel*. Yet you can tell what it means just by using a bit of **common sense.** You ask yourself:

> "How would I behave if I were to carry, or try to carry, something that feels like a ton?"

You realize that you would "sway dizzily," or "stagger." That is exactly what *reel* means.

Can you give a definition of *severed*? Do you know what *pinioned* means? If not, you should be able to discover their meanings from the following context by applying common sense.

> "...I whirled about, grabbing the razor-sharp knife from my belt sheath, and slashed three or four times with a full sweep of my arms in the direction of the touch. By luck I *severed* two of the lassoing arms that were gripping me; in another instant the octopus would have had my two arms *pinioned* and I should have been helpless."
> —VICTOR BERGE AND HENRY W. LANIER

What would you do to the arms of an octopus if you slashed them three or four times with a razor-sharp knife with a full sweep of your arms? You would *cut them off,* of course. *Severed* means "cut off."

And what would happen to your own arms if they were lassoed and gripped by the arms of an octopus? Obviously, they would be *bound fast,* so that you would not be able to use them. *Pinioned* means "bound fast."

The term *"commonsense" context,* as used in this book, means a context that yields the meaning of an unfamiliar word through clues other than a synonym or antonym. Such contexts, as you have seen, involve a bit of reasoning on your part.

Pretest 3

Try to discover the meaning of the italicized word in each of the following "commonsense" contexts:

1. A child wandering through a department store with its mother is *admonished* over and over again not to touch things.—PAUL GALLICO

admonished means _____

2. My simple *repast* consisted of a sandwich and an apple.

repast means _____

3. Restrictions on the use of water will end as soon as our reservoirs are *replenished.*

replenished means _____

4. A sufferer from *insomnia,* she lies awake most of the night.

insomnia means _____

5. The judge listened to the arguments of both attorneys before *rendering* her decision.

rendering means _____

6. And take from seventy springs a *score,*
It only leaves me fifty more.—A. E. HOUSMAN

score means _____

7. In another year my father will have completed his first *decade* in business; he opened his shop nine years ago.

decade means _____

8. The blade slipped and cut my hand. Two *sutures* were needed to close the wound.

sutures means _____

9. When the bald-headed fellow pretended he was the rightful King of France, Huck and Jim believed him. They were quite *gullible.*

gullible means _____

10. While *confined* here in the Birmingham city jail, I came across your recent statement calling my present activities "unwise and untimely."—MARTIN LUTHER KING, JR.

confined means _____

11. A *probe* into the suspect's financial dealings disclosed evidence of large-scale fraud.

probe means _____

12. The seller asked $400 for the computer, and I gave him his price; we did not *haggle.*

haggle means _____

13. I know you asked for coleslaw, but I forgot to order it. I am sorry for the *lapse.*

lapse means _____

14. We moved into first place, but our glory was *ephemeral.* The next day we lost a doubleheader and dropped to third.

ephemeral means _____

15. It was not that he felt any emotion akin to love for Irene Adler. All emotions, and that one particularly, were *abhorrent* to his cold, precise but admirably balanced mind. —ARTHUR CONAN DOYLE

    abhorrent means _____

16. Jean greeted everyone, but when I said, "Hello," she walked past me as if I did not exist. The *snub* bothered me the rest of the day.

    snub means _____

17. As I was leaving the meeting, I realized that I had *unwittingly* taken someone else's coat. Embarrassed, I ran back and apologized.

    unwittingly means _____

18. Construction workers safely cleared the area before the explosive detonated.

    detonated means _____

19. I *immersed* my hands in warm soapy water to loosen the dirt.

    immersed means _____

20. Perhaps in heaven, but certainly not until then, shall I ever taste anything so *ambrosial* as that fried chicken and coffee ice cream!—DOROTHY CANFIELD FISHER

    ambrosial means _____

Study Your New Words, **Group 3**

You have just attempted to learn the meanings of twenty words from "commonsense" clues in their contexts. Now, for a firmer grasp of these words, study the following:

WORD	MEANING	TYPICAL USE
abhorrent (*adj.*) əb-ʹhȯr-ənt	(followed by *to*) in conflict; utterly opposed; loathsome; repugnant; odious; abominable (*ant.* **admirable**)	Please do not ask me to tell an untruth; lying is *abhorrent* to me.
abhor (*v.*) əb-ʹhȯr	utterly detest; loathe; hate	
admonish (*v.*) ad-ʹmä-nish	reprove gently but seriously; warn of a fault; caution (*ant.* **commend**)	The teacher *commended* me on my improvement in writing, but *admonished* me for my lateness to class.
admonition (*n.*) ˌad-mə-ʹni-shən	gentle warning; friendly reproof	

ambrosial (*adj.*) am-'brō-zh(ē-)əl	extremely pleasing to taste or smell; delicious; like *ambrosia* (the food of the gods); heavenly	Taste this ripe pineapple; it has an *ambrosial* flavor.
confine (*v.*) kən-'fīn	shut up; imprison; keep in narrow, cramped quarters (*ant.* **free**)	On July 14, 1789, a Paris mob freed the prisoners *confined* in the Bastille.
confinement (*n.*) kən-'fīn-mənt	imprisonment	
decade (*n.*) 'de-,kād	period of ten years	In the United States, the 1930s were the *decade* of the Great Depression.
detonate (*v.*) 'de-tən-,āt	explode with suddenness and violence; cause (something) to explode	Fallout showed that a nuclear device had probably been *detonated.*
detonation (*n.*) ,de-tən-'ā-shən	explosion	
ephemeral (*adj.*) i-'fem-ə-rəl	lasting one day only; fleeting; transitory; short-lived; transient (*ant.* **permanent; perpetual**)	Day-lily blossoms are *ephemeral;* they last only for a day.
gullible (*adj.*) 'gə-lə-bəl	easily deceived or cheated; credulous (*ant.* **astute**)	The worthless stock was bid up by the *gullible,* spurned by the *astute.*
gull (*v.*) 'gəl	deceive; cheat	
haggle (*v.*) 'ha-gəl	dispute or argue over a price in a petty way; bargain; wrangle	Have they agreed on a price yet, or are they still *haggling*?
immerse (*v.*) i-'mərs	1. plunge or place into a liquid; dip; duck	I filled a basin with lukewarm water and *immersed* my foot in it.
	2. engross; absorb	She is *immersed* in her book.
immersion (*n.*) i-'mər-zhən	state of being deeply engrossed; absorption	
insomnia (*n.*) in-'säm-nē-ə	inability to sleep; abnormal wakefulness; sleeplessness	The former hostages now get a normal amount of sleep; their confinement plagued them with *insomnia.*
insomniac (*n.*) in-'säm-nē-,ak	person suffering from insomnia	
lapse (*n.*) 'laps	1. slip; error; accidental mistake; trivial fault	I wrote your name with one *t,* instead of two. Please forgive the *lapse.*
	2. interval	He returned after a *lapse* of ten years.
lapse (*v.*)	cease being in force; become invalid	

probe (*n.*)
ˈprōb

critical inquiry into suspected illegal activity; investigation

A *probe* is being conducted to learn what happened to the missing funds.

prober (*n.*)
ˈprō-bər

investigator

render (*v.*)
ˈren-dər

hand down officially; deliver (as a verdict); give

Tension was high in the courtroom as the jury filed in to *render* its verdict.

rendering (*n.*)
ˈren-dər-iŋ

presentation; interpretation

The most famous *rendering* of the "Last Supper" was painted by Leonardo.

repast (*n.*)
ri-ˈpast

food for one occasion of eating; meal

Lunch on some fad diets would hardly make a *repast* for a sparrow.

replenish (*v.*)
ri-ˈple-nish

bring back to condition of being full; refill

Every 200 miles we stopped at a service station to *replenish* the gas tank.

score (*n.*)
ˈskȯ(ə)r

group or set of twenty; twenty

We have nineteen signatures already, and if we get one more, we'll have an even *score*.

snub (*n.*)
ˈsnəb

act or instance of *snubbing* (treating with contempt); rebuff; slight; insult

Why did Sharon invite everyone but me? Was it just an oversight, or a deliberate *snub*?

snub (*v.*)

treat with disdain or contempt; slight

suture (*n.*)
ˈsü-chər

strand or fiber used to sew parts of the living body; also, stitch made with such material

A few days after the cut finger was sewn together, the patient returned for the removal of the *sutures*.

unwittingly (*adv.*)
ən-ˈwit-iŋ-lē

unintentionally; by accident; inadvertently; unknowingly (*ant.* **intentionally**)

I *unwittingly* opened a letter addressed to you. I'm sorry.

Apply What You Have Learned

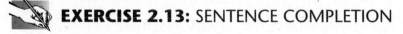 **EXERCISE 2.13:** SENTENCE COMPLETION

Which choice, A or B, makes the sentence correct? Write the *letter* of your answer in the space provided.

1. When you _____, your body is totally immersed.

(A) take a shower   (B) swim underwater

2. A probe of the corporation is under way; several of its top officers have been _____.

   (A) questioned   (B) promoted

3. Dawson entered the House in _____ and served for a score of years until his defeat in 2000.

   (A) 1980   (B) 1960

4. The guests _____ about the ambrosial food.

   (A) raved   (B) complained

5. Shoppers will find the selection _____ because the shelves have been replenished.

   (A) poor   (B) excellent

6. If you regularly watch TV at 3 _____, you may be an insomniac.

   (A) A.M.   (B) P.M.

7. Your snub has upset me: when I offered my hand, you _____ it.

   (A) shook   (B) spurned

8. Did you _____ by yourself, or did someone join you in your repast?

   (A) study   (B) dine

9. For the first decade of her life, she lived on a farm. After those _____ years were over, her family moved to the city.

   (A) ten   (B) eleven

10. They haggled. Keisha wanted twenty dollars for the used book, and Audrey thought that was _____.

    (A) too high   (B) a fair price

EXERCISE 2.14: CONCISE WRITING

Express the thought of each sentence below in no more than four words.

1. The fame that they achieved lasted only for a very short time.

   _____

2. She stays awake most of the night because she has a great deal of trouble falling asleep.

   _____

3. Some shoppers enjoy arguing over a price in a petty way.

   _____

4. Were the stitches that were used to sew up the wound removed?

   _____

5. No one who is serving a prison term likes being kept in narrow, confined quarters.

   _____

6. It is hard to believe how easy it is for others to cheat him.

_____

7. Without realizing what I was doing, I treated you with contempt.

_____

8. We utterly detest the way they have been behaving themselves.

_____

9. Has the policy that you own ceased to be in force?

_____

10. The people who had committed the offenses were reproved in a gentle but firm manner.

_____

EXERCISE 2.15: SYNONYMS AND ANTONYMS

A. In the blank space, insert a SYNONYM from group 3 for the italicized word.

_____ 1. We *bargained* for more than ten minutes.

_____ 2. She took it as an *insult*.

_____ 3. Has your glass been *refilled*?

_____ 4. What causes *sleeplessness*?

_____ 5. A mental *slip* prevented me from recalling your name.

B. In the blank space, insert an ANTONYM from group 3 for the italicized word.

_____ 6. It was a *permanent* friendship.

_____ 7. Your opponent was quite *astute*.

_____ 8. Did she step on your foot *intentionally*?

_____ 9. The chief *commended* us.

_____ 10. On what grounds can the suspect be *freed*?

EXERCISE 2.16: CLOSE READING

Carefully read the statements below and answer the questions.

STATEMENTS

As a child, Roy believed that there were lions, tigers, and fire-breathing dragons in the woods near his home, as well as buried pirate treasure.

Andy consumed a seven-course dinner, but Margie had only a thin slice of cantaloupe.

Louise did not reach her cousin in her first try because she dialed 555-8439 instead of 555-8349.

The florist did exceptionally well on opening day, but after that there were so few customers that he had to go out of business.

Rivers favored an investigation, but Thompson said it would be a waste of time and money.

When Gail was gently reminded that it was getting late and that the bus would soon arrive, she shouted, "Mom, I'll be right down."

Olga had to invent an excuse for her friend, though it was something that she loathed doing.

The payroll clerk was given an office that was scarcely larger than a closet.

While Chuck and Jim were hesitating, wondering about the water temperature, Estelle dived in and swam two laps.

Evan sold forty-two tickets, Stella twenty-nine, and Terry nineteen.

QUESTIONS

1. Who enjoyed ephemeral success? _____
2. Who must have felt confined? _____
3. Who admonished someone? _____
4. Who had an abhorrent experience? _____
5. Who was gullible? _____
6. Who opposed a probe? _____
7. Who had a meager repast? _____
8. Who was short of a score? _____
9. Who was immersed? _____
10. Who committed a lapse? _____

 **EXERCISE 2.17:** COMPOSITION

Answer in a sentence or two.

1. Should employees be required to reach the age of threescore and ten before becoming eligible to retire? Why, or why not?

   _____

   _____

   _____

2. Which could you more readily forgive, a snub or a lapse? Why?

   _____

   _____

   _____

3. Why is a gullible customer not likely to haggle?

   _____

   _____

   _____

4. Should someone who detonates firecrackers on the Fourth of July be admonished? Explain.

   _____

   _____

   _____

5. Describe one of the most ambrosial repasts you ever had.

   _____

   _____

   _____

EXERCISE 2.18: BRAINTEASERS

Fill in the missing letters.

1. We respected them, but they treated us with __ __ __ t e m p t.

2. If yellow is __ o a t h __ __ __ __ to you, choose another color.

3. Many windows were shattered by the __ __ t o n __ __ __ __ __ .

4. Liz read the poem beautifully, but your __ e n d __ __ __ __ __ was even better.

5. Gregg was so __ __ **g r o s s** __ __ in his book that he didn't see us enter.

6. A team of experienced __ **r o b** __ __ __ is investigating the crash.

7. If you are king or queen for a day, your glory will be __ __ **h e m** __ __ __ __ .

8. Most authors are soon forgotten, but a few achieve __ __ __ **m a n** __ __ __ fame.

9. The rebellious inmate was put into solitary __ __ __ **f i n** __ __ __ __ __ .

10. It was his first warning. Never before had he been __ __ __ __ __ __ **s h e d**.

Part

4

Mixed Contexts

This is a review section. It contains contexts of all the types you have met up to now—those with a contrasting word, or a similar word, or a commonsense clue. By this time, you should be able to deal with any of these contexts.

Pretest 4

Try to discover the meaning of the italicized word, and write its meaning in the space provided.

1. . . . then we examined the house itself. We divided its entire surface into compartments, which we numbered, so that none might be missed; then we *scrutinized* each individual square inch throughout the premises, including the two houses immediately adjoining, with the microscope, as before.—EDGAR ALLAN POE

   scrutinized means _____

2. "The two houses adjoining!" I exclaimed. "You must have had a great deal of trouble." "We had; but the reward offered is *prodigious*."—Edgar Allan Poe

   prodigious means _____

3. They meant to be of help, but they *hampered* us by getting in our way.

   hampered means _____

4. The vacation *rejuvenated* her. She returned looking years younger.

   rejuvenated means _____

5. If *acquitted,* the accused will walk out of the courtroom a free person.

   acquitted means _____

6. ...I have known since childhood that faced with a certain kind of simple problem I have sometimes made it so *complex* that there is no way out.—LILLIAN HELLMAN

   complex means _____

7. We were able to peel away the old wallpaper, but it left a sticky *residue.*

   residue means _____

8. Each of us carried a small cylinder of oxygen in his pack, but we used it only in emergencies and found that, while its immediate effect was *salutary,* it left us later even worse off than before.—JAMES RAMSEY ULLMAN

   salutary means _____

9. In many libraries, computer systems have *superseded* the old card catalogs.

   superseded means _____

10. I would never have had the *effrontery* to do what they did. What nerve they had!

    effrontery means _____

11. When he *withdrew* his hands from his gloves, the cold wind seemed to leap forward and grasp his unprotected fingers in an iron grip.—EDWARD A. HERRON

    withdrew means _____

12. There is great hardship in times of inflation and unemployment; they are *nettlesome* problems.

    nettlesome means _____

13. I was about to leave for the beach, *oblivious* of my appointment with the dentist, when Mom reminded me.

    oblivious means _____

14. They do some *zany* things. For example, in one scene, having lost their employer's shopping money, they try to steal a chunk of meat from the cage of a hungry lion at the zoo.

    zany means _____

15. When the neighbor mainland would be *sweltering,* day and night alike, under a breathless heat, out here on the island there was always a cool wind blowing.—SIR CHARLES G. D. ROBERTS

    sweltering means _____

16. It was an *excruciating* headache. I had to stay in bed.

    excruciating means _____

17. The package was so *unwieldy* that it was hard to get a grip on it, and I dreaded taking it on the bus.

unwieldy means _____

18. We have not complained up to now; but our *forbearance* is coming to an end.

forbearance means _____

19. I thought you would be nervous when you were unexpectedly asked to give the first talk, but you were *unruffled*.

unruffled means _____

20. It was even whispered that Whymper and the Taugwalders had deliberately cut the rope, *consigning* their companions to death to save their own skins.—JAMES RAMSEY ULLMAN

consigning means _____

Study Your New Words, **Group 4**

WORD	MEANING	TYPICAL USE
acquit (*v.*) ə-'kwit	1. relieve from an accusation; pronounce not guilty; discharge; exculpate; exonerate (*ant.* **convict**)	Two of the defendants were *convicted* of first-degree murder; the third was *acquitted*.
	2. perform one's part; conduct oneself	The G.I.'s who planted the flag at Iwo Jima *acquitted* themselves superbly.
acquittal (*n.*) ə-'kwi-tᵊl	exculpation; discharge (*ant.* **conviction**)	
complex (*adj.*) käm-'pleks	having varied interrelated parts, and therefore hard to understand; complicated; intricate (*ant.* **simple**)	Many modern appliances are *complex* electronic devices that only trained technicians can repair.
complexity (*n.*) ˌkəm-'plek-sə-tē	difficulty; intricacy (*ant.* **simplicity**)	
consign (*v.*) kən-'sīn	give, transfer, or deliver, as if by signing over; hand over; commit	After they were sentenced, the two convicts were *consigned* to prison.
consignee (*n.*) ˌkän-sə-'nē	person to whom something is shipped	
effrontery (*n.*) i-'frən-tə-rē	shameless boldness; insolence; gall; temerity; nerve; chutzpah	Though uninvited, Dale had the *effrontery* to come to the party.
excruciating (*adj.*) ik-'skrü-shē-ˌāt-iŋ	causing great pain or anguish; agonizing; unbearably painful	I had feared that the drilling of the tooth would be *excruciating*, but I barely felt any pain.

forbearance (*n.*)
fòr-'bar-əns

act of forbearing (refraining); abstaining; leniency; patience (*ant.* **anger**)

If you stepped on my foot by accident, I would show *forbearance.* But if you tripped me on purpose, I would not be able to repress my *anger.*

hamper (*v.*)
'ham-pər

interfere with; hinder; impede (*ant.* **aid**)

We tried to leave the stadium quickly, but the dense crowd *hampered* our progress.

nettlesome (*adj.*)
'ne-tᵊl-səm

literally, full of *nettles* (plants with stinging hairs); irritating; causing annoyance or vexation

How can we safely dispose of nuclear wastes? So far, no satisfactory answer has been found to this *nettlesome* question.

oblivious (*adj.*)
ə-'bli-vē-əs

(usually followed by *of*) forgetful; unmindful; not aware; unwitting

She had promised to wait, but she walked off without me, *oblivious* of her promise.

  oblivion (*n.*)
  ə-'bliv-ē-ən

condition of being forgotten or unknown; forgetfulness

A deep sleep brought the sufferer sweet *oblivion.*

prodigious (*adj.*)
prə-'di-jəs

extraordinary in amount or size; enormous; gigantic; huge; colossal (*ant.* **tiny**)

In one year, there was a *prodigious* increase in the cost of oil; prices nearly tripled.

  prodigy (*n.*)
  'prä-də-jē

person of extraordinary talent or ability; wonder

rejuvenate (*v.*)
ri-'jü-və-,nāt

make young or youthful again; give new vigor to; reinvigorate; refresh

A good night's sleep will *rejuvenate* you, and you will awaken refreshed.

residue (*n.*)
're-zə-,d(y)ü

whatever is left after a part is taken, disposed of, or gone; remainder; rest

The floodwater receded, leaving a *residue* of mud in the streets.

  residual (*adj.*)
  ri-'zi-jə-wəl

remaining after a part is used or taken

salutary (*adj.*)
'sal-yə-,ter-ē

favorable to health; healthful; curative; beneficial; salubrious (*ant.* **deleterious**)

A winter in the South had a *salutary* effect on Manny; his cough disappeared. The icy North would have been *deleterious* to his health.

scrutinize (*v.*)
'skrü-tᵊn-,īz

examine very closely; inspect; vet

After *scrutinizing* our tax returns and other financial documents, the bank approved our loan application.

  scrutiny (*n.*)
  'scrü-tᵊn-ē

examination; inspection; review

supersede (*v.*)
,sü-pər-'sēd

force out of use; displace; supplant; replace

In many businesses, paper wrapping has been *superseded* by plastic.

sweltering (*adj.*) 'swel-tər-iŋ	oppressively hot; torrid; sultry (*ant.* **frigid**)	It was a *sweltering* day; everyone was perspiring.
swelter (*v.*) 'swel-tər	suffer from oppressive heat	
unruffled (*adj.*) ən-'rə-fəld	not upset or agitated; calm; cool; unflustered; imperturbable; collected (*ant.* **discomposed**)	Most of us were *discomposed* by the new developments, but Dulce remained *unruffled*.
unwieldy (*adj.*) ən-'wēl-dē	hard to *wield* (handle) because of size or weight; unmanageable; bulky; cumbersome	Will you please help me dispose of the empty refrigerator carton? It is too *unwieldy* for one person to carry out.
unwieldiness (*n.*) ,ən-'wēl-dē-nəs	bulkiness	
withdraw (*v.*) wi<u>th</u>-'drȯ	1. take back; remove (*ant.* **deposit**)	I *deposited* a check for $87.50 and *withdrew* $50 in cash.
	2. draw back; go away; retreat; leave (*ant.* **advance**)	As the officers *advanced* toward the scene, the mob *withdrew*.
withdrawal (*n.*) wi<u>th</u>-'drȯ(-ə)l	1. taking back; removal	
	2. drawing back; retreat; departure (*ant.* **approach**)	
zany (*adj.*) 'zā-nē	having the characteristics of a clown; mildly insane; crazy; clownish; loony	Warren would squirt you with a water pistol for a laugh; he has a *zany* sense of humor.
zany (*n.*)	clown; buffoon	

Apply What You Have Learned

EXERCISE 2.19: SENTENCE COMPLETION

Which choice, A or B, makes the sentence correct? Write the *letter* of your answer in the space provided.

1. Your zany brother came to the meeting _____.

   (A) with a list of complaints   (B) in a gorilla costume

2. The treatments were salutary; the patient's condition _____.

   (A) improved   (B) worsened

3. Someone in the sweltering auditorium suggested that we turn off the _____.

   (A) air conditioning   (B) heat

4. After saying the pie you baked was not so delicious, Margo had the effrontery to _____.

    (A) apologize for her remark   (B) ask for a second helping

5. They thought that when they found _____, they would become rejuvenated.

    (A) Captain Kidd's treasure   (B) the Fountain of Youth

6. A superseded regulation _____.

    (A) is still in effect   (B) should be disregarded

7. In the imaginary country of Lilliput, where people were no more than six _____ tall, an ordinary human like Gulliver must have seemed prodigious.

    (A) inches   (B) feet

8. After his acquittal, the suspect _____.

    (A) requested a new trial   (B) thanked the jury

9. When your sister is criticized, she shows forbearance; she _____.

    (A) becomes enraged   (B) listens patiently

10. Oblivious of the sudden drop in temperature, I left the house _____.

    (A) without taking a sweater   (B) thinking it would snow

EXERCISE 2.20: CONCISE WRITING

Express the thought of each sentence below in no more than four words.

1. The instructions that you have drawn up are not easy to understand.

_____

2. Who is the person to whom the goods are to be shipped?

_____

3. What are the reasons for their being found not guilty?

_____

4. She examined very closely the application that you sent in.

_____

5. Some packages are hard to handle because they are too big or too heavy.

_____

6. The pain that he had was so agonizing that he could not bear it.

_____

7. The forces that have invaded the country must draw back.

_____

8. She has problems that are causing her a great deal of vexation.

_____

9. The part that is left is not of much importance.

_____

10. Everyone looks with contempt on the shamelessly bold manner in which they behave themselves.

_____

EXERCISE 2.21: SYNONYMS AND ANTONYMS

A. In the blank space, insert a SYNONYM from group 4 for the italicized word.

_____ 1. They remained _cool_ throughout the crisis.

_____ 2. She chose wallpaper with an _intricate_ pattern.

_____ 3. The situation is rapidly becoming _unmanageable_.

_____ 4. Would you have had the _temerity_ to open someone else's mail?

_____ 5. He ordered the most expensive dinner, _unmindful_ of the cost.

B. In the blank space, insert an ANTONYM from group 4 for the italicized word.

_____ 6. The company ended the year with a _tiny_ profit.

_____ 7. Why should the suspect have been _convicted_?

_____ 8. The suggested remedy may have _deleterious_ effects.

_____ 9. We cannot remain in this _frigid_ room.

_____ 10. The security staff _aided_ our efforts to gain admission.

EXERCISE 2.22: CLOSE READING

Carefully read the statements below and answer the questions.

STATEMENTS

When Martin asked permission to look through the files for the missing information, Muriel said, "Not now. Come back next week."

My aunt is more relaxed now that she has given up smoking, and her health has improved.

The recreation supervisor was able to find a way to stop the almost daily bitter fights we were having over the use of the tennis courts.

Though Simpson is still on the payroll, someone else has been put in charge.

Paul had been on the committee for a year, and we wanted him to stay, but he left.

When Jason's father died, Medea, an enchantress, brought him back to life and made him young again.

Humming the "Blue Danube Waltz," Tony danced around the room with a mopstick for a partner.

When the carpenter had finished, his helper swept up the sawdust and tossed it into the fireplace.

Valerie has not repaid the money she borrowed from Eva last month, but so far Eva has said nothing.

In his poem about the outlaw Jesse James, William Rose Benét wrote, "He was ten foot tall when he stood in his boots."

QUESTIONS

1. Who was superseded? _____
2. Who withdrew? _____
3. Who disposed of a residue? _____
4. Who was alleged to be of prodigious stature? _____
5. Who hampered someone? _____
6. Who resolved a nettlesome problem? _____
7. Who was rejuvenated? _____
8. Who acted zany? _____
9. Who showed forbearance? _____
10. Who made a salutary move? _____

EXERCISE 2.23: COMPOSITION

Answer in a sentence or two.

1. How much forbearance should we have with a zany driver? Explain.

_____
_____
_____

2. May we conclude that a person who seems unruffled has no nettlesome problems? Explain.

_____
_____
_____

3. Is it salutary to sunbathe for hours under a sweltering sun? Why, or why not?

_____

_____

_____

4. Should an official who hampers an investigation be superseded? Explain.

_____

_____

_____

5. Would you be joking or serious if you said that a friend who is oblivious of faces, names, and appointments has a prodigious memory? Why?

_____

_____

_____

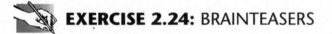 **EXERCISE 2.24:** BRAINTEASERS

Fill in the missing letters.

1. Greasy foods leave a(n) __ __ __ __ **d u a l** film on dishes and silverware.

2. While we are sweltering here, people are shivering in __ **r i g** __ __ temperatures up north.

3. There is still plenty of life left in the old car. It is much too early to __ __ __ **s i g n** it to the scrap heap.

4. We cannot get Olly to stop clowning. He enjoys making a **b u f f** __ __ __ of himself.

5. Our national debt has reached __ __ __ **d i g** __ __ __ __ proportions, and it is still soaring.

6. Because of flaws in the evidence against the defendants, the jury __ __ __ __ __ **p a t** __ __ them.

7. After spurning our offers of assistance, the members of the committee had the __ __ **m e r i t** __ to say that we had never offered to help them.

8. Some of the concepts in advanced physics may be hard to understand at first because of their __ __ __ __ __ **e x i t** __.

9. One way to find a lost needle in a pile rug is to __ __ **r u t** __ __ __ __ __ the area where it was dropped.

10. Her brother was **d i s c o** __ __ __ __ __ __. Obviously, something had upset him.

EXERCISE 2.25: SIMILAR AND CONTRARY

Fill in the missing letters so that each line contains three words or phrases with similar meanings and one with a contrary meaning.

Similar Meaning	Similar Meaning	Similar Meaning	Contrary Meaning
Sample: f _o_ rmer	pr _e_ _v_ ious	pre _c_ _e_ _d_ ing	l _a_ _t_ ter
1. amelior __ te	b __ __ ter	im __ __ __ ve	wor __ __ n
2. uninj __ red	wh __ __ e	in __ __ ct	imper __ __ ct
3. lethar __ ic	ind __ __ __ nt	__ __ le	ac __ __ ve
4. invali __ ate	ab __ __ ish	an __ __ l	__ __ __ idate
5. pars __ __ ony	st __ __ __ iness	cheap __ __ ss	gen __ __ osity
6. demo __ ish	dest __ __ __	r __ __ e	er __ __ t
7. uncommunic __ __ ive	sec __ __ __ ive	re __ __ cent	fr __ __ __ __
8. under __ ine	sub __ __ __ __ t	sa __ __ tage	s __ __ port
9. cont __ __ llable	yi __ __ __ ing	do __ __ le	intrac __ __ ble
10. tr __ __ quillity	har __ __ ny	ag __ __ ement	conf __ __ __ __ t
11. b __ __ fle	bew __ __ __ __ er	conf __ __ __	clari __ __
12. con __ emptible	desp __ __ able	loath __ __ me	ad __ __ rable
13. ex __ berance	eb __ __ __ ience	ent __ __ siasm	ind __ __ __ __ nce
14. par __ __ cular	fin __ __ ky	__ ussy	__ __ s __ to please
15. b __ __ dness	g __ ll	ner __ __	me __ kness
16. p __ __ ntless	in __ __ e	in __ __ __ id	sign __ __ icant
17. str __ ggle	sc __ __ __ le	br __ __ l	c __ __ perate
18. d __ __ dain	rej __ __ t	sp __ __ __	ac __ __ pt
19. unenth __ siastic	tep __ __	luke __ __ rm	eb __ __ lient
20. dw __ __ dle	d __ __ line	w __ __ e	__ row
21. sn __ b	re __ __ __ f	sl __ __ __ t	res __ __ __ t
22. ab __ __ r	l __ __ __ he	h __ __ e	ad __ __ __ e
23. unw __ __ ting	un __ __ owing	acc __ dental	on pur __ __ s __

24. admo __ ish   __ __ ution   re__ __ __ __ e   com __ __ __ d
25. ep __ __ __ eral   __ __ eet __ __ g   trans __ tory   __ __ __ manent
26. lap __ __   fa __ __ t   __ __ __ or   __ __ provement
27. __ __ ll   che __ __   dece __ __ __   undece __ __ e
28. gull __ __ le   __ __ __ dulous   f __ __ __ ish   as __ __ __ __ __
29. im __ __ __ se   d __ __   d __ __ k   take o __ __
30. __ __ __ gle   bar __ __ __ __ __   wr __ __ gle   ag __ __ __
31. exc __ lpate   ac __ __ __ __   d __ __ charge   con __ __ __ t
32. compl __ cated   compl __ __   __ __ tricate   s __ __ __ le
33. forbear __ __ ce   leni __ __ cy   __ __ __ ience   an __ __ r
34. int __ __ fere with   h __ __ der   im __ __ __ e   a __ __
35. prod __ __ ious   en __ __ mous   gig __ __ __ ic   t __ __ y
36. benef __ __ ial   sa __ __ __ ary   cur __ __ ive   dele __ __ rious
37. ex __ mine closely   scru __ __ __ ize   ins __ __ __ t   __ __ nore
38. oppress __ vely hot   s __ __ __ tering   t __ __ rid   f __ __ __ id
39. discom __ __ sed   fl __ stered   ruff __ __ __   c __ __ m
40. c __ __ bersome   unwi __ __ __ y   b __ __ ky   __ __ __ ageable

EXERCISE 2.26: SENTENCE COMPLETION

Write the letter of the word or words that best complete the sentence(s).

___ 1. How soon favors are forgotten! How quickly gratitude _____.

A. wanes

B. is replenished

C. is indemnified

D. is abhorred

___ 2. As Archimedes' principle says, a 50 pound force will lift a 200 pound treasure chest, if the _____ chest is resting on the ocean floor and is displacing 150 pounds of water.

A. immersed

B. valuable

C. abandoned

D. bulky

___ **3.** The undercover detective posed as an easy mark, a(n) _____ tourist for some _____ to peddle the Brooklyn Bridge to.

    A. gullible . . con artist

    B. reticent . . fast talker

    C. astute . . guide

    D. impressionable . . good samaritan

___ **4.** Falstaff, a prodigiously brazen coward, was not a bit _____ when his boasts about his heroics were exposed as lies. What _____!

    A. despised . . nerve

    B. unruffled . . gall

    C. unflustered . . effrontery

    D. discomposed . . temerity

___ **5.** Feeding data and programs into the mainframe computer of the 1960s meant inputting a stack of punched cards (and woe to the user if even one card was out of sequence!), a(n) _____ procedure that has been _____ by such devices as the ubiquitous keyboard.

    A. unwieldy . . followed

    B. intricate . . replaced

    C. cumbersome . . superseded

    D. manageable . . supplanted

EXERCISE 2.27: MATCHMAKING

Write the letter of the word or words best matching the italicized expression(s).

___ **1.** Edgar Allan Poe's Fortunato *affronts* Montresor, who exacts revenge, *immuring* Fortunato behind a wall of stone and mortar.

    A. gulls . . placing

    B. insults . . confining

    C. impedes . . withdrawing

    D. confronts . . replenishing

___ **2.** The inhumanity of the Nazi air attack—machine guns strafing away, bombs *blowing up*—on the defenseless Spanish citizens of Guernica is *portrayed* in Pablo Picasso's painting named after that city.

    A. imploding . . probed

    B. detonating . . rendered

    C. subverting . . despised

    D. retorting . . detrimental

___ **3.** As a burning sun rose in the skies over Krina, so did the *merciless* temperature and the ferocity of the battle, till at last Sundiata forced the *flight* of Soumaoro's army.

    A. sweltering . . withdrawal

    B. unseasonable . . retreat

    C. abnormal . . march

    D. oppressive . . advance

___ **4.** Sancho Panza quit his governorship because its cares were *too staggering a burden* for his shoulders and *too prickly* to give a moment's peace of mind.

    A. troublesome . . irksome

    B. unwieldy . . prodigious

    C. vexatious . . burdensome

    D. cumbersome . . nettlesome

___ **5.** Sancho had, however, nobly *acted so as to bring credit on* himself in executing his duties, despite his deputies' deliberate, repeated efforts to *strew obstacles in the way of* his success.

    A. comported . . undertake

    B. aggrandized . . hinder

    C. acquitted . . impede

    D. exculpated . . hamper

Chapter 3

Building Vocabulary Through Central Ideas

One way to expand your vocabulary is to study words related to a central idea. For example, you can learn **bliss**, **delectable**, **ecstasy**, **elation**, and **jubilation** as "joy" words, and **chagrin**, **compunction**, **dejected**, **disconsolate**, and **lamentable** as "sorrow" words. Grouping lesson words in this way may make vocabulary study easier and more interesting.

Here are a few suggestions for getting the most out of this chapter.

1. Pay careful attention to each illustrative sentence. Then construct, at least in your mind, a similar sentence of your own.

2. Do the drill exercises thoughtfully, not mechanically. Review the words you miss.

3. Deliberately use your new vocabulary as soon as possible in appropriate situations—in chats with friends, class discussions, letters, and compositions. Only by exercising new words will you succeed in making them part of your active vocabulary. (For the meaning of the pronunciation symbols, see the list on the inside back cover.)

1. Joy, Pleasure

WORD	MEANING	TYPICAL USE
bliss (*n.*) 'blis	perfect happiness	The young movie star could conceive of no greater *bliss* than winning an Oscar.
blissful (*adj.*) 'blis-fəl	very happy	The soldiers' reunion with their families was a *blissful* occasion.

blithe (*adj.*)
ˈblīth

1. merry; joyous

Our friends' *blithe* looks signaled that the final had been easy.

2. heedless

He was so enraptured with the scenery that he drove right through the intersection in *blithe* disregard of the Stop sign.

buoy (*v.*)
bȯi

keep afloat; raise the spirits of; encourage

Your encouragement *buoyed* us and gave us hope.

buoyant (*adj.*)
ˈbȯi-ənt

1. cheerful

We need your *buoyant* companionship to lift us from boredom.

2. able to float

The raft is sinking; it is not *buoyant*.

complacency (*n.*)
kəm-ˈplā-sᵊn-sē

self-satisfaction; smugness

Don't be too pleased with yourself; *complacency* is dangerous.

complacent (*adj.*)
kəm-ˈplā-sᵊnt

too pleased with oneself—often without awareness of possible dangers or defects; self-satisfied; smug

We should not be *complacent* about our security; we must be alert to potential threats.

convivial (*adj.*)
kən-ˈviv-ē-əl

fond of eating and drinking with friends; sociable

Our *convivial* host hates to dine alone.

conviviality (*n.*)
ˌkən-ˌviv-ē-ˈal-ə-tē

sociability

We enjoy the *conviviality* of holiday get-togethers.

delectable (*adj.*)
di-ˈlek-tə-bəl

very pleasing; delightful

The food was *delectable*; we enjoyed every morsel.

ecstasy (*n.*)
ˈek-stə-sē

state of overwhelming joy; rapture

If we win tomorrow, there will be *ecstasy*; if we lose, gloom.

ecstatic (*adj.*)
ek-ˈsta-tik

in ecstasy; enraptured

The victors were *ecstatic*.

elated (*adj.*)
i-ˈlāt-əd

in high spirits; joyful

Except for my sister, who misses the old neighborhood, the family is *elated* with our new living quarters.

elation (*n.*)
i-ˈlā-shən

state of being elated; euphoria

Unfortunately, our *elation* was shortlived.

frolic (*v.*)
ˈfrä-lik

play and run about happily; have fun; romp

Very young children need a safe place to *frolic*.

frolicsome (*adj.*)
ˈfrä-lik-səm

full of merriment; playful

The clown's *frolicsome* antics amused the children.

gala (*adj.*) 'gā-lə	characterized by festivity	The annual Mardi Gras in New Orleans is a *gala* carnival of parades and merriment.
jocund (*adj.*) 'jä-kənd	merry; cheerful; lighthearted	Our neighbor is a *jocund* fellow who tells amusing anecdotes.
jubilant (*adj.*) 'jü-bə-lənt	showing great joy; rejoicing; exultant	The defendant's friends are *jubilant* over her acquittal.
jubilation (*n.*) ,jü-bə-'lā-shən	rejoicing; exultation	On election night, *jubilation reigned* at the victor's headquarters.

2. Sadness

ascetic (*adj.*) ə-'se-tik	shunning pleasures; self-denying; austere	The *ascetic* Puritans rigidly suppressed many forms of recreation.
ascetic (*n.*)	person who shuns pleasures and lives simply	Carl never goes to the movies, plays, or parties. He must be an *ascetic*.
chagrin (*n.*) shə-'grin	embarrassment; mortification; disappointment	Imagine my *chagrin* when I learned that I had not been invited to the party!
chagrined (*adj.*) shə-'grind	ashamed; mortified	When my blunder was pointed out to me, I was deeply *chagrined*.
compunction (*n.*) kəm-'pəŋ(k)-shən	regret; remorse; misgiving; qualm; scruple	We had no *compunction* about turning in the old car because it had become undependable.
contrite (*adj.*) kən-'trīt	showing deep regret and sorrow for wrongdoing; deeply penitent; repentant; remorseful	Believing the young offender to be *contrite,* the dean decided to give him another chance.
contrition (*n.*) kən-'trish-ən	repentance; remorse; penitence	The ringleader showed no *contrition,* but his accomplices have expressed sorrow for their misdeeds.
dejected (*adj.*) di-'jek-təd	sad; in low spirits; depressed; downcast	We are elated when our team wins, but *dejected* when it loses.
dejection (*n.*) di-'jek-shən	lowness of spirits; sadness; depression	Cheer up. There is no reason for *dejection*.
disconsolate (*adj.*) dis-'kän-sə-lət	cheerless; inconsolable	The mother could not stop her *disconsolate* son from sobbing over the loss of his dog.

disgruntled (*adj.*)
dis-'grən-t°ld

in bad humor; displeased; discontented

From her *disgruntled* expression, I could tell she was not satisfied with my explanation.

doleful (*adj.*)
'dōl-fəl

causing grief or sadness; mournful; dolorous; lugubrious

The refugee told a *doleful* tale of hunger and persecution.

glum (*adj.*)
'gləm

moody; gloomy; dour

Emerging from the strike talks, the Mayor was *glum* and refused to talk to reporters.

lament (*v.*)
lə-'ment

mourn; deplore

We *lament* the loss of life, and we sympathize with the victims' families.

lamentable (*adj.*)
'la-mən-tə-bəl

pitiable; rueful

The reporter described the *lamentable* hardships of families living in war-torn Afghanistan.

maudlin (*adj.*)
'mȯd-lən

weakly sentimental and tearful

After singing a couple of *maudlin* numbers, the quartet was asked for something more cheerful.

nostalgia (*n.*)
nä-'stal-jə

1. homesickness

Toward the end of a vacation away from home, we usually experience a feeling of *nostalgia.*

2. yearning for the past

In moments of *nostalgia,* I long for the good old days.

nostalgic (*adj.*)
nä-'stal-jik

homesick

When away from home for too long, we tend to become *nostalgic.*

pathetic (*adj.*)
pə-'the-tik

arousing pity

Despite his *pathetic* condition, the released hostage had a ready smile.

pathos (*n.*)
'pā-thäs

quality in events or in art (literature, music, etc.) that arouses our pity

The young seamstress who precedes Sydney Carton to the guillotine adds to the *pathos* of A TALE OF TWO CITIES.

pensive (*adj.*)
'pen-siv

thoughtful in a sad way; melancholy

Unlike her cheerful, outgoing sister, Elizabeth was *pensive* and shy.

plight (*n.*)
'plīt

unfortunate state; predicament

Numerous offers of assistance were received after the *plight* of the distressed family was publicized.

poignant (*adj.*)
'pȯi-nyənt

painfully touching; piercing

One of the most *poignant* scenes in MACBETH occurs when Macduff learns that his wife and children have been slaughtered.

sullen (*adj.*) 'sə-lən	resentfully silent; glum; morose; gloomy	The *sullen* suspect refused to give his name and address.
throes (*n. pl.*) 'thrōz	anguish; pangs	Fortunate are those who have never experienced the *throes* of separation from a loved one.
tribulation (*n.*) ,tri-byə-'lā-shən	suffering; distress	The 1845 potato famine was a time of great *tribulation* in Ireland.

3. Stoutness

burly (*adj.*) 'bər-lē	strongly and heavily built; husky (*ant.* **lank**)	Extra-large football uniforms were ordered to outfit our *burly* linemen.
buxom (*adj.*) 'bək-səm	plump and attractive	Next to her thin city cousin, the farm girl looked radiant and *buxom*.
cherubic (*adj.*) chə-'rü-bik	chubby and innocent-looking; like a *cherub* (angel in the form of a child)	Your well-nourished nephew, despite his *cherubic* face, can be quite mischievous.
obese (*adj.*) ō-'bēs	extremely overweight; corpulent; portly (*ant.* **skinny**)	For a long, healthy life, one should give up smoking and avoid becoming *obese*.
obesity (*n.*) o-'bē-sə-tē	excessive body weight; corpulence	Dieting under professional guidance may help reduce *obesity*.
pudgy (*adj.*) 'pə-jē	short and plump; chubby	This ring is too small for a *pudgy* finger.

4. Thinness

attenuate (*v.*) ə-'ten-yə-,wāt	make thin; weaken	Photographs of President Lincoln reveal how rapidly the cares of leadership aged and *attenuated* him.
emaciated (*adj.*) i-'mā-shē-,āt-əd	made unnaturally thin; abnormally lean because of starvation or illness (*ant.* **fleshy**)	*Emaciated* by his illness, the patient found, on his recovery, that his clothes were too big.
haggard (*adj.*) 'ha-gərd	careworn; gaunt	*Haggard* from their long ordeal, the rescued mountain climbers were rushed to the hospital for treatment and rest.

| **lank** (*adj.*)
ˈlaŋk | lean; ungracefully tall; lanky
(*ant.* **burly**) | Every basketball team longs for a *lank*, agile center who can control the boards. |
| **svelte** (*adj.*)
ˈsvelt | slender; lithe | Ballet dancers observe a strict diet to maintain their *svelte* figures. |

5. Flattery

adulation (*n.*) ˌa-jə-ˈlā-shən	excessive praise; flattery	True leaders can distinguish sincere praise from blind *adulation*.
blandishment (*n.*) ˈblan-dish-mənt	word or deed of mild flattery; allurement; enticement	With terms of endearment, flowers, and other *blandishments*, Brian won Aliya over to his side.
cajole (*v.*) kə-ˈjōl	persuade by pleasant words; wheedle; coax	My sister *cajoled* Dad into raising her allowance.
cajolery (*n.*) kə-ˈjō-lə-rē	persuasion by flattery; wheedling; coaxing	The sly fox used *cajolery* to gain his ends.
curry (*v.*) **favor** (*n.*) ˈkər-ē ˈfā-və(r)	seek to gain favor by flattery	The candidate *curried favor* with the voters by praising their intelligence and patriotism.
fulsome (*adj.*) ˈfu̇l-səm	offensive because of insincerity; repulsive; disgusting	The new chief basks in the *fulsome* praises of his deputy, who raves over his every decision, right or wrong.
ingratiate (*v.*) in-ˈgrā-shē-ˌāt	work (oneself) into favor	By trying to respond to every question, the new pupil tried to *ingratiate* herself with the teacher.
lackey (*n.*) ˈla-kē	follower who carries out another's wishes like a servant; toady	The queen could never get a frank opinion from the *lackeys* surrounding her, for they would always agree with her.
obsequious (*adj.*) əb-ˈsē-kwē-əs	showing excessive willingness to serve; subservient; fawning	The *obsequious* subordinates vied with one another in politeness and obedience, each hoping to win the director's favor.
sycophant (*n.*) ˈsi-kə-fənt	parasitic flatterer; truckler	*Many sycophants* live off celebrities who enjoy flattery.
truckle (*v.*) ˈtrə-kəl	submit in a subservient manner to a superior; fawn; make a doormat of oneself	Some employees, unfortunately, gain promotion by *truckling* to their supervisors.

Apply What You Have Learned

EXERCISE 3.1: SYNONYMS

In the space before each word or expression in column I, write the *letter* of its correct synonym from column II.

COLUMN I	COLUMN II
___ 1. delightful	(A) predicament
___ 2. arousing pity	(B) attenuated
___ 3. plight	(C) nostalgia
___ 4. mild flattery	(D) haggard
___ 5. careworn	(E) delectable
___ 6. self-denying	(F) bliss
___ 7. perfect happiness	(G) lackey
___ 8. weakened	(H) blandishment
___ 9. subservient follower	(I) pathetic
___ 10. homesickness	(J) ascetic

EXERCISE 3.2: UNRELATED WORDS

Write the *letter* of the word unrelated in meaning to the other words on the line.

___ 1.	(A) ecstatic	(B) jubilant	(C) rapturous	(D) pensive
___ 2.	(A) svelte	(B) slender	(C) slippery	(D) lithe
___ 3.	(A) comedian	(B) lackey	(C) flatterer	(D) sycophant
___ 4.	(A) tribulation	(B) insincerity	(C) suffering	(D) pangs
___ 5.	(A) cajolery	(B) gloominess	(C) dejection	(D) melancholy
___ 6.	(A) elation	(B) frolicsomeness	(C) euphoria	(D) adulation
___ 7.	(A) wheedle	(B) attenuate	(C) ingratiate	(D) fawn
___ 8.	(A) pathos	(B) pity	(C) complacency	(D) compassion
___ 9.	(A) portly	(B) burly	(C) buxom	(D) contrite
___ 10.	(A) jovial	(B) jocund	(C) blithe	(D) disconsolate

EXERCISE 3.3: CONCISE WRITING

Express the thought of each sentence below in no more than four words. The first sentence has been rewritten as a sample.

1. What is the reason for your being in bad humor?

    Why are you disgruntled?

2. I was deeply regretful and full of sorrow for what I had done.

    _____

3. We look down on praise that is offered without sincerity.

    _____

4. Mom excels in the art of using pleasant words to persuade others.

    _____

5. They are altogether too willing to serve and obey their superiors.

    _____

6. The one who does the carpentry work is strongly and sturdily built.

    _____

7. Those who survived were little more than skin and bones.

    _____

8. The encouragement that we received from you brought our spirits up high.

    _____

9. A large number refused to take notice of the unfortunate situation that they saw we were in.

    _____

10. It is dangerous to be in a state of mind in which one is too satisfied with oneself.

    _____

EXERCISE 3.4: BRAINTEASERS

Fill in the missing letters.

1. The workers are __ __ __ __ __ __ **t e n t** __ __ because they did not get a raise.

2. No one smiled. It was a(n) __ __ __ __ __ __ **h o l y** occasion.

3. Whenever they try to __ __ __ **r a t** __ __ __ __ themselves with us, we suspect they are looking for a favor.

4. I was __ __ __ **g r i n** __ __ , when I went to pay for my lunch, to find that I had left my money at home.

5. We have no __ __ __ **p u n** __ __ __ __ __ about not waiting for Sally because she has never waited for us.

6. The stolen car was in such **l a m e** __ __ __ __ __ __ condition when it was recovered that its owner was moved to tears.

7. Anyone who enjoys adulation is an easy prey for __ __ __ __ __ __ **a n t s**.

8. Don't expect them to cater to your wishes like servants. They are not your __ __ __ **k e y s**.

9. This shop specializes in clothes for the tall and the __ **o r** __ __ __.

10. It is unwise to adopt a(n) __ __ __ __ **t i c** lifestyle of "all work and no play."

EXERCISE 3.5: SENTENCE COMPLETION

Fill each blank with the most appropriate word from the vocabulary list below.

VOCABULARY LIST

poignant	cajole	tribulation
buxom	burly	emaciated
throes	pathos	gala
fulsome	jubilation	elated
obesity	remorse	glum

1. The _____ movers lifted the piano with surprising ease.

2. After the game, there was wild _____ as supporters rushed onto the field to congratulate their heroes.

3. Announcing the disappointing news, the President looked _____.

4. To a young child, a birthday is certainly a(n) _____ occasion.

5. Newspapers reported the _____ details of the futile rescue attempt.

6. The new supervisor was repelled by the _____ compliments of some of her subordinates.

7. When Mr. Norwood was stopped for a traffic violation, he tried to _____ the officer into not writing a ticket.

8. The _____ appearance of the liberated prisoners shocked the world.

9. At the trial, one of the suspects wept repeatedly; the other showed no _____.

10. Many people watch their diets and exercise regularly to avoid _____.

EXERCISE 3.6: COMPOSITION

Answer in a sentence or two.

1. Who is more likely to do well in a marathon, a lank runner or a burly one? Why?

_____

_____

_____

_____

2. Give an example of something that can be done to buoy the spirits of a dejected friend.

_____

_____

_____

_____

3. Name two delectable foods that may have to be given up for a svelte waistline, and suggest substitutes for those foods.

_____

_____

_____

_____

4. If you accidentally hurt someone, would you be complacent or contrite? Explain.

_____

_____

_____

_____

5. Would you enjoy working for a company where some of the employees are obsequious and truckle to the boss? Explain.

_____

_____

_____

_____

 **EXERCISE 3.7:** ANALOGIES

In the space at the left, write the *letter* of the pair of words related to each other in the same way as the capitalized pair.

SAMPLE

_d_   ECSTASY : JOY

   a. thrift : wealth   *d.* terror : fear
   b. certainty : doubt   *e.* frigid : cold
   c. fondness : adoration

SOLUTION

The first step is to find the relationship in the capitalized pair. As you have learned, ECSTASY is a state of overwhelming JOY. If you designate ECSTASY by the letter X, and JOY by the letter Y, you can express the ECSTASY : JOY relationship by saying, "X is a state of overwhelming Y."

The second step is to check if this relationship holds in pairs *a, b, c, d,* or *e.* Here's how you might check each choice.

a. thrift : wealth
Thrift is a means by which one may acquire *wealth. Thrift* is NOT a state of overwhelming *wealth.*

b. certainty : doubt
Certainty is the opposite of *doubt.* It is definitely NOT a state of overwhelming *doubt.*

c. fondness : adoration
Fondness is a much milder expression of liking than *adoration.* Note that the trouble with this pair is the order. If it were reversed (adoration : fondness), this pair would be a correct answer because *adoration* is a state of overwhelming *fondness.*

d. terror : fear
Terror is a state of overwhelming *fear.* This choice looks very good; even so, check the final pair.

e. frigid : cold
Frigid is overwhelmingly *cold.* The relationship is correct, making both *d* and *e* "finalists."

So, here, a third step is needed: find a way in which one "finalist" better mirrors the original, capitalized pair. Thus, in the original pair, note that ECSTASY and JOY are nouns. But in *e, frigid* and *cold* are adjectives. On the other hand, *terror* and *fear* in *d* are both nouns. This, plus the fact that *terror* is a state of overwhelming *fear,* makes *d* the correct choice.

    __ **1.** NOSTALGIA : PAST

         a. regret : deed   *d.* absence : presence

         b. yearning : eternity   *e.* memory : forgetfulness

         c. anticipation : future

    __ **2.** SYCOPHANT : SINCERITY

         a. thief : cleverness   *d.* friend : loyalty

         b. deceiver : truth   *e.* hero : courage

         c. coward : fear

    __ **3.** ASCETIC : PLEASURE

         a. politician : votes   *d.* root : water

         b. plant : light   *e.* hermit : society

         c. scientist : truth

    __ **4.** FOOD : OBESITY

         a. slip : fall   *d.* rainfall : flood

         b. spark : explosion   *e.* landslide : earthquake

         c. fatigue : work

    __ **5.** DISCONSOLATE : CHEER

         a. intrepid : fear   *d.* frolicsome : merriment

         b. compassionate : sympathy   *e.* plaintive : sorrow

         c. repentant : regret

GOING OVER THE ANSWERS

    Since this is the first exercise in analogies, check your answers with the following, paying careful attention to the reasoning involved.

RELATIONSHIP OF X AND Y	ANSWER AND EXPLANATION
1. *Nostalgia* is a yearning for the *past*.	*c.* *Anticipation* is a yearning for the *future*.
2. A *sycophant* makes a pretense of *sincerity*.	*b.* A *deceiver* makes a pretense of *truth*.
3. An *ascetic* shuns *pleasure*.	*e.* A *hermit* shuns *society*.
4. *Food* in excess may cause *obesity*.	*d.* *Rainfall* in excess may cause a *flood*.
5. A *disconsolate* person is without *cheer*.	*a.* An *intrepid* person is without *fear*.

6. Animal

WORD	MEANING	TYPICAL USE
apiary (*n.*) 'ā-pē-,er-ē	place where bees are kept	A beekeeper maintains an *apiary*.
aviary (*n.*) 'ā-vē-,er-ē	place where birds are kept	Don't miss the birds-of-prey exhibit in the zoo's *aviary*.
badger (*v.*) 'ba-jər	tease; annoy; nag (originally to harass a trapped badger)	*Badgered* by the children's persistent pleas, their parents finally relented and allowed them to go to the movies.
halcyon (*adj.*) 'hal-sē-ən	calm; peaceful (from *halcyon,* a bird thought to calm the waves)	Most adults nostalgically recall the *halcyon* days of their youth.
lionize (*v.*) 'lī-ə-,nīz	treat as highly important	With the first publication of his poems, Robert Burns gained immediate fame and was *lionized* by Edinburgh society.
menagerie (*n.*) mə-'naj-ə-rē	place where animals are kept and trained; collection of wild animals	P. T. Barnum called his traveling circus, museum, and *menagerie* "the greatest show on earth."
molt (*v.*) 'mōlt	shed feathers, skin, hair, etc.	Birds, mammals, and snakes *molt* periodically.
ornithology (*n.*) ,ȯr-nə-'thä-lə-jē	study of birds	John Burroughs' writings on birds inspired Aja's interest in *ornithology*.
parasite (*n.*) 'par-ə-,sīt	animal, plant, or person living on others; freeloader	Shunning employment, he preferred to live as a *parasite* on his sister.
parasitic (*adj.*) ,par-ə-'si-tik	living at the expense of another; sponging	Fleas are *parasitic* insects.
parrot (*v.*) 'par-ət	repeat mechanically, like a parrot (tropical bird that imitates human speech)	Does he really understand what he is saying, or is he merely *parroting* his teacher?
scavenger (*n.*) 'ska-vən-jər	animal or person removing refuse, decay, etc.	Sea gulls are useful harbor *scavengers,* since they feed on garbage.

7. Health, Medicine

antidote (*n.*) 'an-ti-,dōt	remedy for a poison or evil	A bottle containing poison must have the *antidote* specified on the label.
astringent (*n.*) ə-'strin-jənt	substance that shrinks tissues and checks flow of blood	This after-shave lotion acts as an *astringent* by helping to check the bleeding of nicks and scrapes.
astringent (*adj.*)	1. severe; stern 2. causing contraction	Instead of mild criticism, I got an *astringent* rebuke.
benign (*adj.*) bi-'nīn	1. not dangerous (*ant.* **malignant**) 2. gentle; kindly	The patient was relieved to learn that his tumor was *benign,* not *malignant.* The principal's *benign* smile reassured us.
convalesce (*v.*) ,kän-və-'les	recover health after illness; recuperate	After the appendectomy you will have to *convalesce* for about a week before returning to school.
convalescent (*n.*) ,kän-və-'le-sᵊnt	person recovering from sickness	A *convalescent* should not be taxed with chores.
fester (*v.*) 'fes-tər	form pus; rankle; rot; putrefy	When a wound *festers,* it becomes inflamed, swollen, and painful.
hypochondriac (*n.*) ,hī-pə-'kän-drē-,ak	one who is morbidly anxious about personal health, or suffering from imagined illness	The *hypochondriac* often interprets a normal condition as a symptom of serious illness.
immunity (*n.*) i-'myü-nə-tē	1. resistance (to a disease) 2. freedom (as from an obligation); exemption	Most people acquire life-long *immunity* to German measles once they have had that disease. Federal properties within the city limits enjoy *immunity* from taxation.
immunize (*v.*) 'i-myə-,nīz	make *immune* (e.g., resistant to a disease)	Infants receive a series of injections to *immunize* them against serious childhood diseases.
lesion (*n.*) 'lē-zhən	injury; hurt	The slightest *lesion* on a tree's bark, if left untended, may kill the tree.

malignant (*adj.*)
mə-'lig-nənt

1. threatening to cause death (*ant.* **benign**)

An emergency operation was scheduled to remove the *malignant* growth.

2. very evil

Ray's parents considered their son's new friend a *malignant* influence, someone sure to get Ray into serious trouble.

morbid (*adj.*)
'mȯr-bəd

1. gruesome

In describing his accident, he discreetly omitted the *morbid* details.

2. having to do with disease

One sign of Lady Macbeth's *morbid* condition is that hallucinations and fantasies trouble her.

pestilential (*adj.*)
,pes-tə-'lent-shəl

1. morally harmful

Parents, teachers, and spiritual leaders have attacked certain TV programs as *pestilential*.

2. pertaining to a *pestilence* (plague); deadly

The flu is a *pestilential* disease.

regimen (*n.*)
're-jə-mən

set of rules, esp. to improve health

After the operation, I followed the *regimen* of diet and exercise drawn up by my physician.

salubrious (*adj.*)
sə-'lü-brē-əs

healthful

Southern Florida's *salubrious* climate attracts many convalescents.

sebaceous (*adj.*)
si-'bā-shəs

greasy; secreting *sebum* (fatty matter secreted by the glands of the skin)

The *sebaceous* glands in the skin secrete an oily substance essential for skin health.

therapeutic (*adj.*)
,ther-ə-'pyü-tik

curative

The "get-well" cards have been *therapeutic* for the hospitalized patient.

toxic (*adj.*)
'täk-sik

poisonous

Idling a car in a closed garage may cause death, as the exhaust fumes are dangerously *toxic*.

unguent (*n.*)
'əŋ-gwənt

salve; ointment

Flora's skin irritation was relieved after she applied the *unguent* prescribed by her dermatologist.

viral (*adj.*)
'vī-rəl

caused by a *virus*

The flu is a *viral* disease.

virulent (*adj.*)
'vir-(y)ə-lənt

1. extremely poisonous; deadly; venomous

Some insecticides and weed killers contain arsenic, a *virulent* substance.

2. very bitter

The rebels show a *virulent* antagonism to the present ruler.

virus (*n.*) 'vī-rəs	1. disease-causing substance too small to be seen through a microscope	Diseases like AIDS, rabies, smallpox, and polio are caused by *viruses*.
	2. corruptive force	What further measures are needed to combat the *virus* of prejudice?

8. Praise

acclaim (*v.*) ə-'klām	welcome with approval; applaud loudly	I did not enjoy that novel although many leading reviewers *acclaimed* it.
encomium (*n.*) en-'kō-mē-əm	speech or writing of high praise; tribute; eulogy; panegyric	Lincoln's "Gettysburg Address" is, in part, an *encomium* of those who fought at the Battle of Gettysburg.
eulogize (*v.*) 'yü-lə-,jīz	praise; extol; laud; glorify (*ant.* **vilify**)	The late composer was *eulogized* for his contributions to American music.
kudos (*n.*) 'kü-,däs	fame or praise due to achievement	David Russell won *kudos* early in his career for his guitar virtuosity.
laudable (*adj.*) 'lȯ-də-bəl	praiseworthy; commendable	Although the track star did not succeed in breaking the world's record, she did make a *laudable* attempt.
laudatory (*adj.*) 'lȯ-də-,tȯr-ē	expressing praise; eulogistic	Six reviews of the new film were *laudatory*, one was tepid, and one negative.
plaudit (*n.*) 'plȯ-dət	(used mainly in the plural) applause; enthusiastic praise; acclaim	Reappearing, the quartet rewarded their admirers' *plaudits* with an encore.

9. Defamation

calumnious (*adj.*) kə-'ləm-nē-əs	falsely and maliciously accusing; defamatory; slanderous	Witnesses who heard the *calumnious* attack offered to testify in behalf of the slandered person.
derogatory (*adj.*) di-'rä-gə-,tȯr-ē	expressing low esteem; belittling; disparaging (*ant.* **complimentary**)	Despite *derogatory* comments by some critics, the film is a box office hit.

imputation (*n.*) ,im-pyə-'tā-shən	charge, esp. an unjust or false charge; insinuation; accusation	My rival has tried to besmirch my character with the cowardly *imputation* that I am untrustworthy.
libel (*n.*) 'lī-bəl	false and defamatory printed (or written) statement	We shall sue the newspaper that printed this *libel* against our company.
libelous (*adj.*) 'lī-bə-ləs	injurious to reputation; defamatory; calumnious	
malign (*v.*) mə-'līn	speak evil of; vilify; traduce	I cannot bear to hear you *malign* so good a man.
slander (*n.*) 'slan-dər	false and defamatory spoken statement; calumny	The rumor that she was fired is a foul *slander*; the fact is, she resigned.
stigma (*n.*) 'stig-mə	mark of disgrace	The *stigma* of a prison record hampered the ex-convict's search for a job.
stigmatize (*v.*) 'stig-mə-,tīz	brand with a mark of disgrace	Surely no one would enjoy being *stigmatized* by a nickname like "Dopey."

10. Jest

banter (*n.*) 'ban-tər	playful teasing; joking; raillery	The retiring employees were subjected to gentle *banter* about their coming life of ease.
caricature (*n.*) 'kar-i-kə-,chủr	drawing, imitation, or description that ridiculously exaggerates peculiarities or defects	The Class Night skit that drew the loudest plaudits was a *caricature* of the first day in high school.
droll (*adj.*) 'drōl	odd and laughter-provoking	"On Eating Crackers in Bed" is surely a *droll* title for an essay.
facetious (*adj.*) fə-'sē-shəs	1. in the habit of joking	Our *facetious* coach likes turning almost every comment into a joke.
	2. said in jest without serious intent	When you are carrying a heavily loaded lunch tray, some joker may try to upset you with a *facetious* remark, like "Hey, do you have a pen?"

flippant (*adj.*)
'fli-pənt

treating serious matters lightly

One should not be so *flippant* about the need for studying; it is a serious matter that may affect your graduation.

harlequin (*n.*)
'här-li-k(w)ən

buffoon; clown

The *harlequin's* clowning endeared him to all.

hilarious (*adj.*)
hi-'lar-ē-əs

boisterously merry; very funny

The comedian was *hilarious*.

hilarity (*n.*)
hi-'lar-ə-tē

noisy gaiety; mirth; jollity; glee

The laughter and shouting made passersby wonder what all the *hilarity* was about.

ironic or **ironical**
(*adj.*) ‚ī-'rän-ik
‚ī-'rän-i-kəl

containing or expressing irony

It is *ironic* that a fire broke out in the fire station.

irony (*n.*)
'ī-rə-nē

1. species of humor whose intended meaning is the opposite of the words used

In *irony*, the team named its black cat mascot "Snowball."

2. state of affairs contrary to what would normally be expected

The breakdown occurred just after the car was inspected and found to be in perfect condition. What *irony*!

jocose (*adj.*)
jō-'kōs

given to jesting; playfully humorous; jocular

Some columnists write in a *jocose* vein; others are inclined to be serious.

levity (*n.*)
'le-və-tē

lack of proper seriousness; trifling gaiety; frivolity

Some of us felt that George's giggling during the ceremony was an unforgivable *levity*.

ludicrous (*adj.*)
'lü-də-krəs

exciting laughter; ridiculous; farcical; absurd

Pie-throwing, falling down stairs, and similar *ludicrous* antics were common in early film comedies.

parody (*n.*)
'par-ə-dē

humorous imitation

The Washington press corps entertained the Chief Executive with a *parody* of a Presidential message to Congress.

sarcasm (*n.*)
'sär-‚ka-zəm

sneering and often ironic language intended to hurt a person's feelings

Instead of helping, he offered such *sarcasm* as "You're such a genius, you'll find a solution."

sarcastic (*adj.*)
sär-'kas-tik

given to or expressing sarcasm

Sarcastic language can deeply hurt a person.

sardonic (*adj.*) sär-ʹdä-nik	bitterly sarcastic; mocking; sneering	Villains are often portrayed with a *sardonic* grin that suggests contempt for others.
satire (*n.*) ʹsa-ˌtīr	language or writing that exposes follies or abuses by holding them up to ridicule	Jonathan Swift's GULLIVER'S TRAVELS is a brilliant *satire* on human follies.
satiric or **satirical** (*adj.*) sə-ʹtir-ik sə-ʹtir-i-kəl	given to or expressing satire	In CATCH-22, a *satirical* novel, Joseph Heller ridicules the inflexibility of military bureaucrats.
travesty (*n.*) ʹtra-və-stē	imitation that makes a serious thing seem ridiculous; mockery	It is a *travesty* of justice that a notorious criminal should escape trial because of a technicality.

Apply What You Have Learned

EXERCISE 3.8: ANTONYMS

Each word or expression in column I has an ANTONYM (opposite) in column II. Insert the *letter* of the correct ANTONYM in the space provided.

COLUMN I	COLUMN II
___ **1.** mark of honor	(A) complimentary
___ **2.** susceptible	(B) poisonous
___ **3.** nontoxic	(C) halcyon
___ **4.** treat (someone) as unimportant	(D) doleful
___ **5.** hilarious	(E) levity
___ **6.** derogatory	(F) stigma
___ **7.** turbulent	(G) encomium
___ **8.** seriousness	(H) lionize
___ **9.** denunciation	(I) vilify
___ **10.** extol	(J) immune

EXERCISE 3.9: DEFINITIONS

In the space provided, write the *letter* of the word or expression that best defines the italicized word.

___ 1. *Astringent* rebuke   (A) mild   (C) undeserved
                                        (B) friendly   (D) stern

___ 2. Effective *antidote*   (A) harlequin   (C) remedy
                                        (B) punishment   (D) precaution

___ 3. *Derogatory* comment   (A) unfair   (C) congratulatory
                                        (B) belittling   (D) false

___ 4. *Benign* ruler   (A) healthful   (C) kindly
                                        (B) aging   (D) tyrannical

___ 5. *Ironical* development   (A) contrary to expectation   (C) discouraging
                                        (B) very sudden   (D) unfortunate

___ 6. *Festering* slums   (A) decaying   (C) poverty-stricken
                                        (B) crime-ridden   (D) spreading

___ 7. Utterly *farcical*   (A) hopeless   (C) irresponsible
                                        (B) incompetent   (D) absurd

___ 8. Prescribed *regimen*   (A) rules   (C) dose
                                        (B) medicine   (D) enforcement

___ 9. *Venomous* fangs   (A) vigorous   (C) dangerous
                                        (B) virulent   (D) pointed

___ 10. *Halcyon* atmosphere   (A) cloudy   (C) calm
                                        (B) noisy   (D) clear

EXERCISE 3.10: CONCISE WRITING

Express the thought of each sentence below in no more than four words. The first sentence has been rewritten as a sample.

1. We look down with contempt on those who live on others.

> *We despise parasites.*

_____

2. Who is the person who wrote that false and defamatory statement?

_____

3. He deliberately uses sneering language that can hurt people's feelings.

_____

4. Those who suffer from imaginary illnesses are in urgent need of help.

_____

5. They visited a place where animals are kept and trained.

_____

6. At the present time, she is recovering from an illness.

_____

7. He makes remarks that are meant as jokes and are not intended to be taken seriously.

_____

8. The outcome was the opposite of what one would normally have expected.

_____

9. Some tumors do not threaten the life of the patient.

_____

10. At no time in the past did she speak evil of anyone.

_____

EXERCISE 3.11: SENTENCE COMPLETION

Write the *letter* of the word or set of words that best completes the sentence.

___ 1. Newspapers generally withhold the names of criminal offenders under sixteen so as not to _____ them.

   (A) popularize   (C) stigmatize   (E) traduce
   (B) libel   (D) slander

___ 2. DON QUIXOTE, a _____ novel by Cervantes, ridicules exaggerated notions of chivalry.

   (A) satirical   (C) historical   (E) eulogistic
   (B) sentimental   (D) realistic

___ 3. The _____ currently being exhibited in the _____ have attracted numerous students of ornithology.

   (A) apes . . aviary   (C) bees . . menagerie   (E) vultures . . aviary
   (B) parrots . . apiary   (D) monkeys . . apiary

___ 4. The Olympic medal winner was _____ by the citizens of her hometown.

   (A) badgered   (C) maligned   (E) caricatured
   (B) parodied   (D) lionized

___ 5. Winston Churchill _____ the heroes of the Battle of Britain in this memorable _____: "Never was so much owed by so many to so few."

   (A) congratulated . . travesty (C) vilified . . plaudit   (E) extolled . . oration
   (B) defended . . encomium   (D) acclaimed . . tribute

EXERCISE 3.12: BRAINTEASERS

Fill in the missing letters.

1. At the dedication ceremony, the mayor will **e __ l o g __ __ __** the scientist for whom the school is being named.

2. Fearing that failure to win a promotion might __ __ __ __ __ **m a t __ __ __** her, Margaret did her best to succeed on the job.

3. It is **i r o n __ __ __ __** that the pneumonia patient's name is Hale, which means "healthy."

4. Swimming is believed to have __ __ __ __ **a p e __ __ __ __** benefits for people who suffer from arthritis.

5. **F a c e __ __ __ __ __** remarks on solemn occasions are entirely inappropriate.

6. The person who accidentally swallowed the poison was given a(n) __ __ __ __ **d o t __** and rushed to the hospital.

7. Several newspapers commended the governor for his __ __ __ **d a b __ __** efforts to prevent the strike.

8. Beneath the outer layer of the skin are the __ __ __ **a c e __ __ __** glands, which secrete oil to lubricate the skin and the hair.

9. Many a life has been saved by the timely surgical removal of a(n) __ __ __ __ __ __ **a n t** growth.

10. Though responsible for the fatal collision, the envoy could not be arrested because of diplomatic __ __ __ **u n i t __**.

EXERCISE 3.13: COMPOSITION

Answer in a sentence or two.

1. Is badgering a convalescent forgivable? Explain.

_____

_____

_____

2. Would you feel maligned if someone called you a hypochondriac when you were not feeling well? Why, or why not?

_____

_____

_____

3. Is it a travesty for suspects who testify against fellow suspects to receive immunity from prosecution? Explain.

_____

_____

_____

4. Why is it derogatory to be called a "parasite"?

_____

_____

_____

5. Why would it be ironical for an ordinary high-school tennis player to win a match against an acclaimed world champion?

_____

_____

_____

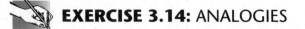 **EXERCISE 3.14**: ANALOGIES

Write the *letter* of the word that best completes the analogy.

SAMPLE

__e__   *Aviary* is to *birds* as *apiary* is to _____.
     a. flowers *b.* apes *c.* worms *d.* reptiles *e.* bees

EXPLANATION

The first step is to find the relationship of *aviary* and *birds*. As you have learned, an *aviary* is a "place where birds are kept." The second step is to say to yourself, "An *apiary* is a place in which what is kept?" The answer, of course, is *e, bees*.

____ **1.** *Invalid* is to *hypochondriac* as *real* is to _____.
    a. sickly *b.* genuine *c.* healthful *d.* imagined *e.* impossible

____ **2.** *Birds* are to *ornithologist* as *poisons* are to _____.
    a. bacteriologist *b.* pharmacist *c.* toxicologist *d.* physician *e.* coroner

____ **3.** *Waste* is to *scavenger* as *dirt* is to _____.
    a. oil *b.* parasite *c.* cleanser *d.* ant *e.* weed

— **4.** *Photograph* is to *caricature* as *fact* is to _____.
　　a. drawing *b.* exaggeration *c.* sketch *d.* truth *e.* description

— **5.** *Ludicrous* is to *laugh* as *dolorous* is to _____.
　　a. weep *b.* laud *c.* exult *d.* condemn *e.* smile

11. *Willingness—Unwillingness*

WORD	MEANING	TYPICAL USE
alacrity (*n.*) ə-'la-krə-tē	cheerful willingness; readiness; liveliness	Dr. Burke's class is one which pupils attend with *alacrity* and leave with reluctance.
aversion (*n.*) ə-'vər-zhən	strong dislike; repugnance; antipathy	Philip's *aversion* to work led to his dismissal.
involuntary (*adj.*) in-'vä-lən-,ter-ē	not done of one's own free will; automatic; unintentional; spontaneous (*ant.* **voluntary**)	Sneezing is *involuntary*.
loath (*adj.*) 'lōth	unwilling; averse; disinclined; reluctant	We were *loath* to leave our friends, but my father's transfer to California left us no choice.
loathe (*v.*) 'lōth	have an intense aversion to; detest	We *loathe* liars.
volition (*n.*) vō-'li-shən	will	Were you fired, or did you leave of your own *volition*?

12. *Height*

WORD	MEANING	TYPICAL USE
acclivity (*n.*) ə-'kli-və-tē	upward slope (*ant.* **declivity**)	Our marathon's last mile, a prolonged *acclivity,* tests the fittest runner.
acme (*n.*) 'ak-mē	highest point; pinnacle; summit	Many believe that Shakespeare reached his *acme* as a playwright when he wrote HAMLET.

apogee (*n.*)
'ap-ə-jē

1. farthest point from the earth in the orbit of a heavenly body (*ant.* **perigee**)

At its *apogee,* the satellite was 560 miles (903 kilometers) from the earth, and at its *perigee,* 150 miles (242 kilometers).

2. highest point; culmination

The use of solar energy, though increasing, is still exceedingly far from its *apogee.*

climactic (*adj.*)
klī-'mak-tik

arranged in order of increasing force and interest (*ant.* **anticlimactic**)

Notice the *climactic* order of ideas in this sentence: "Swelled by heavy rains, brooks became creeks, creeks rivers, and rivers torrents."

consummate (*adj.*)
kən-'sə-mət

perfect; superb; carried to the highest degree

The pilot guided the plane onto the runway with *consummate* skill.

eminence (*n.*)
'e-mə-nəns

high rank

Raised suddenly to an *eminence* for which he was ill-qualified, the executive antagonized his new subordinates.

eminent (*adj.*)
'e-mə-nənt

standing out; notable; famous

Our local grade school's name honors an *eminent* poet, Gwendolyn Brooks.

ethereal (*adj.*)
i-'thir-ē-əl

of the heavens; celestial; airy; delicate; intangible

Charles was told by his employer, "Get rid of your *ethereal* notions, and come down to earth."

exalt (*v.*)
ig-'zȯlt

1. lift up with joy, pride, etc.; elate (*ant.* **humiliate**)

My parents were *exalted* to learn that I had won a scholarship.

2. raise in rank, dignity, etc.; extol; glorify

Some films have *exalted* criminals to the level of heroes.

precipice (*n.*)
'pre-sə-pəs

very steep or overhanging place; cliff

An insurmountable *precipice* forced the climbers to make a lengthy detour.

precipitous (*adj.*)
pri-'si-pə-təs

1. steep as a precipice

2. hasty; rash

She descended from the summit in low gear, using her brakes all the way, since the road was so *precipitous.*

Don't rush into a *precipitous* action that you may later regret. Take your time.

preeminent (*adj.*)
prē-'e-mə-nənt

standing out above others; superior

As a violinmaker, Stradivarius remains *preeminent.*

sublimate (*v.*) 'səb-lə-,māt	1. redirect the energy of a person's bad impulses into socially and morally higher channels	Working with a psychologist, the child was able to *sublimate* his destructive impulses into positive activities.
	2. purify; refine	The alchemists failed in their efforts to *sublimate* baser metals, such as lead and copper, into gold.
sublime (*adj.*) sə-'blīm	elevated; noble; exalted; uplifting	The Grand Canyon's *sublime* scenery inspires and refreshes.
vertex (*n.*) 'vər-,teks	farthest point opposite the base, as in a triangle or pyramid; apex	The *vertex* of the largest Egyptian pyramid was originally 482 feet (147 meters) from the base.
zenith (*n.*) 'zē-nəth	1. highest point; culmination; peak (*ant.* **nadir**)	Her election to the Senate marked the *zenith* of her long career in politics.
	2. point in the heavens directly overhead	The North Star approaches the *zenith* as you approach the North Pole.

13. Lowness, Depth

abject (*adj.*) 'ab-,jekt	deserving contempt; sunk to a low condition; wretched	For your *abject* submission to your tyrannical associate, we have the utmost contempt.
abysmal (*adj.*) ə-'biz-məl	deep; profound; immeasurably great	I was ashamed of my *abysmal* ignorance.
abyss (*n.*) ə-'bis	bottomless depth; immeasurably great space	The sudden death of his closest friend threw Tennyson into an *abyss* of despair.
anticlimax (*n.*) ,an-ti-'klī-,maks	abrupt decline from the dignified or important to the trivial or ludicrous; comedown; bathos (*ant.* **climax**)	Sal used *anticlimax* in saying that Tito has a boundless appetite for classical music, Renaissance painting, and roasted peanuts.
chasm (*n.*) 'ka-zᵊm	deep breach; wide gap or rift	Prospects for a settlement became remote as the *chasm* between the rival parties deepened.
declivity (*n.*) di-'kliv-ət-ē	downward slope (*ant.* **acclivity**)	The hill was ideal for beginning skiers because of its gentle *declivity*.
dregs (*n. pl.*) 'dregz	most worthless part; sediment at the bottom of a liquid	Drug pushers are among the *dregs* of society.

earthy (*adj.*) ˈər-thē	down-to-earth; realistic; coarse; low	The 2 A.M. comedy show attracts audiences with a taste for *earthy* humor.
humble (*adj.*) ˈhəm-bəl	1. of low position or condition	Despite his *humble* origin, Lincoln rose to the highest office in the land.
	2. not proud; unpretentious; modest; courteously respectful	Though Stella has done far more than anyone else, she has never boasted of her achievement; she is *humble*.
humiliate (*v.*) hyü-ˈmi-lē-ˌāt	lower the pride, position, or dignity of; abase; degrade; mortify (*ant.* **exalt**)	Ted feels that I *humiliated* him at the meeting when I said that his motion was unnecessary.
humility (*n.*) hyü-ˈmi-lət-ē	freedom from pride; humbleness; lowliness; modesty	Boasters and braggarts need a lesson in *humility*.
menial (*adj.*) ˈmē-nē-əl	low; mean; subservient; servile	Some might consider mowing lawns *menial* work, but Harvey loves it.
nadir (*n.*) ˈnā-ˌdir	lowest point (*ant.* **zenith**)	The hopes of the American Revolutionary forces were at their *nadir* in the bitter winter of 1777–78 at Valley Forge.
plumb (*v.*) ˈpləm	get to the bottom of; ascertain the depth of; fathom	Sherlock Holmes's ability to *plumb* the deepest mysteries amazes readers.
profound (*adj.*) prə-ˈfaund	very deep; deeply felt; intellectually deep	Einstein's theories are so *profound* that only a few people are able to understand them.
ravine (*n.*) rə-ˈvēn	deep, narrow gorge worn by running water	Survivors of the plane that crashed in the mountain *ravine* were rescued by helicopter.

14. Relatives

consanguinuity (*n.*) ˌkän-ˌsan-ˈgwi-nə-tē	blood relationship	Grandchildren have *consanguinuity* of the second degree with their grandparents, and vice versa.
filial (*adj.*) ˈfil-ē-əl	of or like a son or daughter	Cordelia was the only one of King Lear's daughters who showed him *filial* affection.

fraternal (*adj.*)
frə-'tər-nᵊl

of or like a brother

A *fraternal* spirit from sharing the perils of combat sprang up between the two soldiers.

genealogy (*n.*)
,jē-nē-'ä-lə-jē

a person's or family's descent; lineage; pedigree

Most people can trace their *genealogy* back to a grandparent, or a great-grandparent, but they know almost nothing about their earlier ancestors.

gentility (*n.*)
jen-'ti-lə-tē

1. good manners

George Bernard Shaw's PYGMALION shows how an unrefined flower girl quickly acquires the *gentility* necessary to pass as a duchess.

2. gentry; upper class

The duke scandalized many of the *gentility* by marrying a commoner.

kith and kin (*n. pl.*)
'kith; 'kin

friends and relatives; kindred

Because he married in a distant state, the soldier had few of his *kith and kin* at the wedding.

maternal (*adj.*)
mə-'tər-nᵊl

of or like a mother

The kindergarten teacher has a kindly, *maternal* concern for each pupil.

nepotism (*n.*)
'ne-pə-,ti-zəm

favoritism to relatives by those in power

Whenever a President appoints a relative to a government position, the cry of *nepotism* is raised by the opposition party.

paternal (*adj.*)
pə-'tər-nᵊl

of or like a father

The molding of a child's character is an important maternal and *paternal* obligation.

progenitor (*n.*)
prō-'je-nə-tə(r)

forefather

Adam is the Biblical *progenitor* of the human race.

progeny (*n.*)
'prä-jən-ē

offspring; children; descendants

The fifteenth of Josiah Franklin's seventeen *progeny* was his son Benjamin.

sibling (*n.*)
'si-bliŋ

one of two or more children of a family

Jennifer has three *siblings*—two younger brothers and an older sister.

15. Smell

aroma (*n.*)
ə-'rō-mə

pleasant odor; bouquet

What a smoker may describe as a rich tobacco *aroma*, a nonsmoker may consider a disgusting stench.

aromatic (*adj.*)
ˌar-ə-'ma-tik

sweet-scented; fragrant

Honeysuckle is *aromatic*.

fragrant (*adj.*)
'frā-grənt

having a pleasant odor; pleasantly odorous or odoriferous

A florist's shop is a *fragrant* place.

fusty (*adj.*)
'fəs-tē

1. stale-smelling; musty; moldy

To rid the unused room of its *fusty* smell, we opened the windows and let the fresh air in.

2. old-fashioned

The *fusty* tenant refused to allow any modern appliance to be installed in the apartment.

incense (*n.*)
'in-ˌsens

substance yielding a pleasant odor when burned

Ancient Greek and Roman worshipers often burned *incense* to please their gods.

malodorous (*adj.*)
mal-'ō-də-rəs

ill-smelling; stinking; fetid; unpleasantly odorous

The air was *malodorous* with the smell of burning rubber carried by the wind.

noisome (*adj.*)
'nȯi-səm

1. offensive to smell; disgusting

The bus discharged *noisome* exhaust fumes that offended our nostrils.

2. harmful; noxious

"Stay indoors till the *noisome* fog has lifted," the TV news advised.

olfactory (*adj.*)
äl-'fak-t(ə-)rē

pertaining to the sense of smell

Because of their superior *olfactory* sense, bloodhounds can pick up the trails of fleeing criminals.

pungent (*adj.*)
'pən-jənt

sharp in smell or taste; acrid; biting; stimulating

When you slice onions, the *pungent* fumes may cause your eyes to tear.

putrid (*adj.*)
'pyü-trəd

1. stinking from decay

A rinse with a soapy solution rids garbage cans of *putrid* odors.

2. extremely bad; corrupt

Any system that requires applicants for promotion to pay bribes is *putrid*.

rancid (*adj.*)
'ran-səd

unpleasant to smell or taste from being spoiled or stale

Butter or fish that has a *rancid* odor is unfit to eat.

rank (*adj.*) 'raŋk	1. having a strong, bad odor or taste; offensively gross or coarse	When threatened, a skunk protects itself effectively by emitting a *rank* odor.
	2. extreme	Many felt that the murderer's acquittal on the grounds of insanity was a *rank* injustice.
reek (*v.*) 'rēk	emit a strong, disagreeable smell; be permeated with	Even after the fire was extinguished and the tenants were allowed to return, the building *reeked* of smoke.
scent (*n.*) 'sent	smell; perfume	The room was fragrant with the *scent* of freshly cut lilacs.
scent (*v.*)	get a suspicion of	When I saw my two rivals putting their heads together in a whispered conference, I *scented* a plot.
unsavory (*adj.*) 'ən-'sā-və-rē	1. unpleasant to taste or smell	The *unsavory* odor was traced to a decaying onion in the vegetable bin.
	2. morally offensive	Was the nominee—as opponents hinted—an *unsavory* character with connections to organized crime?

Apply What You Have Learned

EXERCISE 3.15: SYNONYMS

In the space before each word or expression in column I, write the *letter* of its correct synonym from column II.

COLUMN I

___ 1. spicy

___ 2. most worthless part

___ 3. chasm

___ 4. consummate

___ 5. disinclined

___ 6. humiliated

___ 7. descent

___ 8. high rank

___ 9. hasty

___ 10. freedom from pride

COLUMN II

(A) abyss

(B) eminence

(C) humility

(D) precipitous

(E) dregs

(F) loath

(G) pungent

(H) lineage

(I) humbled

(J) perfect

EXERCISE 3.16: UNRELATED WORDS

Write the *letter* of the word unrelated in meaning to the other words on the line.

___ 1. (A) contemptible   (B) abject   (C) reluctant   (D) wretched   (E) low

___ 2. (A) putrid   (B) unsavory   (C) involuntary   (D) fusty   (E) malodorous

___ 3. (A) children   (B) offspring   (C) scent   (D) progeny   (E) descendants

___ 4. (A) vertex   (B) apex   (C) climax   (D) acme   (E) base

___ 5. (A) rank   (B) position   (C) gross   (D) offensive   (E) coarse

___ 6. (A) abyss   (B) precipice   (C) elevation   (D) peak   (E) cliff

___ 7. (A) modesty   (B) humility   (C) unpretentiousness   (D) pride
       (E) humbleness

___ 8. (A) unwillingness   (B) repugnance   (C) antipathy   (D) aversion   (E) alacrity

___ 9. (A) rift   (B) acclivity   (C) breach   (D) ravine   (E) gorge

___ 10. (A) servile   (B) paternal   (C) obsequious   (D) submissive   (E) subservient

EXERCISE 3.17: SENTENCE COMPLETION

Fill each blank with the most appropriate word or expression from the vocabulary list below.

VOCABULARY LIST

maternal	progeny	exalted
rancid	bathos	kith and kin
attraction	aversion	chasm
gentility	delectable	humiliated
filial	climax	declivity

1. Janet's _____ to the water made her dread our swimming class.

2. It is only natural that we should be _____ by our successes.

3. Mother's Day gives children an opportunity to express their _____ love.

4. The gripping suspense at the _____ of the play held the audience breathless.

5. As we came down the steep _____, the speed of our car increased sharply.

6. The meal was wholesome and delicious except for the butter, which was

   _____ .

7. Total strangers treated the youngsters more kindly than their own _____ .

8. Coming after three excellent skits, the dull final number was a(n) _____ .

9. Your companion's earthy manner of speaking suggests a lack of _____.

10. I felt _____ when I failed my driving test a second time.

EXERCISE 3.18: CONCISE WRITING

Express the thought of each sentence below in no more than four words. The first sentence has been rewritten as a sample.

1. Does the soap that you use have a pleasant odor?

   Is your soap fragrant?
   _____

2. This downward slope is as steep as a precipice.

   _____

3. The American people look down on favoritism to relatives by those in power.

   _____

4. Hell is an immeasurably deep place that has no bottom.

   _____

5. We saw no sediment at the bottom of the liquid.

   _____

6. Look at the point in the heavens directly over your head.

   _____

7. Their freedom from pride is something that is worthy of praise.

   _____

8. The record that she has compiled stands out above that of others.

   _____

9. This cheese is stale, and it has an unpleasant odor.

   _____

10. The yawning that I did was beyond the control of my will.

    _____

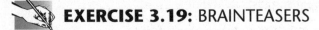

EXERCISE 3.19: BRAINTEASERS

Fill in the missing letters.

1. One whiff of that __ __ __ **s o m e** air made us hold our noses.

2. The eminent guitarist displayed her usual __ __ __ **s u m** __ __ __ __ control of her instrument.

3. After an occasional short trip to Earth, the king of the gods would return to his __ __ **h e r e** __ __ palace.

4. In comparison with a mansion, a log cabin is a **h u m** __ __ __ dwelling.

5. We want no part of that deal! It is corrupt! It is __ __ __ **r i d**!

6. Destructive energy can be __ __ __ __ __ **m a t** __ __ toward constructive ends.

7. In a world torn by war and dissension, wouldn't peace and harmony be __ __ __ **l i m e**?

8. No one forced us to do it. We did it of our own __ __ **l i t** __ __ __ .

9. The __ __ **a s** __ between the opposing sides is widening.

10. For a scientist, the award of a Nobel Prize is the __ __ **m e** of fame.

EXERCISE 3.20: COMPOSITION

Answer in two or three sentences.

1. Describe a noisome situation to which you had a strong aversion.

_____

_____

_____

2. Give an example of a necessary menial task that you were not loath to do.

_____

_____

_____

3. Tell how a parent succeeded or failed to bridge a chasm between siblings.

_____

_____

_____

4. Would you feel humiliated if someone said you were a student of consummate intelligence? Explain.

_____

_____

_____

5. Is it the acme of praise to be called an eminent zany? Why, or why not?

_____

_____

_____

EXERCISE 3.21: ANALOGIES

In the space at the left, write the *letter* of the pair of words that most nearly approaches the relationship between the capitalized words.

___ 1. INFINITE : END

    a. wealthy : money   *d.* contrite : repentance

    b. blithe : happiness   *e.* delectable : delight

    c. abysmal : bottom

___ 2. AUDITORY : HEARING

    a. keen : observing   *d.* olfactory : smelling

    b. gustatory : touching   *e.* irritable : feeling

    c. tactile : tasting

___ 3. VERTEX : TRIANGLE

    a. peak : mountain   *d.* hill : ravine

    b. summit : foot   *e.* index : preface

    c. slope : base

___ 4. PROGENY : PROGENITOR

    a. root : branch   *d.* bricks : house

    b. river : source   *e.* orchestra : conductor

    c. genius : protector

___ 5. FETID : FRAGRANT

    a. imperfect : consummate   *d.* fresh : stale

    b. humble : pretentious   *e.* reeking : aromatic

    c. shallow : profound

16. Age

WORD	MEANING	TYPICAL USE
adolescent (*adj.*) ˌa-dᵊl-ʼe-sᵊnt	growing from childhood to adulthood; roughly, of the teenage period	Boys and girls undergo many changes in their *adolescent* years.
adolescent (*n.*)	teenager	As *adolescents* develop into adults, they tend to become more self-confident.
antediluvian (*adj.*) ˌan-ti-də-ʼlü-vē-ən	antiquated; belonging to the time before the Biblical Flood (when all except Noah and his family perished)	Compared with today's sophisticated aircraft, the plane the Wright brothers flew in 1903 seems *antediluvian*.
archaic (*adj.*) är-ʼkā-ik	no longer used, except in a special context; old-fashioned	An *archaic* meaning of the word "quick" is "living," as in the Biblical phrase "the quick and the dead."
callow (*adj.*) ʼka-lō	young and inexperienced; unfledged	No prudent executive would entrust the management of a company to a *callow* youth just out of college.
contemporary (*adj.*) kən-ʼtem-pə-ˌrer-ē	1. of the same period or duration	The English Renaissance was not *contemporary* with the Italian Renaissance, but came two centuries later.
	2. modern; up-to-date	Rapid changes in taste mark the *contemporary* popular music scene.
contemporary (*n.*)	person who lives at the same time as another	Benjamin Franklin was Thomas Jefferson's *contemporary*.
crone (*n.*) ʼkrōn	withered old woman	The use of the word *crone* is unfair to women because there is no corresponding word for a "withered old man."
decrepit (*adj.*) di-ʼkre-pət	weakened by old age	The *decrepit* wooden shack collapsed under the weight of the heavy snow.
defunct (*adj.*) di-ʼfəŋkt	dead; deceased; extinct	Acme Lumber is still in business, but Equity Fixtures has long been *defunct*.
forebear (*n.*) ʼfȯr-ˌbar	forefather; ancestor; progenitor	The world of our *forebears* centuries ago was much less polluted.

hoary (*adj.*) ˈhȯr-ē	1. white or gray with age	Santa Claus is usually portrayed as a stout oldster with a *hoary* beard.
	2. ancient	The novel's plot is based on one of the *hoary* legends of Ancient Greece.
infantile (*adj.*) ˈin-fən-ˌtīl	of or like an infant or infancy; childish	A child may revert to the *infantile* act of thumb-sucking when insecure.
inveterate (*adj.*) in-ˈve-tə-rət	1. firmly established by age; deep-rooted	From their ancestors, Americans inherit an *inveterate* dislike of tyranny.
	2. habitual	Hats off to the *inveterate* smokers struggling to give up cigarettes!
juvenile (*adj.*) ˈjü-və-ˌnīl	1. of or for youth; youthful	The *juvenile* section of the library houses books for grade-schoolers.
	2. immature	Jody wants to play hide-and-seek? How *juvenile*!
longevity (*n.*) län-ˈje-və-tē	1. long life	Methuselah is renowned for his *longevity;* according to the Bible, he lived for 969 years.
	2. length of life	Medical advances are prolonging the average person's *longevity.*
matriarch (*n.*) ˈmā-trē-ˌärk	1. mother and ruler of a family or tribe; founder	Mama, in A RAISIN IN THE SUN, is the *matriarch* of the Younger family.
	2. highly respected old woman	A concert hall at Lincoln Center is named in honor of the *matriarch* Alice Tully.
mature (*adj.*) mə-ˈt(y)ùr	1. full-grown; ripe	Rita, 19, was not appointed manager because the employer wanted a more *mature* person in that position.
	2. carefully thought out	These are *mature* plans; they were not devised hastily.
nonage (*n.*) ˈnä-nij	legal minority; period before maturity	On his twenty-first birthday, the heir assumed control of his estate from the trustees who had administered it during his *nonage.*
nonagenarian (*n.*) ˌnō-nə-jə-ˈner-ē-ən	person 90–99 years old (Note also **octogenarian**, person 80–89 years old, and **septuagenarian**, person 70–79 years old.)	George Bernard Shaw, among his many other distinctions, was a *nonagenarian,* for he lived to be 94.

obsolescent (*adj.*) ˌäb-sə-ˈle-sᵊnt	going out of use; becoming obsolete	The company will soon have to replace its *obsolescent* machinery to compete successfully with rivals having state-of-the-art equipment.
obsolete (*adj.*) ˌäb-sə-ˈlēt	no longer in use; out-of-date	Have computers and word processing software made typewriters *obsolete*?
patriarch (*n.*) ˈpā-trē-ˌärk	1. father and ruler of a family or tribe; founder	According to the Bible, Adam is the *patriarch* and Eve the matriarch from whom the human family descends.
	2. highly respected old man	The acclaimed *Star Wars* epics crown the cinematic career of film *patriarch* George Lucas.
posthumous (*adj.*) ˈpäs-chə-məs	1. published after the author's death	Only two of Emily Dickinson's poems were published before her death; the rest are *posthumous*.
	2. occurring after death	*Posthumous* fame is of no use to an artist who struggles for a lifetime and dies unknown.
prelapsarian (*adj.*) ˌprē-ˌlap-ˈser-ē-ən	of the time or state before the fall of mankind (*ant.* **postlapsarian**)	In PARADISE LOST, Milton's Satan works to destroy Adam's and Eve's *prelapsarian* bliss.
primeval (*adj.*) prī-ˈmē-vəl	pertaining to the world's first ages; primitive	The Grand Canyon's exposed rock strata have taught scientists much about *primeval* life on Earth.
primordial (*adj.*) prī-ˈmȯr-dē-əl	1. existing at the very beginning	Humanity's *primordial* conflict with the environment has continued to the present day.
	2. elementary; primary; first in order	One of the *primordial* concepts of science is that light travels at the rate of 186,000 miles per second.
pristine (*adj.*) ˈpris-ˌtēn	in original, long-ago state; uncorrupted	The antique chair is in its *pristine* state—it has not been painted or refinished.
puberty (*n.*) ˈpyü-bər-tē	physical beginning of manhood (at about age 14) or womanhood (at about age 12)	Among the changes in boys at *puberty* are a deepening of the voice and the growth of hair on the face.
puerile (*adj.*) ˈpyu̇(-ə)r-əl	foolish for a grown person to say or do; childish	Some think it fun to play practical jokes, while others consider it *puerile*.

senile (*adj.*) 'sē-ˌnīl	showing the weakness of age	Grandfather no longer has the energy he used to have. He often forgets things. He is becoming *senile*.
superannuated (*adj.*) ˌsü-pər-'an-yə-wāt-əd	1. retired on a pension; advanced in years; very old	Many *superannuated* individuals can outproduce some workers who are still in the work force.
	2. incapacitated by age	Some *superannuated* citizens suffer from Alzheimer's disease.
venerable (*adj.*) 've-nər(-ə)-bəl	worthy of respect because of advanced age, achievement, virtue, or historical importance	At family reunions, our *venerable* grandmother, now past 80, sits at the head of the table.
veteran (*n.*) 've-tə-rən	1. person experienced in some occupation, art, or profession	In her bid for reelection, the mayor—a *veteran* of twenty years in public service—cited her opponent's lack of experience.
	2. ex-member of the armed forces	Many Vietnam War *veterans* found it hard to readjust to civilian life.
yore (*n.*) 'yȯr	(always preceded by *of*) long ago	In days of *yore,* knights engaged in tournaments.

17. Sobriety—Intoxication

abstemious (*adj.*) ab-'stē-mē-əs	sparing in eating and drinking; temperate; abstinent	Employers usually do not hire known alcoholics, preferring personnel who are *abstemious* in their habits.
carousal (*n.*) kə-'raȯ-zəl	drinking party; drunken revelry	While the enemy was celebrating Christmas Eve in a merry *carousal,* Washington and his troops—quite sober—crossed the Delaware and took them by surprise.
dipsomania (*n.*) ˌdip-sə-'mā-nē-ə	abnormal, uncontrollable craving for alcohol; alcoholism	An organization that has helped many persons to overcome *dipsomania* is Alcoholics Anonymous.
inebriated (*adj.*) i-'nē-brē-ˌāt-əd	drunk; intoxicated	Captain Billy Bones, *inebriated* from too much rum, terrorized the other patrons of the Admiral Benbow Inn.

sober (*adj.*) 'sō-bər	1. not drunk; temperate (*ant.* **drunk; intoxicated**)	Driver-education programs must emphasize the motorist's responsibility to be *sober*.
	2. serious; free from excitement or exaggeration	My immediate thought was to leave; however, after *sober* consideration, I decided not to.
sobriety (*n.*) sə-'brī-ə-tē	temperance; abstinence	*Sobriety* is a virtue.
sot (*n.*) 'sät	person made foolish by excessive drinking; drunkard	Don't ask a *sot* for directions; consult someone whose mind is clear.
teetotaler (*n.*) 'tē-'tō-t°l-ər	person who totally abstains from intoxicating beverages (*ant.* **dipsomaniac**)	Former dipsomaniacs who are now *teetotalers* deserve admiration for their courage and willpower.

18. Sea

bow (*n.*) 'baů	forward part of a ship; prow (*ant.* **stern**)	A search from *bow* to *stern* before sailing revealed no stowaways.
brine (*n.*) 'brīn	1. salty water	*Brine* can be converted to drinking water, but at high cost.
	2. ocean; sea; the deep	Anything on deck that was not firmly secured blew into the *brine*.
doldrums (*n. pl.*) 'dōl-drəmz	1. calm, windless part of the ocean near the equator	Becalmed in the *doldrums,* the sailing vessel was "As idle as a painted ship/ Upon a painted ocean."
	2. listlessness	The rise in sales and employment showed that America was emerging from the economic *doldrums*.
flotsam (*n.*) 'flät-səm	wreckage of a ship or its cargo found floating on the sea; driftage	*Flotsam* from the sunken freighter littered the sea for miles around.
jetsam (*n.*) 'jet-səm	goods cast overboard to lighten a ship in distress	*Jetsam* washed ashore indicated that frantic efforts had been made to lighten the ship's cargo.
jettison (*v.*) 'je-tə-sən	throw (goods) overboard to lighten a ship or plane; discard	The pilot of the distressed plane *jettisoned* surplus fuel before attempting an emergency landing.

leeward (*adj.*) ˈlē-wərd	in the direction away from the wind (*ant.* **windward**)	To avoid the wind, we chose deck chairs on the *leeward* side of the ship.
marine (*adj.*) mə-ˈrēn	of the sea or shipping; nautical; maritime	If you are fascinated by undersea plants and animals, you may want to study *marine* biology.
mariner (*n.*) ˈmar-ə-nər	sailor; seaman	Verne's Captain Nemo, master of the *Nautilus*, is an experienced *mariner*.
starboard (*adj.*) ˈstär-bərd	pertaining to the right-hand side of a ship when you are on deck and facing the bow (forward) (*ant.* **port**)	When a ship follows a southerly course, sunrise is on the *port* side and sunset on the *starboard* side.

19. Cleanliness—Uncleanliness

carrion (*n.*) ˈkar-ē-ən	decaying flesh of a carcass	Having eaten their fill, the lions left the *carrion* for the vultures to feed on.
contaminate (*v.*) kən-ˈta-mə-ˌnāt	make impure by mixture; pollute; defile (*ant.* **decontaminate**)	Many of our rivers have been *contaminated* by sewage.
dross (*n.*) ˈdräs	waste; refuse	When you revise your composition, eliminate all meaningless expressions, repetitions, and similar *dross*.
expurgate (*v.*) ˈek-spər-ˌgāt	remove objectionable material from a book; bowdlerize; purify	In his FAMILY SHAKESPEARE (published 1818), Bowdler *expurgated* Shakespeare's works, removing words and expressions that he considered improper for reading aloud in a family.
immaculate (*adj.*) i-ˈma-kyə-lət	spotless; absolutely clean; pure; faultless	Four hours of vacuuming, dusting, and scrubbing left the house *immaculate*.
offal (*n.*) ˈȯ-fəl	waste parts of a butchered animal; refuse; garbage	Sea gulls hovered about the wharf where fish was being sold, waiting to scoop up any *offal* cast into the water.
purge (*v.*) ˈpərj	cleanse; purify; rid of undesired element or person	The candidate vowed if elected to *purge* the county administration of corruption and inefficiency.

slatternly (*adj.*) 'sla-tərn-lē	untidy; dirty from habitual neglect; slovenly	There were cobwebs on the walls, dust on the shelves, and dirty dishes in the sink; it was a *slatternly* kitchen.
sloven (*n.*) 'slə-vən	person habitually untidy, dirty, or careless in dress, habits, etc.	It is difficult for an immaculate person to share a room with a *sloven*.
sordid (*adj.*) 'sȯr-dəd	filthy; vile	As soon as the athlete received the bribe offer, he informed his coach of the *sordid* affair.
squalid (*adj.*) 'skwä-ləd	filthy from neglect; dirty; degraded	The *squalid* streets of the poverty-stricken town were a depressing sight.
squalor (*n.*) 'skwä-lər	filth; degradation; sordidness	People do a great deal of washing, vacuuming, and mopping because they do not want to live in *squalor*.
sully (*v.*) 'sə-lē	tarnish; besmirch; defile	The celebrity felt that her name had been *sullied* by the publicity given her son's arrest for speeding.

20. Nearness

adjacent (*adj.*) ə-'jā-sᵊnt	lying near or next to; bordering; adjoining	Alaska is *adjacent* to northwestern Canada.
approximate (*adj.*) ə-'präk-sə-mət	nearly correct (*ant.* **exact**; **precise**)	The *approximate* length of a year is 365 days; its *exact* length is 365 days, 5 hours, 48 minutes, and 46 seconds.
contiguous (*adj.*) kən-'ti-gyə-wəs	touching; adjoining	England and France are not *contiguous*; they are separated by the English Channel.
environs (*n. pl.*) in-'vī-rənz	districts surrounding a place; suburbs	Many of the city's former residents now live in its immediate *environs*.
juxtapose (*v.*) 'jək-stə-ˌpōz	put side by side; put close together	If you *juxtapose* the two cabinets, you will see that one is slightly taller.
juxtaposition (*n.*) ˌjək-stə-pə-'zi-shən	close or side-by-side position	Soap should not be placed in *juxtaposition* with foods because it may impart its scent to them.

propinquity (*n.*)
prə-'piŋ-kwə-tē

1. kinship

Disregarding *propinquity*, the executive hired a highly recommended stranger rather than his own nephew.

2. nearness of place; proximity

There were large shrubs too close to the house, and their *propinquity* added to the dampness indoors.

Apply What You Have Learned

EXERCISE 3.22: ANTONYMS

Each word in column I has an *antonym* in column II. Insert the *letter* of that antonym in the space provided.

COLUMN I	COLUMN II
___ 1. full-fledged	(A) teetotaler
___ 2. sturdy	(B) abstinent
___ 3. dipsomaniac	(C) filthy
___ 4. right	(D) callow
___ 5. intemperate	(E) bow
___ 6. windward	(F) approximate
___ 7. exact	(G) intoxication
___ 8. immaculate	(H) leeward
___ 9. stern	(I) decrepit
___ 10. sobriety	(J) port

EXERCISE 3.23: SYNONYMS

Select the *synonym* of the italicized word and enter its *letter* in the space provided.

___ 1. *Unexpurgated* edition
   (A) abbreviated   (C) purified
   (B) unpurified   (D) bowdlerized

___ 2. Jefferson's *forebears*
   (A) contemporaries   (C) ancestors
   (B) rivals   (D) followers

___ 3. *Defunct* princess
   (A) dead   (C) intemperate
   (B) infantile   (D) slatternly

___ 4. *Inveterate* latecomer

(A) strange
(B) extinct
(C) juvenile
(D) habitual

___ 5. *Sober* estimates

(A) approximate
(B) calm
(C) exaggerated
(D) inaccurate

___ 6. Venerable *patriarch*

(A) founder
(B) martyr
(C) monument
(D) philosopher

___ 7. *Jettisoned* cargo

(A) surplus
(B) wrecked
(C) discarded
(D) loaded

___ 8. *Primordial* rights

(A) inherited
(B) secondary
(C) elementary
(D) royal

___ 9. Surface *dross*

(A) waste
(B) flotsam
(C) dregs
(D) polish

___ 10. *Contiguous* properties

(A) sordid
(B) contagious
(C) noxious
(D) touching

EXERCISE 3.24: SENTENCE COMPLETION

Fill each blank with the most appropriate word from the vocabulary list below.

VOCABULARY LIST

juxtaposition	puberty	primeval
obsolescent	abstemious	dross
squalid	puerile	obsolete
senility	immaculate	nonage
longevity	jetsam	carrion

1. Aunt Matilda thinks it childish for grown-ups to yell and boo at ball games. She cannot understand their _____ behavior.

2. When individuals distinguished for their advanced age are interviewed by the press, they are usually asked for the secret of their _____.

3. As a means of transportation, the horse-drawn carriage has long been _____.

4. In the hospital, every room was spotless. The corridors, too, were _____.

5. During his legal minority, the young monarch had heeded his advisers, but, once past his _____, he took absolute personal control.

6. Most eighth-graders have reached the stage of development known as _____.

7. The two troublemakers sat side by side. This _____ gave them ample opportunity to create disturbances.

8. Jackals feed on the decaying flesh of a carcass. Kites, hawks, and buzzards also subsist on _____.

9. By studying fossils, scientists have learned a great deal about _____
plants and animals.

10. When pedestrians track in mud from dirty streets, the custodial staff has to mop the halls
and stairways frequently to keep them from becoming _____.

EXERCISE 3.25: CONCISE WRITING

Express the thought of each sentence below in no more than four words. The
first sentence has been rewritten as a sample.

1. Some former members of the armed forces are between eighty and eighty-nine years of age.
   Some veterans are octogenarians.
   _____

2. Our uniforms are so clean that there is not a spot on them.

   _____

3. Was Shakespeare living at the time that Elizabeth was alive?

   _____

4. Most of the men and women in their seventies no longer go to work.

   _____

5. We know several men and women who totally abstain from alcohol.

   _____

6. The computer that we own is going out of use.

   _____

7. Was this play published after the death of its author?

   _____

8. Move those two tables so that one is right alongside the other.

   _____

9. She had a craving for intoxicating beverages that she could not control.

   _____

10. Wreckage from the ship and its cargo is drifting ashore.

    _____

EXERCISE 3.26: BRAINTEASERS

Fill in the missing letters.

1. The office staff consists of three newcomers and one __ __ __ __ **r a n**.

2. The guests helped themselves generously, except for a few noticeably __ __ **s t e m** __ __ __ __ dieters.

3. What Mom says goes in this house. She is the __ __ __ __ __ __ **a r c h** of the family.

4. The city is congested, but its __ __ __ **i r o n** __ are sparsely populated.

5. Merchants are complaining that business has been in the __ **o l d** __ __ __ __.

6. Thanks to the cleanup sponsored by the Block Association, the vacant lot is now __ __ __ __ __ __ **l a t e**.

7. The edifice is still called the Price Corporation Building, even though that company has long been __ __ **f u n** __ __.

8. This must be the room of a(n) __ __ **o v e n**; it is so untidy!

9. She can play tennis almost every day because of the __ __ **o x** __ __ __ __ __ of her house to the courts.

10. The __ __ __ __ __ **t a l e** __ next to us didn't even taste his champagne.

EXERCISE 3.27: COMPOSITION

Answer in two or three sentences.

1. What can apartment house dwellers do to prevent an adjacent vacant lot from becoming squalid?

_____

_____

_____

2. Is it puerile for a mature person to play chess? Explain.

_____

_____

_____

3. If you were an employer, would you hire a former dipsomaniac? Why, or why not?

_____

_____

_____

4. Suggest one thing you can do to ease the plight of a grandparent who is becoming senile.

_____

_____

_____

5. How does the jettisoning of sludge by oil tankers affect marine plant and animal life?

_____

_____

_____

EXERCISE 3.28: ANALOGIES

Write the *letter* of the word that best completes the analogy.

___ **1.** *Invalid* is to *hypochondriac* as *real* is to _____.
a. sickly   b. genuine   c. healthful   d. imagined   e. impossible

___ **1.** *Drought* is to *rain* as *doldrums* is to _____.
a. sea   b. calm   c. sails   d. sunshine   e. wind

___ **2.** *Refrigerator* is to *chill* as *brine* is to _____.
a. moisten   b. preserve   c. spoil   d. fill   e. spill

___ **3.** *Employed* is to *salary* as *superannuated* is to _____.
a. bonus   b. wages   c. pension   d. royalties   e. commission

___ **4.** *Banana* is to *peel* as *carcass* is to _____.
a. offal   b. meat   c. game   d. hunter   e. carrion

___ **5.** *Front* is to *rear* as *bow* is to _____.
a. leeward   b. prow   c. port   d. stern   e. starboard

21. *Reasoning*

WORD	MEANING	TYPICAL USE
analogy (*n.*) ə-'na-lə-jē	likeness in some respects between things otherwise different; similarity; comparison	An *analogy* is frequently made between the human heart and a pump because the heart pumps blood through the body.
arbitrary (*adj.*) 'är-bə-,trer-ē	autocratic; despotic; tyrannical; proceeding from a whim or fancy (*ant.* **legitimate**)	A promotion should depend on an employee's record rather than on some official's *arbitrary* decision.
arbitrate (*v.*) 'är-bə-,trāt	1. decide a dispute, acting as an *arbiter* or *arbitrator* (judge)	When the opposing claimants asked me to *arbitrate*, it was understood they would abide by my decision.
	2. submit a dispute to arbitration	Neither side has shown any eagerness to *arbitrate*.
axiom (*n.*) 'ak-sē-əm	self-evident truth; maxim	It is an *axiom* that practice makes perfect.
axiomatic (*adj.*) ,ak-sē-ə-'ma-tik	self-evident; universally accepted as true	It is *axiomatic* that expenditures should not exceed income.
bias (*n.*) 'bī-əs	opinion formed before there are grounds for it; prejudice; predilection; partiality	Prospective jurors with a *bias* for or against the defendant were not picked for the jury.
bigoted (*adj.*) 'bi-gə-təd	intolerant; narrow-minded	It is futile to argue with *bigoted* persons; they hold stubbornly to their prejudices.
bigotry (*n.*) 'bi-gə-trē	views or behavior of a *bigot* (one intolerantly devoted to one's own beliefs and prejudices); narrow-mindedness; intolerance	Found guilty, the defendant accused the judge and the jury of *bigotry*.
cogitate (*v.*) 'kä-jə-,tāt	think over; consider with care; ponder; deliberate	Since the matter is important, I must have time to *cogitate* before announcing my decision.
criterion (*n.*) krī-'tir-ē-ən	standard; rule or test for judging (*pl.* **criteria**)	Two of the *criteria* that experts consider in judging an automobile are fuel consumption and frequency of repair.
crux (*n.*) 'krəks	most important point; essential part	Skip over the minor points, and get to the *crux* of the matter.

deduce (*v.*)
di-'düs

derive by reasoning; infer

The intruder's approximate weight was *deduced* from the depth of footprints in the moist sand.

dilemma (*n.*)
də-'le-mə

situation requiring a choice between two equally bad alternatives; predicament

With so few jobs available, Greg faced the *dilemma* of taking a job he didn't want or remaining unemployed.

dogmatic (*adj.*)
dȯg-'ma-tik

asserting opinions as if they were facts; opinionated; asserted without proof; doctrinaire

If, without offering any proof at all, you keep insisting that the plan will not work, you are being *dogmatic*.

eclectic (*adj.*)
e-'klek-tik

choosing (ideas, methods, etc.) from various sources; selective

In some matters, I follow the progressives and in others, the conservatives; you may consider me *eclectic*.

fallacious (*adj.*)
fə-'lā-shəs

based on a *fallacy* (erroneous idea); misleading; deceptive (*ant.* **sound; valid**)

For centuries people held the *fallacious* view that the sun revolves around the earth.

fallible (*adj.*)
'fa-lə-bəl

liable to be mistaken (*ant.* **infallible**)

Umpires occasionally make mistakes; like other human beings, they too are *fallible*.

heterodox (*adj.*)
'he-tə-rə-,däks

rejecting regularly accepted beliefs or doctrines; heretical; nonconformist (*ant.* **orthodox**)

Political dissenters in dictatorships are often persecuted for their *heterodox* beliefs.

hypothetical (*adj.*)
,hī-pə-'the-ti-kəl

supposed; having the characteristics of a *hypothesis*, a supposition made as a basis for reasoning or research. (If supported by considerable evidence, a hypothesis becomes a *theory*, and eventually, if no exceptions are found, a *law*.)

The detective investigated each employee because of a *hypothetical* notion that the robber had received "inside" information.

illusion (*n.*)
i-'lü-zhən

misleading appearance; false impression; misconception

Jordan had thought that working in a restaurant would be fun, but eight hours on her feet shattered that *illusion*.

indubitable (*adj.*)
in-'dü-bə-tə-bəl

certain; incontrovertible; indisputable (*ant.* **questionable; doubtful**)

The defendant's confession, added to the witnesses' testimony, makes his guilt *indubitable*.

orthodox (*adj.*)
'ȯr-thə-,däks

generally accepted, especially in religion; conventional; approved (*ant.* **heterodox; unorthodox**)

At the dinner table, it is *orthodox* to use a knife and fork instead of your fingers.

paradoxical (*adj.*)
,par-ə-'däk-si-kəl

having the characteristics of a *paradox* (a self-contradictory statement which may nevertheless be true)

It is *paradoxical* but true that teachers may be taught by their pupils.

plausible (*adj.*)
'plȯ-zə-bəl

apparently trustworthy; superficially true or reasonable

The suspects' alibis are all *plausible*. Will all survive closer scrutiny?

preposterous (*adj.*)
pri-'päs-t(ə-)rəs

senseless; absurd; irrational

The choice of Stella for the leading role is *preposterous*; she can't act.

rational (*adj.*)
'rash-ə-nᵊl

1. able to think clearly; having the power to reason

Humans are *rational*; animals have little power of reason.

2. based on or agreeable to reason; intelligent; sensible; sane (*ant.* **absurd; irrational**)

Mobs, as a rule, do not make *rational* decisions.

rationalize (*v.*)
'rash-ə-nᵊl-,īz

invent excuses for one's actions, desires, failures, etc.

The fox in the fable *rationalized* his failure to get at the grapes by claiming that they were sour.

sophistry (*n.*)
'sä-fə-strē

clever but deceptive reasoning

Imagine the *sophistry* of that child! He denied having a water pistol because, as he later explained, he had two!

specious (*adj.*)
'spē-shəs

superficially true, reasonable, attractive, or just, but not really so

Expert Contracting's ad that its employees' experience averages five years is *specious*: one employee has worked there nineteen years, but the other three only four months each.

speculate (*v.*)
'spe-kyə-,lāt

1. reflect; meditate; conjecture

Space exploration may solve a problem we have long *speculated* about—whether intelligent life exists elsewhere in the universe.

2. buy or sell with the hope of profiting by price fluctuations

Aunt Tahaira never invests in risky stocks; she does not *speculate*.

tenable (*adj.*)
'te-nə-bəl

capable of being maintained or defended; defensible (*ant.* **untenable**)

An argument backed by facts is more *tenable* than one based on hearsay.

22. Shape

amorphous (*adj.*)
ə-'mȯr-fəs

shapeless; having no definite form; unorganized

At first my ideas for a term paper were *amorphous,* but now they are beginning to assume a definite shape.

concave (*adj.*)
kän-'kāv

curved inward, creating a hollow space (*ant.* **convex**)

In its first and last quarters, the moon is crescent-shaped; its inner edge is *concave* and its outer *convex.*

contour (*n.*)
'kän-,túr

outline of a figure

The *contour* of our Atlantic coast is much more irregular than that of our Pacific coast.

distort (*v.*)
di-'stȯrt

1. twist out of shape

My uncle suffered a minor stroke that temporarily *distorted* his face.

2. change from the true meaning

To describe a pleasure trip to Hawaii as a "fact-finding mission" is to *distort* the truth.

malleable (*adj.*)
'ma-lē-ə-bəl

1. capable of being shaped by hammering, as a metal

Copper is easily shaped into thin sheets because it is very *malleable.*

2. adaptable; pliant

Had they asked me, I would not have cut the price, but they bargained with my partner, who is more *malleable.*

rotund (*adj.*)
rō-'tənd

1. rounded out; plump

Santa Claus has a *rotund* figure.

2. full-toned

The announcer introduced each of the players in a clear, *rotund* voice.

sinuous (*adj.*)
'sin-yə-wəs

bending in and out; winding; serpentine

Signs that forewarn motorists of a *sinuous* stretch of road often indicate a safe speed for negotiating the curves.

symmetrical (*adj.*)
sə-'me-tri-kəl

balanced in arrangement; capable of division by a central line into similar halves (*ant.* **asymmetrical**)

This badly misshapen bumper was perfectly *symmetrical* before the accident.

symmetry (*n.*)
'si-mə-trē

balance; harmony

It is amazing how a flock of wild geese can maintain perfect *symmetry* in flight.

23. *Importance—Unimportance*

grave (*adj.*)
'grāv
deserving serious attention; weighty; momentous
The President summoned the cabinet into emergency session on receipt of the *grave* news.

nugatory (*adj.*)
'nü-gə-,tȯr-ē
of little or no value; trifling; worthless; useless
My last-minute cramming was *nugatory*; at the examination, I didn't remember a thing.

paltry (*adj.*)
'pȯl-trē
practically worthless; trashy; piddling; petty
I complain not because of the *paltry* few pennies I was overcharged but because of the principle involved.

paramount (*adj.*)
'par-ə-,maunt
chief; above others; supreme
The *paramount* concern of the parents is the welfare of their children.

relevant (*adj.*)
're-lə-vənt
bearing upon the matter in hand; pertinent (*ant.* **irrelevant; extraneous**)
The prosecutor objected that the witness's testimony had nothing to do with the case, but the judge ruled that it was *relevant*.

24. *Modesty*

coy (*adj.*)
'kȯi
pretending to be shy
Annabelle's shyness was just a pretense; she was being *coy*.

demure (*adj.*)
di-'myur
1. falsely modest or serious; coy
The children giggled behind the teacher's back, but as soon as he turned around they looked *demure*.

2. grave; prim
Who would have guessed that so *demure* a person as Mr. Lewis was addicted to betting on horse races?

diffident (*adj.*)
'di-fə-dənt
lacking self-confidence; unduly timid; shy (*ant.* **confident**)
Though Carla's coach was confident she would make the finals, she herself was *diffident*.

modest (*adj.*)
'mä-dəst
not thinking too highly of one's merits; unpretentious; humble (*ant.* **ambitious**)
Joe is the real hero, but he is too *modest* to talk about it.

modesty (*n.*)
'mä-də-stē
freedom from conceit or vanity; unpretentiousness; humility
Modesty prevents Donna from wearing any of the medals she has won.

staid (*adj.*)
'stād
settled; of quiet disposition; sedate
To seem more *staid*, the applicant wore gray—not shocking pink!

25. *Vanity*

brazen (*adj.*) ′brā-z°n	1. shameless; impudent	Two persons in the audience were smoking in *brazen* defiance of the "No Smoking" sign.
	2. made of brass or bronze	We have a pair of *brazen* candlesticks.
egoism (*n.*) ′ē-gə-,wi-zəm	excessive concern for oneself; selfishness; conceit (*ant.* **altruism**)	*Oscar* winners avoid the charge of *egoism* by giving others much credit.
ostentatious (*adj.*) ,äs-tən-′tā-shəs	done to impress others; showy; pretentious	Parked next to our staid family car was an *ostentatious* red convertible.
overweening (*adj.*) ,ō-vər-′wē-niŋ	thinking too highly of oneself; arrogant; presumptuous	After four victories, the *overweening* wrestler boasted he was invincible.
pert (*adj.*) ′pərt	1. too free in speech or action; bold; saucy; impertinent	Most of us addressed the speaker as "Dr. Bell," but one sophomore began a question with a *pert* "Doc."
	2. lively; spirited	Dana's *pert* delivery of her speech kept the audience's attention.
vain (*adj.*) ′vān	1. conceited; excessively proud or concerned about one's personal appearance or achievements	Al boasts about his awards to everyone, even strangers. I have never seen such a *vain* person.
	2. empty; worthless	We have had enough of your *vain* promises; you never keep your word.
	3. futile	Anna made a valiant but *vain* effort to get her sister to stop smoking.
vainglorious (*adj.*) vān-′glōr-ē-əs	excessively proud or boastful; elated by vanity	*Vainglorious* Ozymandias had these words inscribed on the pedestal of his statue, now shattered: "Look on my works, ye Mighty, and despair!"
vanity (*n.*) ′va-nə-tē	condition of being too vain about one's appearance or achievements; conceit (*ant.* **humility**)	If you are free of *vanity*, you will not be fooled by flatterers.

Apply What You Have Learned

EXERCISE 3.29: ANTONYMS

Each italicized word in column I has an *antonym* in column II. Insert the *letter* of that antonym in the space provided.

COLUMN I	COLUMN II
___ 1. *confident* outlook	(A) altruism
___ 2. *legitimate* ruling	(B) fallacious
___ 3. shows *vanity*	(C) diffident
___ 4. *questionable* evidence	(D) arbitrary
___ 5. example of *egoism*	(E) rational
___ 6. *sound* reasoning	(F) indubitable
___ 7. *ambitious* expectations	(G) concave
___ 8. *absurd* conclusion	(H) humility
___ 9. *relevant* details	(I) modest
___ 10. *convex* surface	(J) extraneous

EXERCISE 3.30: UNRELATED WORDS

Write the *letter* of the word unrelated in meaning to the other words on the line.

___ 1. (A) deceptive   (B) infallible   (C) erroneous   (D) fallacious

___ 2. (A) bold   (B) immodest   (C) pertinent   (D) impudent

___ 3. (A) intolerance   (B) prejudice   (C) impartiality   (D) bias

___ 4. (A) concave   (B) buxom   (C) rotund   (D) corpulent

___ 5. (A) unrelated   (B) impertinent   (C) rude   (D) irrelevant

___ 6. (A) petty   (B) piddling   (C) paltry   (D) prim

___ 7. (A) heretical   (B) paradox   (C) heterodox   (D) unorthodox

___ 8. (A) preposterous   (B) vain   (C) proud   (D) conceited

___ 9. (A) shy   (B) diffident   (C) arrogant   (D) coy

___ 10. (A) indisputable   (B) axiomatic   (C) incontrovertible   (D) hypothetical

EXERCISE 3.31: SENTENCE COMPLETION

Fill each blank with the most appropriate word from the vocabulary list below.

VOCABULARY LIST

axiomatic	analogy	saucy
dilemma	staid	hypothesis
theory	paradox	dogmatic
paramount	illusion	speculating
sophistry	relevant	ostentatious

1. Scientific research usually begins with a(n) _____.

2. Grandmother and Grandfather look dignified and _____ in their wedding picture.

3. Jack never wears any of his medals because he doesn't want to appear _____.

4. On a sinking ship, saving the lives of the passengers is the _____ consideration.

5. When exasperated with my little brother, I call him a "snake," but my parents do not like the _____.

6. It is _____ that the shortest distance between any two points on a plane surface is a straight line.

7. As we were discussing tomorrow's picnic, Dinah interrupted with a(n) _____ question about the weather forecast.

8. The company faces the _____ of going into bankruptcy or seeing its debts mount further.

9. _____ always involves risk, as prices fluctuate.

10. What I had been reasonably certain was a ship approaching on the horizon turned out to be a mere _____.

EXERCISE 3.32: CONCISE WRITING

Express the thought of each sentence below in no more than four words. The first sentence has been rewritten as a sample.

1. His weakness is that he is excessively concerned about his personal appearance.
   His weakness is vanity.
   _____

2. People dislike commands that proceed from someone's whim or fancy.

   _____

3. We're in a situation in which we must make a choice between two equally bad alternatives.

_____

4. The reasons that he gave seemed reasonable, but they really were not.

_____

5. She sometimes expresses opinions without offering proof to support them.

_____

6. The questions you are asking have no bearing on the matter in hand.

_____

7. What is the supposition on which she is basing her research?

_____

8. Traders like to buy or sell with the expectation of making profits from price fluctuations.

_____

9. The thoughts that I had in my brain had no definite shape or form.

_____

10. What is the reason for your lack of confidence in yourself?

_____

EXERCISE 3.33: BRAINTEASERS

Fill in the missing letters.

1. The __ __ __ __ **o u r** of the distant peak grew more distinct in the sky.

2. Why must you insist that you are always right? Don't you know that everyone is __ **a l l** __ __ __ __ ?

3. These __ __ **t e n t** __ __ __ __ __ __ furnishings were meant to impress guests.

4. This deer's antlers are perfectly __ __ __ **m e t** __ __ __ __ __ .

5. It is __ __ __ __ **m a t** __ __ that opposites attract.

6. The older settlers found it hard to adapt to the new circumstances; the younger ones were much more __ **a l l** __ __ __ __ __ .

7. It is a maxim that a person with __ __ __ __ __ **w e e** __ __ __ __ ambitions is almost surely headed for a downfall.

8. The path was so **s i n** __ __ __ __ __ that we soon lost our sense of direction.

9. Most investors were dissatisfied with their __ __ __ **a t** __ __ __ gains.

10. Are you so wrapped up in your own __ **g o** __ __ __ that you give no thought to others?

EXERCISE 3.34: COMPOSITION

Answer in two or three sentences.

1. Why is it difficult for vain individuals to admit that they are fallible?

_____

_____

_____

2. Who is more likely to be popular—a modest champion or an overweening one? Why?

_____

_____

_____

3. What would be your most important criterion in arbitrating a dispute between two members of your family? Explain.

_____

_____

_____

4. Would you regard it as nugatory if your opponent in an election distorted one of your statements? Why, or why not?

_____

_____

_____

5. Someone with a bias against consumers heads a consumer-protection agency. In what sense is this situation preposterous? But what might be a rational explanation for it?

_____

_____

_____

EXERCISE 3.35: ANALOGIES

In the space at the left, write the *letter* of the pair of words that most nearly approaches the relationship between the capitalized words.

____   1. CONTOUR : STATUE

      a. shadow : body   *d.* area : surface

      b. coastline : island   *e.* original : imitation

      c. peak : mountain

____   2. CRUX : ARGUMENT

      a. title : book   *d.* door : house

      b. bridge : river   *e.* costume : actor

      c. kernel : nut

____   3. CONCAVE : CONVEX

      a. bowl : platter   *d.* cavity : swelling

      b. bulge : dent   *e.* building : dome

      c. cup : saucer

____   4. HYPOTHESIS : TRUTH

      a. supposition : fact   *d.* folly : wisdom

      b. proof : conclusion   *e.* guess : blunder

      c. deceit : honesty

____   5. RATIONALIZING : SELF-DECEPTION

      a. speculating : thrift   *d.* brazenness : courtesy

      b. egoism : shyness   *e.* boasting : vanity

      c. cogitating : brain

EXERCISE 3.36: SIMILAR AND CONTRARY

Fill in the missing letters so that each line contains three words or phrases with similar meanings and one with a contrary meaning.

Similar Meaning	Similar Meaning	Similar Meaning	Contrary Meaning
Sample: s _y_ mmetry	bal _a_ _n_ ce	harm _o_ _n_ y	_a_ symmetry
1. dej __ __ ted	s __ d	dep __ __ ssed	el __ __ ed
2. ga __ __ t	emaci __ __ __ d	l __ an	b __ __ ly
3. melan __ __ __ ly	sadly tho __ __ __ tful	pen __ __ ve	buo __ __ __ t
4. c __ __ pulent	o __ __ se	p __ __ tly	th __ __

5. re __ __ __ tant	cont __ __ __ e	reg __ __ __ ful	imp __ __ itent
6. po __ __ nant	pi __ __ cing	pat __ __ __ ic	m __ __ ry
7. sv __ __ te	s __ __ __ der	l __ the	bux __ __
8. gl __ __	gl __ __ my	mo __ __ y	bl __ __ he
9. f __ __ n	fl __ __ ter	whe __ __ le	in __ __ lt
10. conv __ __ ial	jo __ __ al	joc __ __ __	uns __ __ iable
11. pr __ ise	e __ tol	l __ __ d	bl __ __ e
12. ben __ __ n	not d __ __ gerous	g __ __ __ le	m __ __ ignant
13. cal __ mnious	de __ __ matory	sl __ __ __ erous	e __ __ ogistic
14. conv __ __ esce	rec __ __ er	re __ __ __ erate	w __ __ sen
15. de __ __ gatory	bel __ __ tling	d __ __ paraging	__ __ __ __ plimentary
16. lev __ __ y	tr __ __ ling	fri __ __ lity	ser __ __ __ __ sness
17. pes __ __ __ __ ential	h __ __ mful	__ __ adly	he __ __ __ __ hful
18. encomi __ __	t __ __ __ ute	eu __ __ __ y	vil __ __ ication
19. __ __ lign	sl __ __ __ er	tr __ __ uce	l __ __ __ ize
20. p __ __ sonous	ve __ __ mous	t __ __ ic	ther __ __ __ utic
21. av __ __ sion	rep __ __ nance	an __ __ __ athy	l __ __ ing
22. cons __ mmate	p __ __ __ ect	sup __ __ b	im __ __ __ fect
23. ethere __ l	__ __ __ icate	cel __ __ __ ial	t __ __ gible
24. h __ __ ble	m __ __ est	unpre __ __ __ tious	ex __ __ __ ed
25. auto __ __ __ ic	un __ __ tentional	spon __ __ __ eous	vol __ __ tary
26. lo __ __ h	dis __ __ clined	reluct __ __ t	incl __ __ ed
27. mal __ __ orous	re __ __ ing	f __ tid	f __ __ __ rant
28. antic __ imax	c __ __ edown	bath __ __	cli __ __ __
29. n __ isome	un __ __ __ lesome	n __ __ ious	sal __ brious
30. zen __ __ h	highest p __ __ nt	cul __ __ __ ation	n __ __ ir
31. s __ __ did	f __ lthy	v __ __ e	sp __ __ less
32. sob __ __ ety	tem __ __ __ ance	abs __ __ __ ence	in __ __ riation
33. immac __ __ ate	un __ __ llied	__ __ ultless	de __ __ led
34. inex __ __ __ ienced	unfl __ __ __ __ d	c __ __ low	v __ __ eran
35. sul __ __ ed	t __ __ nished	__ __ smirched	pur __ __ d

36. ju __ enile	pue __ __ le	ch __ __ __ ish	ma __ __ re
37. pur __ __ y	ex __ __ __ gate	b __ __ dlerize	cont __ __ inate
38. uncor __ __ __ ted	un __ __ lluted	pr __ __ tine	imp __ re
39. dec __ __ __ __ d	def __ nct	ext __ __ ct	li __ ing
40. slatt __ __ nly	squ __ __ id	slo __ __ __ ly	t __ dy
41. arb __ __ rary	aut __ __ ratic	des __ __ __ ic	l __ __ itimate
42. f __ __ __ acious	mis __ __ ading	de __ __ __ tive	val __ __
43. he __ __ tical	hetero __ __ __	non __ __ __ formist	__ __ thodox
44. in __ __ bitable	incon __ __ __ vertible	indis __ __ table	qu __ __ tionable
45. p __ __ posterous	s __ __ seless	abs __ __ d	__ __ __ ional
46. mod __ __ ty	un __ __ __ tentiousness	h __ __ ility	v __ __ ity
47. e __ __ ism	__ __ __ fishness	c __ __ __ eit	__ __ truism
48. __ __ alogy	s __ __ __ __ arity	c __ __ parison	d __ __ __ __ imilarity
49. __ etty	trif __ __ __ __	p __ __ dling	mo __ __ __ tous
50. dif __ __ __ ent	t __ __ id	sh __	bra __ __ n

EXERCISE 3.37: SENTENCE COMPLETION

Write the *letter* of the set of words that best completes the sentence(s).

___ 1. Othello, provoked by patriotic animosity against anyone viciously disposed to his adopted city-state, Venice, kills "a _____ and a turbaned Turk" who "beat a Venetian and _____ the state."

A. libelous . . insulted

B. calumnious . . lauded

C. malignant . . traduced

D. maleficent . . lionized

___ 2. Now that Venus is enamored of Adonis, who is the go-between she sends to whisper in his ear the sweet _____ of love? None but her darling little angel, her very own infant son, _____ Cupid.

A. blandishments . . cherubic

B. allurements . . jovial

C. enticements . . svelte

D. ironies . . troublemaking

___ 3. Thus, as memories of the Roman Republic grew ever dimmer, "Law is the will of the ruler" came to be the _____ of the Roman emperors, of their sycophants and apologists, and of their countless despotic spawn down through our present millenium, heirs to this hand-me-down of _____ government.

    A. fallacy . . tyrannical

    B. axiom . . legitimate

    C. misconception . . autocratic

    D. maxim . . arbitrary

___ 4. Lean year keeps following lean year, killing hopes the famine will abate. So Jacob has a _____. Should he risk starvation? That will come if he refuses to part with Benjamin, his youngest child (and his favorite, since the loss of Joseph, foolishly entrusted to jealous older brothers). Or should he risk bereavement? That may come if he consigns his lamb to those very same brothers to take to Egypt, as demanded by Pharoah's _____ deputy, who alone is empowered to sell them food.

    A. challenge . . supreme

    B. predicament . . jocose

    C. problem . . haggard

    D. dilemma . . paramount

___ 5. By and large, Shakespeare's _____ attended the theater not in the evening, as we tend to, but at midday, and not by coming into the heart of a big city, as we tend to, but by leaving it, crossing the Thames River to slum it in London's _____ _____, where comedies and tragedies could be put on beyond the jurisdiction of the city's magistrates, _____ men who held that stage plays, by portraying immorality, encouraged it.

    A. contemporaries . . squalid environs . . stern

    B. forebears . . primordial countryside . . dour

    C. audiences . . pristine suburbs . . convivial

    D. patrons . . adjoining districts . . decrepit

EXERCISE 3.38: MATCHMAKING

Write the *letter* of the set of words best matching the italicized words.

___ 1. The magnitude of the moon's velocity *attains its maximum value* at its *closest approach to the Earth.*

    A. reaches its zenith . . apogee

    B. climaxes . . perihelion

    C. culminates . . aphelion

    D. peaks . . perigee

___ 2. Uriah Heep, the hypocritical villain of DAVID COPPERFIELD, hides overweening schemes behind his *nauseating* pretense of abject *abasement*.

    A. fulsome . . humility

    B. malevolent . . insincerity

    C. convincing . . humiliation

    D. offensive . . mortification

___ 3. "Better thou hadst not been born than not t' have pleased me better," thunders King Lear at his youngest daughter, Cordelia, who won't *kowtow to* him by exaggerating her filial affection. Lear then turns her out, but the French King, stirred to love by Cordelia's integrity, rescues her from this *misfortune*.

    A. eulogize . . predicament

    B. curry favor with . . situation

    C. ingratiate herself with . . plight

    D. acclaim . . embarrassment

___ 4. Whenever Hercules threw giant Antaeus to the ground, Earth, Antaeus's mother, renewed his strength. What prodigious *restorative* powers! But they could not *thwart every measure that might render him susceptible to* defeat, for then Hercules crushed the life out of Antaeus while holding him aloft.

    A. maternal . . bar all gates to

    B. ameliorative . . desensitize him to

    C. nugatory . . protect him from

    D. recuperative . . immunize him to

___ 5. When the dreaded bubonic plague struck a major city, often one-third of the population would die—a *macabre* statistic indeed—before the *lethal* attack ceased.

    A. morbid . . pestilential

    B. pathetic . . epidemic

    C. grave . . deadly

    D. mortal . . sordid

Chapter 4

Words Derived From Greek

A great revival of interest in ancient Greek and Latin civilizations took place in England during the years 1500–1650, a period known as the Renaissance. At that time, numerous ancient Greek and Latin words and their derivatives were incorporated into our language. This pattern of language growth has continued to the present day. When modern scientists need to name a new idea, process, or object, they tend to avoid existing English words because these already may have several other meanings. Instead, they prefer to construct a new English word out of one or more ancient Greek or Latin words. Ancient Greek has been especially preferred as a source of new words in the scientific and technical fields.

Here are twenty-five ancient Greek prefixes and roots that have enriched our language. Each one, as you can see, has produced a group of useful English words.

1. PHOBIA: "fear," "dislike," "aversion"

WORD	MEANING
acrophobia (*n.*) ˌa-krə-ˈfō-bē-ə	fear of being at a great height
agoraphobia (*n.*) ˌa-g(ə-)rə-ˈfō-bē-ə	fear of open spaces
Anglophobia (*n.*) ˌaŋ-glə-ˈfō-bē-ə	dislike of England or the English (*ant.* **Anglophilia**)
claustrophobia (*n.*) ˌklȯ-strə-ˈfō-bē-ə	fear of enclosed or narrow spaces

Germanophobia (*n.*)   dislike of Germany or the Germans (*ant.* **Germanophilia**)
jer-,man-ə-'fō-bē-ə

hydrophobia (*n.*)   1. dread of water
,hī-drə-'fō-bē-ə   2. rabies

monophobia (*n.*)   fear of being alone
,mä-nō-'fō-bē-ə

phobia (*n.*)   fear; dread; aversion
'fō-bē-ə

photophobia (*n.*)   aversion to light
'fō-tə-,fō-bē-ə

xenophobia (*n.*)   aversion to foreigners
,ze-nə-'fō-bē-ə

The form *phobe* at the end of a word means "one who fears or dislikes." For example:

Russophobe (*n.*)   one who dislikes Russia or the Russians (*ant.* **Russophile**)
'rə-sə-,fōb

Also: **Francophobe, Anglophobe, Germanophobe, computerphobe,** etc.

EXERCISE 4.1

In each blank, insert the most appropriate word from group 1, *phobia.*

1. You would not expect a professional mountain climber to have _____.

2. As we grow up, we overcome our childhood _____ of the dark.

3. Passage of the Chinese Exclusion Act of 1882 proves that some degree of _____ existed in our nation at that time.

4. Crowded elevators are especially avoided by anyone with _____.

5. After many decades of _____ the French joined the West Germans in close economic ties following World War II.

2. PHIL (PHILO): "loving," "fond of"

philanthropist (*n.*)   lover of humanity; person active in promoting human welfare (*ant.*
fə-'lan-thrə-pəst   **misanthrope**)

philanthropy (*n.*)   love of humanity, especially as shown in donations to charitable and
fə-'lan-thrə-pē   socially useful causes (*ant.* **misanthropy**)

philatelist (*n.*) fə-ˈla-tᵊl-əst	stamp collector
philately (*n.*) fə-ˈla-tᵊl-ē	collection and study of stamps
philharmonic (*adj.*) ˌfi-lər-ˈmä-nik	pertaining to a musical organization, such as a symphony orchestra (originally, "loving music")
philhellenism (*n.*) fil-ˈhel-ə-ˌniz-əm	support of Greece or the Greeks
philogyny (*n.*) fə-ˈlä-jə-nē	love of women (*ant.* **misogyny**)
philology (*n.*) fə-ˈlä-lə-jē	study (love) of language and literature
philosopher (*n.*) fə-ˈläs-ə-fə(r)	lover of, or searcher for, wisdom or knowledge; person who regulates his or her life by the light of reason

The form *phile* at the end of a word means "one who loves or supports." For example:

Anglophile (*n.*) ˈaŋ-glə-ˌfīl	supporter of England or the English (*ant.* **Anglophobe**)
audiophile (*n.*) ˈȯd-ē-ō-ˌfīl	one who is enthusiastic about high-fidelity sound reproduction
bibliophile (*n.*) ˈbi-blē-ə-ˌfīl	lover of books (*ant.* **bibliophobe**)
Francophile (*n.*) ˈfraŋ-kə-ˌfīl	supporter of France or the French (*ant.* **Francophobe**)
Sinophile (*n.*) ˈsī-nə-ˌfīl	supporter of China or the Chinese

EXERCISE 4.2

In each blank, insert the most appropriate word from group 2, *phil* (*philo*).

1. Socrates, the great Athenian _____, devoted his life to seeking truth and exposing error.

2. The _____ was proud of his fine collection of beautifully bound volumes.

3. Do you collect stamps? I, too, was once interested in _____.

4. The _____s among the American colonists were opposed to the war with England.

5. In her will, the _____ bequeathed 100 million dollars to charity.

6. _____s are especially eager to listen to newly released recordings by outstanding artists.

3. MIS: *"hate" (MIS means the opposite of PHIL.)*

misandry (*n.*)   hatred of males
'mi-,san-drē

misanthrope (*n.*)   hater of humanity (*ant.* **philanthropist**)
'mi-sᵊn-,thrōp

misanthropy (*n.*)   hatred of humanity (*ant.* **philanthropy**)
mi-'san-thrə-pē

misogamy (*n.*)   hatred of marriage
mə-'säg-ə-mē

misogyny (*n.*)   hatred of women (*ant.* **philogyny**)
mə-'sä-jə-nē

misology (*n.*)   hatred of argument, reasoning, or discussion
mə-'säl-ə-jē

misoneism (*n.*)   hatred of anything new
,mi-sə-'nē-,i-zəm

 **EXERCISE 4.3**

In each blank, insert the most appropriate word from group 3, *mis.*

1. Hamlet's _____ resulted from his suspicion that he had been betrayed by a woman—Ophelia.

2. When Gulliver returned from his travels, he could not endure the sight of fellow humans; he had become a _____.

3. Surprisingly, the first senior to marry had been the loudest advocate of _____.

4. Isabel enjoys discussion and debate; she cannot be accused of _____.

5. Some oppose innovation out of sheer _____; they do not want any change.

4. DYS: "bad," "ill," "difficult"

dysentery (*n.*)　　　　inflammation of the large intestine
'di-s°n-,ter-ē

dysfunction (*n.*)　　　abnormal functioning, as of an organ of the body
dis-'fəŋk-shən

dyslexia (*n.*)　　　　impairment of the ability to read
dis-'lek-sē-ə

dyslogistic (*adj.*)　　expressing disapproval or censure; uncomplimentary (*ant.* **eulogistic**)
,dis-lə-'jis-tik

dyspepsia (*n.*)　　　1. difficult digestion; indigestion (*ant.* **eupepsia**)
dis-'pep-shə　　　　2. ill humor; disgruntlement

dysphagia (*n.*)　　　difficulty in swallowing
dis-'fā-j(ē-)ə

dysphasia (*n.*)　　　speech difficulty resulting from brain injury
dis-'fā-zh(ē-)ə

dysphoria (*n.*)　　　sense of great unhappiness or dissatisfaction (*ant.* **euphoria**)
dis-'fōr-ē-ə

dystopia (*n.*)　　　imaginary place where living conditions are dreadful (*ant.* **utopia**)
dis-'tō-pē-ə

dystrophy (*n.*)　　　1. faulty nutrition
'dis-trə-fē　　　　　2. muscle disorder

✍ EXERCISE 4.4

In each blank, insert the most appropriate word from group 4, *dys*.

1. To aid digestion, eat slowly; rapid eating may cause _____.

2. Those who ate the contaminated food became ill with _____.

3. Injury to the brain may result in _____, a complicated speech disorder.

4. Muscular _____ is a disease in which the muscles waste away.

5. A badly inflamed throat may cause some _____ at mealtime.

6. George Orwell's NINETEEN EIGHTY-FOUR is about a totalitarian _____ where life is incredibly horrible.

5. EU: "good," "well," "advantageous" (EU means the opposite of DYS.)

eugenics (*n.*)
yü-'je-niks
science dealing with improving hereditary qualities (e.g., of the human race)

eulogize (*v.*)
'yü-lə-,jīz
write or speak in praise of someone (*ant.* **vilify**)

eupepsia (*n.*)
yü-'pep-shə
good digestion (*ant.* **dyspepsia**)

euphemism (*n.*)
'yü-fə-,mi-zəm
substitution of a "good" expression for an unpleasant one. Example: *sanitation* for *garbage collection*.

euphonious (*adj.*)
yü-'fō-nē-əs
pleasing in sound (*ant.* **cacophonous**)

euphoria (*n.*)
yü-'fȯr-ē-ə
sense of great happiness or well-being (*ant.* **dysphoria**)

euthanasia (*n.*)
,yü-thə-'nā-zh(ē-)ə
controversial practice of mercifully putting to death a person suffering from an incurable, painfully distressing disease (literally, "advantageous death")

euthenics (*n.*)
yü-'the-niks
science dealing with improving living conditions

 **EXERCISE 4.5**

In each blank, insert the most appropriate word from group 5, *eu.*

1. The audience liked the organist's _____ melodies.

2. Before conferring the award, the presiding officer will _____ the recipient.

3. The employee formerly called a "janitor" is now known by a _____, such as "superintendent" or "custodian."

4. Many believe that anyone who commits _____, regardless of the circumstances, is a murderer.

5. The _____ I felt when my teacher complimented my work this morning stayed with me for the rest of the day.

6. *MACRO: "large," "long"*
7. *MICRO: "small," "minute"*

macro (*n.*)
ˈma-krō

computer instruction standing for a series of steps

macrocosm (*n.*)
ˈma-krə-ˌkä-zəm

great world; universe (*ant.* **microcosm,** ˈmīk-rə-ˌkäz-əm, little world; epitome; reproduction of a larger unity)

macron (*n.*)
ˈmā-ˌkrän

horizontal mark indicating that the vowel over which it is placed is long

macroscopic (*adj.*)
ˌma-krə-ˈskä-pik

large enough to be visible to the naked eye (*ant.* **microscopic**)

microbe (*n.*)
ˈmī-ˌkrōb

microscopic life form; microorganism; germ

microbicide (*n.*)
mī-ˈkrō-bə-ˌsīd

agent that destroys microbes

microdont (*adj.*)
ˈmī-krə-ˌdänt

having small teeth

microfilm (*n.*)
ˈmī-krə-ˌfilm

film of very small size

microgram (*n.*)
ˈmī-krə-ˌgram

millionth of a gram

micrometer (*n.*)
ˈmī-krō-ˌmē-tər
mī-ˈkrä-mə-tər

1. millionth of a meter

2. instrument for measuring small lengths

microorganism (*n.*)
ˌmī-krō-ˈȯr-gə-ˌni-zəm

microscopic animal or plant

microsecond (*n.*)
ˈmī-krə-ˌsek-ənd

millionth of a second

microsurgery (*n.*)
ˌmī-krō-ˈsərj-ə-rē

surgery with the aid of microscopes and minute instruments or laser beams

microvolt (*n.*)
ˈmī-krə-ˌvōlt

millionth of a volt

microwatt (*n.*)
ˈmī-krə-ˌwät

millionth of a watt

microwave (*n.*)
ˈmī-krə-wāv

1. very short electromagnetic wave
2. microwave oven (oven that cooks quickly by using microwaves)

EXERCISE 4.6

In each blank, insert the most appropriate word from groups 6 and 7, *macro* and *micro*.

1. Documents can be recorded in a minimum of space if photographed on _____.

2. Space exploration has made us more aware of the vastness of the _____.

3. A _____ enables us to measure very minute distances that cannot be measured accurately with a ruler.

4. An ant is visible to the naked eye, but an ameba is _____.

5. The dictionary uses a _____ to tell us that the *e* in *eat* (ēt) is long.

6. The miracle of _____ enables reattaching a detached retina.

8. A (AN): "not," "without"

amoral (*adj.*) ā-'mȯr-əl	not moral; without a sense of moral responsibility
amorphous (*adj.*) ə-'mȯr-fəs	without (having no) definite form; shapeless; unorganized
anarchy (*n.*) 'a-nər-kē	total absence of rule or government; confusion; disorder
anemia (*n.*) ə-'nē-mē-ə	lack of a normal number of red blood cells
anesthesia (*n.*) ˌa-nəs-'thē-zhə	loss of feeling or sensation resulting from ether, chloroform, novocaine, etc.
anesthetic (*n.*) ˌa-nəs-'the-tik	drug that produces anesthesia
anhydrous (*adj.*) an-'hī-drəs	destitute of (without) water
anomaly (*n.*) ə-'nä-mə-lē	deviation from the common rule
anomalous (*adj.*) ə-'nä-mə-ləs	not normal; abnormal

anonymous (*adj.*)   nameless; of unknown or unnamed origin
ə-'nä-nə-məs

anoxia (*n.*)   deprivation of (state of being without) oxygen
a-'näk-sē-ə

apnea (*n.*)   temporary cessation of breathing
'ap-nē-ə

aseptic (*adj.*)   free from disease-causing microorganisms
ā-'sep-tik

asymptomatic (*adj.*)   showing no symptoms of disease
ˌā-ˌsim(p)-tə-'ma-tik

atheism (*n.*)   godlessness; denial of the existence of a Supreme Being
'ā-thē-ˌi-zəm

atrophy (*n.*)   lack of growth, as from disuse, disease, or malnourishment (*ant.*
'a-trə-fē   **hypertrophy**, hī-'pər-trə-fē, enlargement of a body part, as from overuse)

atypical (*adj.*)   unlike the typical
ā-'ti-pi-kəl

 **EXERCISE 4.7**

In each blank, insert the most appropriate word from group 8, *a*(*an*).

1. The gift is _____. We have no idea who sent it.

2. In the tropics, a snowstorm would be a(n) _____.

3. The administration of a(n) _____ prevents the patient from feeling pain during and immediately after an operation.

4. Wendy is _____ in one respect: she doesn't care for ice cream.

5. In _____ surgery, rigid precautions aim to exclude disease-causing microbes.

6. Miguel is cured. Medical tests show that he is _____.

9. MONO (MON): "one," "single," "alone"
10. POLY: "many"

monarchy (*n.*)
'mä-nər-kē
rule by a single person (*ant.* **polyarchy**)

monochromatic
(*adj.*)
,mä-nə-krō-'mat-ik
of one color (*ant.* **polychromatic**)

monocle (*n.*)
'mä-ni-kəl
eyeglass for one eye

monogamy (*n.*)
mə-'nä-gə-mē
marriage with one mate at a time (*ant.* **polygamy**)

monogram (*n.*)
'mä-nə-,gram
two or more letters interwoven to represent a name

monograph (*n.*)
'mä-nə-,graf
written account of a single thing or class of things

monolith (*n.*)
'mä-nᵊl-,ith
single stone of large size; obelisk

monolithic (*adj.*)
,mä-nᵊl-'i-thik
massive and rigidly uniform

monolog(ue) (*n.*)
'mä-nᵊl-,og
long speech by one person

monomania (*n.*)
,mä-nə-'mā-nē-ə
excessive concentration on one idea or subject

monomorphic (*adj.*)
,mä-nə-'mȯr-fik
having a single form (*ant.* **polymorphic**)

monosyllabic (*adj.*)
,mä-nə-sə-'la-bik
having one syllable (*ant.* **polysyllabic**)

monotheism (*n.*)
'mä-nə-thē-,i-zəm
belief that there is one God (*ant.* **polytheism**)

monotonous (*adj.*)
mə-'nä-tᵊ-nəs
continuing in an unchanging tone; wearying

polyarchy (*n.*)
'pä-lē-,är-kē
rule by many; government having three or more rulers (*ant.* **monarchy**)

polychromatic (*adj.*)
,pä-lē-krō-'ma-tik
having a variety of colors; multicolored; variegated (*ant.* **monochromatic**)

polygamy (*n.*)   marriage to several people at the same time (*ant.* **monogamy**)
pə-'li-gə-mē

polyglot (*adj.*)   speaking several languages
'pä-lē-,glät

polyglot (*n.*)   person who speaks several languages

polygon (*n.*)   closed plane figure having, literally, many angles and therefore many sides
'pä-lē-,gän

polymorphic (*adj.*)   having various forms (*ant.* **monomorphic**)
,pä-lē-'mȯr-fik

polyphonic (*adj.*)   having many sounds or voices (*ant.* **homophonic**, having the same sound)
,pä-lē-'fä-nik

polysyllabic (*adj.*)   having more than three syllables (*ant.* **monosyllabic**)
,pä-lē-sə-'la-bik

polytechnic (*adj.*)   dealing with many applied sciences and technical arts
,pä-lē-'tek-nik

polytheism (*n.*)   belief that there is a plurality of gods (*ant.* **monotheism**)
'pä-lē-thē-,i-zəm

 **EXERCISE 4.8**

In each blank, insert the most appropriate word from groups 9 and 10,
mono and *poly*.

1. The idea of getting revenge on Moby Dick was never absent from Ahab's mind—it was his _____.

2. Books for beginning readers contain relatively few _____ words.

3. The Romans obviously practiced _____, for they worshiped many gods.

4. A relative gave me a jacket embroidered with my own _____.

5. No one escapes in less than 20 minutes once my boss launches into a _____!

6. Our _____ neighbor speaks French, German, Russian, and English.

7. Professor Shaw's _____ on garden insecticides is being widely read.

8. _____ institutes offer courses in many applied sciences and technical arts.

9. Repetitive work soon becomes _____.

10. A huge _____, the 555-foot Washington Monument dominates the skyline of our nation's capital.

Review Exercises

REVIEW 1: GREEK PREFIXES AND ROOTS

In the space before each Greek prefix or root in column I, write the *letter* of its correct meaning from column II.

COLUMN I	COLUMN II
___ 1. PHOBIA	*a.* bad; ill; difficult
___ 2. MACRO	*b.* small; minute
___ 3. PHIL (PHILO)	*c.* not; without
___ 4. MONO (MON)	*d.* one; single; alone
___ 5. A (AN)	*e.* fear; dislike; aversion
___ 6. DYS	*f.* one who loves or supports
___ 7. POLY	*g.* many
___ 8. PHOBE	*h.* loving; fond of
___ 9. MIS	*i.* large; long
___ 10. MICRO	*j.* good; well; advantageous
___ 11. EU	*k.* hate
___ 12. PHILE	*l.* one who fears or dislikes

REVIEW 2: OPPOSITES

In the blank space, write the word that means the OPPOSITE of the word defined. (The first answer has been filled in as an example.)

DEFINITION	WORD	OPPOSITE
1. belief in God	theism	*atheism*
2. supporter of Russia	Russophile	_____
3. conforming to a type	typical	_____
4. good digestion	eupepsia	_____
5. one who dislikes books	bibliophobe	_____
6. lover of humanity	philanthropist	_____
7. believing there is but one God	monotheistic	_____
8. harsh in sound	cacophonous	_____

9. showing a variety of colors   polychromatic   _____

10. infected   septic   _____

11. without a sense of moral responsibility   amoral   _____

12. married to several people at the same time   polygamous   _____

13. invisible to the naked eye   microscopic   _____

14. enlargement, as from overuse   hypertrophy   _____

15. rule by many   polyarchy   _____

16. sense of great happiness   euphoria   _____

17. expressing censure or disapproval   dyslogistic   _____

18. having but one syllable   monosyllabic   _____

19. the great world; universe   macrocosm   _____

20. having various forms   polymorphic   _____

REVIEW 3: SENTENCE COMPLETION

Fill each blank with the most appropriate word from the vocabulary list below.

VOCABULARY LIST

euphemistic	euphoria	dysentery
monogram	dysphagia	acrophobia
euthanasia	anesthesia	dystrophy
misanthropy	anomalous	philatelist
anonymous	monograph	xenophobia

1. There is a conflict in the minds of many between the commandment "Thou shalt not kill" and the practice of _____.

2. A two-headed horse would be a(n) _____ sight.

3. The new regime dislikes foreigners; it exhibits a profound _____.

4. Though the letter was _____, I was able to discover who had written it.

5. The term "mortician" is a(n) _____ term for "undertaker."

6. The drinking of contaminated water can cause _____, an inflammation of the large intestine.

7. A(n) _____ collects stamps.

8. I had no dread of heights, but my companion's _____ became more severe as we approached the summit.

9. So effective was the local _____ that the patient experienced practically no pain during the surgery.

10. The biology professor is the author of a(n) _____ on earthworms.

REVIEW 4: CONCISE WRITING

Express the thought of each sentence below in no more than four words. The first sentence has been rewritten as a sample.

1. Scrooge has nothing but hate and contempt for other human beings.

    Scrooge is a misanthrope. _____

2. That patient does not have the normal number of red blood cells.

    _____

3. It is impossible to see viruses with the naked eye.

    _____

4. Beret suffered from a fear of being in the midst of open spaces.

    _____

5. It is against the law to be married to several people at the same time.

    _____

6. Clouds in the sky generally have no definite shape or form.

    _____

7. Carnegie used his millions to promote the welfare of his fellow human beings.

    _____

8. Many inhabitants had a disease characterized by an inflammation of the large intestine.

    _____

9. The fear of being at a great height is quite common.

    _____

10. Plato was an individual who lived his life by the light of reason.

    _____

REVIEW 5: BRAINTEASERS

Fill in the missing letters.

1. Stop using __ __ __ __ __ __ __ l a b __ __ words just to impress others.

2. Many __ __ __ l a t e __ __ __ __ __ own stamps from almost every nation.

3. The dog owner used a(n) __ __ __ **h e m** __ __ __ when he told us that his ailing poodle had been "put to sleep" by the veterinarian.

4. One would not expect a **b i b** __ __ __ __ __ __ __ __ to have a library card.

5. If we had no laws or government, there would be total __ __ **a r c** __ __.

6. Is there really a(n) __ **t o p** __ __, where living conditions are ideal?

7. Under favorable conditions, an accident victim's detached limb can be reattached through __ __ __ __ __ __ **u r g e** __ __.

8. My __ __ __ __ **h a g** __ __ has eased, but it is still hard for me to swallow.

9. The star was delighted when critics wrote __ __ **l o g** __ __ __ __ __ reviews about her new film.

10. In heated discussions, people may sometimes lose their heads, call each other names, and __ __ __ **i f** __ each other.

✍ REVIEW 6: COMPOSITION

Answer in two or three sentences.

1. If you were a discussion leader, what could you do to prevent an audience from having to listen to a monotonous monologue?

   _____

   _____

2. How would an invasion by hundreds of cacophonous birds affect the euphoria of people living in the neighborhood?

   _____

   _____

3. Would it be an anomaly for a well-known Francophobe to choose to live permanently in France? Why, or why not?

   _____

   _____

4. In your opinion, has the ready availability of anesthesia affected the phobias that people have about surgery? Explain.

   _____

   _____

5. Is it atypical for an immigrant to encounter no xenophobia whatsoever? Explain.

   _____

   _____

REVIEW 7: ANALOGIES

Write the *letter* of the word that best completes the analogy.

___ 1. *Anemia* is to *red blood cells* as *anoxia* is to _____.
   a. corpuscles   *b.* disease   *c.* oxygen   *d.* tissue   *e.* surgery

___ 2. *Euthenics* is to *environment* as *eugenics* is to _____.
   a. surroundings   *b.* heredity   *c.* nutrition   *d.* health   *e.* education

___ 3. *Dysphagia* is to *swallowing* as *dysphasia* is to _____.
   a. digestion   *b.* hearing   *c.* sight   *d.* speech   *e.* tasting

___ 4. *Misanthropy* is to *humanity* as *misogamy* is to _____.
   a. women   *b.* novelty   *c.* marriage   *d.* argument   *e.* foreigners

___ 5. *Polychromatic* is to *colors* as *polytechnic* is to _____.
   a. arts   *b.* sounds   *c.* forms   *d.* syllables   *e.* angles

11. LOGY: "science," "study," "account"

WORD	MEANING
anthropology (*n.*) ˌan-thrə-ˈpä-lə-jē	science dealing with the origin, races, customs, and beliefs of humankind
bacteriology (*n.*) bak-ˌtir-ē-ˈä-lə-jē	science dealing with the study of bacteria
biology (*n.*) bī-ˈä-lə-jē	science dealing with the study of living organisms
cardiology (*n.*) ˌkär-dē-ˈä-lə-jē	science dealing with the action and diseases of the heart
criminology (*n.*) ˌkri-mə-ˈnä-lə-jē	scientific study of crimes and criminals
dermatology (*n.*) ˌdər-mə-ˈtä-lə-jē	science dealing with the skin and its diseases
ecology (*n.*) i-ˈkä-lə-jē	science dealing with the relation of living things to their environment and to each other

ethnology (*n.*)
eth-'nä-lə-jē

branch of anthropology dealing with human races, their origin, distribution, culture, etc.

genealogy (*n.*)
ˌjē-nē-'ä-lə-jē

account of the descent of a person or family from an ancestor

geology (*n.*)
jē-'ä-lə-jē

science dealing with the earth's history as recorded in rocks

meteorology (*n.*)
ˌmē-tē-ə-'rä-lə-jē

science dealing with the atmosphere and weather

morphology (*n.*)
mȯr-'fä-lə-jē

1. scientific study of the forms and structures of plants and animals
2. form and structure of an organism or any of its parts

mythology (*n.*)
mi-'thä-lə-jē

account or study of myths

necrology (*n.*)
nə-'krä-lə-jē

list of persons who have died recently; obituary

neurology (*n.*)
nu̇-'rä-lə-jē

scientific study of the nervous system and its diseases

paleontology (*n.*)
ˌpā-lē-än-'tä-lə-jē

science dealing with life in the remote past as recorded in fossils

pathology (*n.*)
pə-'thä-lə-jē

1. science dealing with the nature and causes of disease
2. something abnormal

petrology (*n.*)
pə-'trä-lə-jē

scientific study of rocks

physiology (*n.*)
ˌfi-zē-'ä-lə-jē

science dealing with the functions of living things or their organs

psychology (*n.*)
sī-'kä-lə-jē

science of the mind

sociology (*n.*)
ˌsō-sē-'ä-lə-jē

study of the evolution, development, and functioning of human society

technology (*n.*)
tek-'nä-lə-jē

use of science to achieve a practical purpose; applied science; engineering

theology (*n.*)
thē-'ä-lə-jē

study of religion and religious ideas

EXERCISE 4.9

In each blank, insert the most appropriate word from group 11, *logy*.

1. Both ethnology and _____ deal with the origin and races of humankind.

2. The tale of Pyramus and Thisbe is one of the most appealing in Greek _____.

3. Advances in _____ enable industries to lower manufacturing costs.

4. Sherlock Holmes is a fictional character who excels in _____.

5. Sufferers from skin disorders are often referred to a specialist in _____.

6. The good news is that the patient's medical tests show no evidence of _____.

12. BIO: "life"

abiogenesis (*n.*) ,ā-'bī-ō-'je-nə-səs	spontaneous generation (development of life from lifeless matter) (*ant.* **biogenesis**)
amphibious (*adj.*) am-'fi-bē-əs	1. able to live both on land and in water 2. attacking with coordinated land, sea, and air forces
antibiotic (*n.*) ,an-ti-bī-'ä-tik	germ-killing substance produced by or derived from a microorganism
autobiography (*n.*) ,ȯ-tə-bī-'ä-grə-fē	story of a person's life written by that person
biochemistry (*n.*) ,bī-ō-'ke-mə-strē	chemistry dealing with chemical compounds and processes in living plants and animals
biocidal (*adj.*) ,bī-ə-'sī-dᵊl	destructive to life or living things
biodegradable (*adj.*) ,bī-ō-di-'grā-də-bəl	capable of being readily decomposed into harmless substances by microorganisms (*ant.* **nonbiodegradable**)
biogenesis (*n.*) ,bī-ō-'je-nə-səs	development of life from preexisting life (*ant.* **abiogenesis**)
biography (*n.*) bī-'ä-grə-fē	story of a person's life written by another person
biology (*n.*) bī-'ä-lə-jē	science dealing with the study of living organisms

biometry (*n.*) bī-'ä-mə-trē	statistical analysis of biological data
or **biometrics** (*n.*) ,bī-ō-'me-triks	
biopsy (*n.*) 'bī-,äp-sē	diagnostic examination of a piece of tissue from the living body
biota (*n.*) bī-'ō-tə	plants (flora) and animals (fauna) living in a region
microbe (*n.*) 'mī-,krōb	microscopic life form; microorganism; germ
symbiosis (*n.*) ,sim-bi-'ō-səs	living together in mutually helpful association of two dissimilar organisms

 **EXERCISE 4.10**

In each blank, insert the most appropriate word from group 12, *bio*.

1. Fish can live only in water, but frogs are _____.

2. One _____ widely used to arrest the growth of harmful bacteria is penicillin.

3. In his _____, AN AMERICAN DOCTOR'S ODYSSEY, Victor Heiser tells how he survived the Johnstown flood.

4. An example of _____ is provided by the fungus that lives in a mutually beneficial partnership with the roots of an oak tree.

5. A(n) _____ is a microscopic organism.

6. The use of the pesticide DDT was discontinued when it was found to be too _____.

13. TOMY (TOM): "cutting," "operation of incision"

anatomy (*n.*) ə-'na-tə-mē	1. dissection of plants, animals, or other things to study their structure; analysis 2. structure (e.g., of a plant or animal)
appendectomy (*n.*) ,a-pən-'dek-tə-mē	surgical removal of the appendix
atom (*n.*) 'a-təm	smallest particle of an element (literally, "not cut," "indivisible")

atomizer (*n.*) 'a-tə-,mī-zə(r)	device for converting a liquid to a fine spray
dichotomy (*n.*) dī-'kä-tə-mē	cutting or division into two; division
gastrectomy (*n.*) ga-'strek-tə-mē	surgical removal of part or all of the stomach
lobotomy (*n.*) lō-'bä-tə-mē	brain surgery for treatment of certain mental disorders
mastectomy (*n.*) ma-'stek-tə-mē	surgical removal of a breast
phlebotomy (*n.*) fli-'bä-tə-mē	opening of a vein to diminish the blood supply
tome (*n.*) 'tōm	one volume, or "cut," of a work of several volumes; scholarly book
tonsillectomy (*n.*) ,tän-sə-'lek-tə-mē	surgical removal of the tonsils
tracheotomy (*n.*) ,trā-kē-'ä-tə-mē	surgical operation of cutting into the trachea (windpipe)

EXERCISE 4.11

In each blank, insert the most appropriate word from group 13, *tomy (tom)*.

1. Candidates deny any _____ between their promises and their deeds.

2. The _____ was once common to reduce the number of a child's colds.

3. In former times, _____ (usually termed *bleeding*) was used indiscriminately as a treatment for practically all illnesses.

4. You will learn about the structure of the skeleton, the muscles, the heart, and the other parts of the body when you study human _____.

5. Only in certain cases of extremely serious mental illness is a(n) _____ to be considered.

14. POD: "foot"

antipodes (*n. pl.*) an-'ti-pə-,dēz	parts of the globe (or their inhabitants) diametrically opposite to each other (literally, "with the feet opposite")
arthropod (*n.*) 'är-thrə-,päd	invertebrate (animal having no backbone) with jointed legs, e.g., insects.
chiropodist (*n.*) kə-'rä-pə-dist	one who treats ailments of the human foot
dipody (*n.*) 'di-pə-dē	verse (line of poetry) consisting of two feet; a dimeter
podiatrist (*n.*) pə-'dī-ə-trist	chiropodist
podium (*n.*) 'pō-dē-əm	1. dais; raised platform 2. low wall serving as a foundation

pseudopod (*n.*)
'sü-də-,päd
 	
  or **pseudopodium**
  ,sü-də-'pō-dē-əm
	(literally, "false foot") temporary extension of the protoplasm, as in the ameba, to enable the organism to move and take in food

tripod (*n.*) 'trī-,päd	utensil, stool, or caldron having three legs
unipod (*n.*) 'yü-nə-,päd	one-legged support

✍ EXERCISE 4.12

In each blank, insert the most appropriate word from group 14, *pod*.

1. One who treats ailments of the feet is known as a chiropodist or a(n) _____.

2. The English often call Australia and New Zealand the _____, since these countries are almost diametrically opposite England on the globe.

3. As the guest conductor stepped onto the _____, the audience burst into applause.

4. A crab is a(n) _____; so, too, are lobsters, bees, flies, spiders, and other invertebrates with segmented legs.

5. Joined at the top, the three poles supporting a tent form a(n) _____.

15. HOMO: "one and the same," "like"
16. HETERO: "different"

homochromatic (*adj.*)
͵hō-mō-krō-'ma-tik
having the same color; monochromatic; unicolor

heterochromatic
(*adj.*)
͵he-tə-rō-krō-'ma-tik
having different colors

homogeneous (*adj.*)
͵hō-mə-'jē-nē-əs
of the same kind; similar; uniform

heterogeneous (*adj.*)
͵het-ə-rə-'jē-nē-əs
differing in kind; dissimilar; varied

homology (*n.*)
hō-'mä-lə-jē
similarity in structure

heterology (*n.*)
͵he-tə-'rä-lə-jē
dissimilarity in structure

homomorphic (*adj.*)
͵hō-mə-'mȯr-fik
exhibiting similarity of form

heteromorphic (*adj.*)
͵he-tə-rə-'mȯr-fik
exhibiting diversity of form

homonym (*n.*)
'hä-mə-͵nim
word that sounds like another but differs in meaning and spelling, e.g., *principal* and *principle*

heteronym (*n.*)
'he-tə-rə-͵nim
word spelled like another, but differing in sound and meaning, e.g., *bass* (the tone, pronounced "base") and *bass* (the fish, rhyming with "pass").

homocentric (*adj.*)
hō-mō-'sen-trik
having the same center; concentric

homophonic (*adj.*)
͵hä-mə-'fä-nik
having the same sound or voice (*ant.* **polyphonic**)

heteroclite (*adj.*)
'he-tə-rə-͵klīt
deviating from the common rule; abnormal; atypical

heteroclite (*n.*)
person or thing deviating from the common rule

heterodox (*adj.*)
'he-tə-rə-͵däks
opposed to accepted beliefs or established doctrines, especially in religion; unorthodox (*ant.* **orthodox**)

EXERCISE 4.13

In each blank, insert the most appropriate word from groups 15 and 16, *homo* and *hetero.*

1. The butterfly is _____; it goes through four stages in its life cycle, and in each of these it has a different form.

2. An archery target usually consists of several _____ circles.

3. People of many races and religions can be found in the _____ population of large American cities.

4. The words *write* and *right* are _____.

5. The foreleg of a horse and the wing of a bird exhibit _____; they have a fundamental similarity of structure.

6. To escape persecution for his _____ views, Roger Williams fled from Massachusetts Bay Colony and founded the colony of Rhode Island.

7. *Lead,* as in "lead the way," and *lead,* as in "lead pipe," are a pair of _____s.

8. Stained-glass windows are _____; they are composed of glass sections of many colors.

9. The newly admitted students, though fairly _____ in age, were quite heterogeneous in ability.

10. Do not expect heteroclite views from a(n) _____ person.

17. HYPER: "over," "above," "beyond the ordinary"
18. HYPO: "under," "beneath," "less than the ordinary"

hyperacidity (*n.*) ,hī-pər-ə-'si-də-tē	excessive acidity
hypoacidity (*n.*) ,hī-pō-ə-'sid-ət-ē	weak acidity
hyperglycemia (*n.*) ,hī-pər-glī-'sē-mē-ə	excess of sugar in the blood
hypoglycemia (*n.*) ,hī-pō-glī-'sē-mē-ə	abnormally low level of sugar in the blood
hypertension (*n.*) ,hī-pər-'ten-shən	abnormally high blood pressure

hypotension (*n.*)   low blood pressure
,hī-pō-'ten-shən

hyperthermia (*n.*)   especially high fever; hyperpyrexia
,hī-pər-'thər-mē-ə

hypothermia (*n.*)   subnormal body temperature
,hī-pō-'thər-mē-ə

hyperthyroid (*adj.*)   marked by excessive activity of the thyroid gland
,hī-pər-'thī-,ròid

hypothyroid (*adj.*)   marked by deficient activity of the thyroid gland
,hī-pō-'thī-,ròid

hyperactive (*adj.*)   overactive
,hī-pər-'ak-tiv

hyperbole (*n.*)   extravagant exaggeration of statement
hī-'pər-bə-lē

hypercritical (*adj.*)   overcritical
,hī-pər-'kri-ti-kəl

hyperemia (*n.*)   superabundance of blood
,hī-pər-'ē-mē-ə

hyperopia (*n.*)   farsightedness (*ant.* **myopia**)
,hī-pə-'rō-pē-ə

hypersensitive (*adj.*)   excessively sensitive; supersensitive
,hī-pər-'sen-s(ə-)tiv

hypertrophy (*n.*)   excessive growth or development, as of a body part (*ant.* **atrophy**)
,hī-'pər-trə-fē

hypodermic (*adj.*)   injected under the skin
,hī-pə-'dər-mik

hypothesis (*n.*)   theory or supposition assumed as a basis for reasoning (something "placed
,hī-'pä-thə-səs   under")

hypothetical (*adj.*)   assumed without proof for the purpose of reasoning; conjectural
,hī-pə-'the-ti-kəl

EXERCISE 4.14

In each blank, insert the most appropriate word from groups 17 and 18, *hyper* and *hypo*.

1. The more that the members of a cast have devoted themselves to perfecting their roles, the likelier they are to be _____ about criticism of their performances.

2. In _____, the blood pressure is lower than normal.

3. The novel's review was _____; it exaggerated minor faults and gave no credit at all for the author's style and humor.

4. Causing _____, too much lemon juice spoils lemonade.

5. "I've told you a *million* times to buckle up!" is an example of _____.

6. A _____ syringe and needle are used to administer injections under the skin.

7. Billy is a _____ youngster; he won't sit still for a minute.

8. If your _____ is disproved by facts, you should abandon it.

9. In _____, the blood pressure is abnormally high.

10. Excessive activity of the thyroid gland is described as a _____ condition.

19. ENDO: "within"
20. EXO: "out of," "outside"

endocrine (*adj.*) ʹen-də-krən	secreting internally
exocrine (*adj.*) ʹek-sə-krən	secreting externally
endogamy (*n.*) en-ʹdä-gə-mē	marriage within the tribe, caste, or social group
exogamy (*n.*) ek-ʹsä-gə-mē	marriage outside the tribe, caste, or social group
endogenous (*adj.*) en-ʹdä-jə-nəs	produced from within; due to internal causes
exogenous (*adj.*) ek-ʹsäj-ə-nəs	produced from without; due to external causes
endoskeleton (*n.*) ‚en-dō-ʹske-lə-tᵊn	internal skeleton or supporting framework in an animal

exoskeleton (*n.*)   hard protective structure developed outside the body, as the shell of a
,ek-sō-'ske-lə-t°n   lobster

endosmosis (*n.*)   osmosis inward
,en-,däs-'mō-səs

exosmosis (*n.*)   osmosis outward
,ek-,säs-'mō-səs

endocarditis (*n.*)   inflammation of the lining of the heart
,en-dō-kär-'dī-təs

endoderm (*n.*)   membranelike tissue lining the digestive tract
'en-də-,dərm

endoparasite (*n.*)   parasite living on the inside of its host (*ant.* **ectoparasite**)
,en-dō-'par-ə-'sīt

endophyte (*n.*)   plant growing within another plant
'en-də-,fīt

exoteric (*adj.*)   known externally (outside a select group; publicly); readily understandable
,ek-sə-'ter-ik   (*ant.* **esoteric**)

exotic (*adj.*)   1. introduced from another country; foreign (*ant.* **native**)
ig-'zä-tik   2. strikingly unusual; strange

EXERCISE 4.15

In each blank, insert the most appropriate word from groups 19 and 20,
endo and *exo*.

1. Algae that live within other plants are known as _____s.

2. Foreign visitors can often be identified by their _____ dress.

3. _____ glands discharge their secretions externally through ducts
   or tubes.

4. _____ glands, having no ducts or tubes, secrete internally.

5. Some primitive tribes observe _____, forbidding marriage outside
   the tribe.

6. The body louse is a most annoying _____, as it moves freely over the
   body of its host.

7. The lobster has a thick protective shell known as an _____.

8. Unlike lobsters, humans have an internal skeleton called an _____.

9. The tyrant blames "foreign agitators," not _____ rebels, for the riot.

10. Once established in the intestines of its host, an _____ leads a life
    of ease.

21. ARCHY: "rule"

anarchy (*n.*)
ˈa-nər-kē
total absence of rule or government; confusion; disorder

autarchy (*n.*)
ˈȯ-,tär-kē
rule by an absolute sovereign

hierarchy (*n.*)
ˈhī-(ə-),rär-kē
body of rulers or officials grouped in ranks, each being subordinate to the rank above it; pecking order

matriarchy (*n.*)
ˈmā-trē-,är-kē
form of social organization in which the mother rules the family or tribe, descent being traced through the mother

monarchy (*n.*)
ˈmä-nər-kē
state ruled over by a single person, as a king or queen

oligarchy (*n.*)
ˈä-lə-,gär-kē
form of government in which a few people have the power

patriarchy (*n.*)
ˈpā-trē-,är-kē
form of social organization in which the father rules the family or tribe, descent being traced through the father

 **EXERCISE 4.16**

In each blank, insert the most appropriate word from group 21, *archy*.

1. In the naval _____, a rear admiral ranks below a vice admiral.

2. Many a supposedly "democratic" organization is controlled by a(n) _____ of three or four influential members.

3. In a constitutional _____, the power of the king or queen is usually limited by a constitution and a legislature.

4. A family in which the mother alone makes all the final decisions could be called a(n) _____.

5. To advocates of _____, the best government is no government at all.

22. GEO: "earth," "ground"

geocentric (*adj.*)
,jē-ō-ˈsen-trik
measured from the earth's center; having the earth as a center

geodetic (*adj.*)
,jē-ə-ˈde-tik
pertaining to *geodesy* (mathematics dealing with the earth's shape and dimensions)

geography (*n.*)　　　study of the earth's surface, climate, continents, people, products, etc.
jē-'ä-grə-fē

geology (*n.*)　　　science dealing with the earth's history as recorded in rocks
jē-'ä-lə-jē

geometry (*n.*)　　　mathematics dealing with lines, angles, surfaces, and solids (literally,
jē-'ä-mə-trē　　　　"measurement of land")

geomorphic (*adj.*)　　pertaining to the shape of the earth or the form of its surface
‚jē-ə-'mȯr-fik

geophysics (*n.*)　　　science treating of the forces that modify the earth
‚jē-ə-'fi-ziks

geopolitics (*n.*)　　　study of government and its policies as affected by physical geography
‚jē-ō-'pä-lə-‚tiks

geoponics (*n.*)　　　art or science of agriculture (literally, "working of the earth")
‚jē-ə-'pä-niks

georgic (*adj.*)　　　agricultural
‚jȯr-jik

georgic (*n.*)　　　poem on husbandry (farming)

geotropism (*n.*)　　response to earth's gravity, as the growing of roots downward in the ground
jē-'ä-trə-‚pi-zəm

The form *gee* is used at the end of a word. For example:

apogee (*n.*)　　　farthest point from the earth in the orbit of a heavenly body (*ant.* **perigee**);
'ap-ə-jē　　　　　culmination

EXERCISE 4.17

In each blank, insert the most appropriate word from group 22, *geo*.

1. At its apogee, the moon is nearly 252,000 miles from the earth; at its
_____, it is less than 226,000 miles away.

2. Heliotropism attracts leaves to sunlight; _____ draws roots downward in
the earth.

3. Unlike _____ surveying, plane surveying neglects the mathematics that
accounts for the effect of the earth's curved surface.

4. Some earthquakes have little impact on the form of the earth's surface, but others result in
noticeable _____ changes.

5. A force such as a tornado that affects our planet is dealt with in _____.

23. PATH (PATHO, PATHY):
(1) "feeling," "suffering"; (2) "disease"

(1) FEELING, SUFFERING

antipathy (*n.*) aversion ("feeling against"); dislike (*ant.* **sympathy**)
an-'ti-pə-thē

apathy (*n.*) lack of feeling, emotion, interest, or excitement; indifference
'a-pə-thē

empathy (*n.*) complete understanding of another's feelings, motives, etc.
'em-pə-thē

pathetic (*adj.*) arousing pity
pə-'the-tik

pathos (*n.*) quality in drama, speech, literature, music, or events that arouses a feeling
'pā-thäs of pity or sadness

sympathy (*n.*) sharing of ("feeling with") another's trouble; compassion (*ant.* **antipathy**)
'sim-pə-thē

telepathy (*n.*) transference of the thoughts and feelings of one person to another by no
tə-'le-pə-thē apparent means of communication

(2) DISEASE

homeopathy (*n.*) treatment of disease with minute doses of a remedy that, if given in
,hō-mē-'ä-pə-thē massive doses to healthy persons, would produce effects like those of the
disease (*ant.* **allopathy**)

osteopath (*n.*) practitioner of *osteopathy* (treatment of diseases by manipulation of bones,
'äs-tē-ə-,path muscles, nerves, etc.)

pathogenic (*adj.*) causing disease
,pa-thə-'je-nik

pathological (*adj.*) due to disease
,pa-thə-'lä-ji-kəl

psychopathic (*adj.*) 1. pertaining to mental disease
,sī-kə-'pa-thik 2. insane

EXERCISE 4.18

In each blank, insert the most appropriate word from group 23, *path* (*patho, pathy*).

1. _____ bacteria cause such diseases as pneumonia and scarlet fever.

2. Sometimes, as if by _____, one may know the thoughts of an absent friend or relative.

3. The _____ expression on the youngster's face made everyone feel sorry for him.

4. Such intense _____ resulted from their quarrel that the sisters haven't spoken to each other for years.

5. The forced parting of the young lovers was full of _____.

24. MORPH: "form"

amorphous (*adj.*) ə-'mȯr-fəs	having no definite form; shapeless; unorganized
anthropomorphic (*adj.*) ,an-thrə-pə-'mȯr-fik	attributing human form or characteristics to beings not human, especially gods
dimorphous (*adj.*) dī-'mȯr-fəs	occurring under two distinct forms
endomorphic (*adj.*) ,en-də-'mȯr-fik	having a form deriving largely from the embryo's inner layer; having a heavy body build (*ant.* **ectomorphic**)
heteromorphic (*adj.*) ,he-tə-rə-'mȯr-fik	exhibiting diversity of form
metamorphosis (*n.*) ,me-tə-'mȯr-fə-səs	change of form
monomorphic (*adj.*) ,mä-nə-'mȯr-fik	having a single form
morphology (*n.*) mȯr-'fä-lə-jē	1. branch of biology dealing with the form and structure of animals and plants 2. form and structure of an organism or any of its parts

EXERCISE 4.19

In each blank, insert the most appropriate word from group 24, *morph*.

1. As the fog slowly lifted, _____ objects began to assume definite shapes.

2. When you study cell _____, you will learn about the nucleus, the cell membrane, and the other features of cell structure.

3. The drastic _____ from forested area to attractive residential neighborhood was accomplished in less than three years.

4. Individual members of a(n) _____ species are similar in form.

5. The ancient Greeks had a(n) _____ conception of deity; they gave their gods and goddesses the characteristics of men and women.

25. PERI: "around," "about," "near," "enclosing"

pericardium (*n.*) ˌper-ə-ˈkär-dē-əm	membranous sac enclosing the heart
perigee (*n.*) ˈper-ə-jē	nearest point to the earth in the orbit of a heavenly body (*ant.* **apogee**)
perihelion (*n.*) ˌper-ə-ˈhēl-yən	nearest point to the sun in the orbit of a heavenly body (*ant.* **aphelion**)
perimeter (*n.*) pə-ˈri-mə-tər	whole outer boundary or measurement of a surface or figure
periodontics (*n.*) ˌper-ē-ō-ˈdän-tiks	branch of dentistry dealing with diseases of the bone and gum tissues supporting the teeth
peripatetic (*adj.*) ˌper-ə-pə-ˈte-tik	traveling about; itinerant
peripheral (*adj.*) pə-ˈri-fə-rəl	1. on the *periphery* (outside boundary); outside or away from the central part, as in *peripheral* vision 2. only slightly connected with what is essential; merely incidental
peripheral (*n.*)	device that can be attached to or used with a computer, such as a keyboard, monitor, printer, or scanner
periphrastic (*adj.*) ˌper-ə-ˈfras-tik	expressed in a roundabout way; circumlocutory
periscope (*n.*) ˈper-ə-ˌskōp	instrument permitting those in a submarine a view ("look around") of the surface

peristalsis (*n.*)
,per-ə-'stȯl-səs
wavelike contraction of the walls of the intestines, which propels contents onward

peristyle (*n.*)
'per-ə-,stīl
1. row of columns around a building or court
2. the space so enclosed

peritonitis (*n.*)
,per-ə-tᵊn-'ī-təs
inflammation of the *peritoneum* (membrane lining the abdominal cavity and surrounding the organs within it)

EXERCISE 4.20

In each blank, insert the most appropriate word from group 25, *peri*.

1. The _____ of a rectangle is twice its width plus twice its length.

2. At its aphelion, the earth is 152,516,120 kilometers (94,560,000 miles) from the sun; at its _____, it is only 147,496,770 kilometers (91,448,000 miles) away.

3. We will not be able to reach a decision on the main issue if we waste too much time on _____ matters.

4. In _____, wavelike contractions move food through the intestines.

5. Before changing its position, the cautious turtle raised its head like a _____ to survey surrounding conditions.

Review Exercises

REVIEW 8: GREEK PREFIXES AND ROOTS

In the space before each Greek prefix or root in column I, write the *letter* of its correct meaning from column II. (Exercise continues on next page.)

COLUMN I	COLUMN II
___ 1. POD	*a.* different
___ 2. EXO	*b.* life
___ 3. HETERO	*c.* under; beneath; less than ordinary
___ 4. GEO	*d.* one and the same; like
___ 5. LOGY	*e.* rule
___ 6. HYPO	*f.* around; about; near; enclosing
___ 7. BIO	*g.* cutting; operation of incision
___ 8. MORPH	*h.* feeling; suffering; disease
___ 9. PATH (PATHO, PATHY)	*i.* earth; ground

___ **10.** ARCHY	*j.* within
___ **11.** PERI	*k.* foot
___ **12.** TOMY (TOM)	*l.* form
___ **13.** HYPER	*m.* out of; outside
___ **14.** ENDO	*n.* over; above; beyond the ordinary
___ **15.** HOMO	*o.* science; study; account

REVIEW 9: SYNONYMS

In the space provided, write the *letter* of the word that most nearly has the SAME MEANING as the italicized word or expression.

___ **1.** *hypercritical* reviewer: *a.* uncritical   *b.* hypersensitive   *c.* esoteric   *d.* overcritical

___ **2.** complete *metamorphosis*:   *a.* change   *b.* course   *c.* process   *d.* misunderstanding

___ **3.** eminent *foot specialist*:   *a.* criminologist   *b.* world traveler   *c.* podiatrist   *d.* osteopath

___ **4.** trace one's *genealogy*:   *a.* career   *b.* descent   *c.* downfall   *d.* personality

___ **5.** *hypothetical* statement: *a.* conjectural   *b.* introductory   *c.* unbiased   *d.* incontrovertible

___ **6.** *anatomical* defect: *a.* minor   *b.* irremediable   *c.* structural   *d.* inherited

___ **7.** *homogeneous* in size: *a.* different   *b.* perfect   *c.* heteromorphic   *d.* similar

___ **8.** seems *psychopathic*:   *a.* pathetic   *b.* indifferent   *c.* insane   *d.* unsympathetic

___ **9.** *exotic* customs: *a.* native   *b.* foreign   *c.* familiar   *d.* cultured

___ **10.** *amorphous* ideas: *a.* organized   *b.* original   *c.* exaggerated   *d.* shapeless

REVIEW 10: OPPOSITES

In the blank space, write the word that means the OPPOSITE of the word defined.

DEFINITION	WORD	OPPOSITE
1. differing in kind	heterogeneous	_____
2. conforming to an acknowledged standard	orthodox	_____
3. lack of growth from want of nourishment	atrophy	_____
4. feeling of accord	sympathy	_____

5. having many sounds   polyphonic   _____

6. difficult to understand   esoteric   _____

7. similarity in structure   homology   _____

8. parasite living on the exterior of an animal   ectoparasite   _____

9. low blood pressure   hypotension   _____

10. nearsightedness   myopia   _____

11. excessive acidity   hyperacidity   _____

12. osmosis outward   exosmosis   _____

13. secreting internally   endocrine   _____

14. excess of sugar in the blood   hyperglycemia   _____

15. nearest point to the earth in the orbit   perigee   _____
    of a satellite

16. development of life from preexisting life   biogenesis   _____

17. due to external causes   exogenous   _____

18. nearest point to the sun in the orbit   perihelion   _____
    of a planet

19. exhibiting diversity of form   heteromorphic   _____

20. marriage outside the tribe, caste, or   exogamy   _____
    social group

 REVIEW 11: BRAINTEASERS

Fill in the missing letters.

1. Many citizens do not bother to vote on Election Day. What is the reason for
   their __ **p a t h** __?

2. The __ __ **r i m** __ __ __ __ of a 7-inch square is 28 inches.

3. TV weather programs teach us a great deal about __ __ __ __ __ __ __ **l o g** __.

4. A country ruled by a(n) __ __ __ **g a r c h** __ of three powerful officials is not a true
   democracy.

5. Continued progress in __ __ __ __ **n o** __ __ __ __ is enabling factories to turn out more
   and more products with fewer and fewer employees.

6. The feelings of a(n) __ __ __ __ __ __ __ __ **s i t** __ __ __ person are easily hurt.

7. If there were no laws, and we all could do as we pleased, our nation would be in a state
   of **a n** __ __ __ __ __.

8. Some of the lecturer's remarks were so __ s o t __ __ __ __ that nobody but advanced scholars could understand them.

9. When it is noon here, it is midnight in the __ __ t i p __ __ __ __.

10. Frogs are **a m** __ __ __ __ __ __ __ __; they spend part of their time on land.

REVIEW 12: CONCISE WRITING

Express the thought of each sentence below in no more than four words.

1. Shock may cause a person's body temperature to drop to a subnormal level.

   _____

2. Some wastes cannot readily be decomposed into harmless substances by microorganisms.

   _____

3. Galileo had ideas that were contrary to the accepted beliefs of his time.

   _____

4. The science that deals with the study of living things is fascinating.

   _____

5. Some chiefs forbid the marriage of any member of their tribe to an outsider.

   _____

6. Is the supposition that you are making as a basis for your reasoning logical?

   _____

7. The operation for the surgical removal of her appendix was a success.

   _____

8. These very minute organisms are invisible to the naked eye.

   _____

9. We are studying the science that deals with the earth's history as told in rocks.

   _____

10. He goes to a physician who specializes in the treatment of foot problems.

   _____

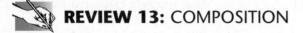

REVIEW 13: COMPOSITION

Answer in two or three sentences.

1. Is our nation's population more homogeneous or more heterogeneous than it was a hundred years ago? Explain.

_____

_____

_____

2. Why would most Americans have an antipathy to the establishment of a monarchy in their country?

_____

_____

_____

3. Would it encourage or discourage apathy in a lesson on amphibious animals if a living frog were brought into the classroom? Why?

_____

_____

_____

4. How would a hypersensitive individual react to criticism by a hypercritical person?

_____

_____

_____

5. Describe one metamorphosis in the way we live that a technological discovery brought on.

_____

_____

_____

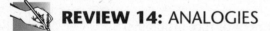

REVIEW 14: ANALOGIES

Write the *letter* of the word that best completes the analogy.

___   1. *Environment* is to *ecology* as *skin* is to _____.
         a. osteopathy   *b.* dermatology   *c.* peritonitis   *d.* neurology   *e.* endoderm

___   2. *Lobotomy* is to *brain* as *phlebotomy* is to _____.
         a. throat   *b.* nerve   *c.* foot   *d.* vein   *e.* muscle

___ 3. *Government* is to *anarchy* as *sympathy* is to _____.
   a. pathos   *b.* compassion   *c.* apathy   *d.* empathy   *e.* telepathy

___ 4. *Pathology* is to *disease* as *morphology* is to _____.
   a. structure   *b.* function   *c.* descent   *d.* health   *e.* race

___ 5. *Animal* is to *tapeworm* as *plant* is to _____.
   a. earthworm   *b.* biota   *c.* microbe   *d.* ectoparasite   *e.* endophyte

REVIEW 15: SIMILAR AND CONTRARY

Fill in the missing letters so that each line contains three words or phrases with similar meanings and one with a contrary meaning.

Similar Meaning	Similar Meaning	Similar Meaning	Contrary Meaning
1. uncompl __ __ entary	dysl __ __ istic	__ __ sapproving	lau __ __ __ ory
2. __ morphous	without f __ __ m	sh __ __ __ less	org __ __ ized
3. con __ __ __ tional	orthod __ __	__ __ cepted	he __ __ __ __ dox
4. mo __ __ tonous	unc __ __ __ __ ing	we __ __ ying	var __ __ ng
5. po __ __ chromatic	m __ __ __ icolored	varie __ __ ted	mono __ hromatic
6. phil __ __ __ hropy	love of __ __ nkind	alt __ __ ism	m __ __ anthropy
7. ph __ __ __ a	an __ __ __ athy	aver __ __ on	pred __ __ ection
8. heterocl __ __ e	un __ __ nventional	unorth __ __ __ x	conf __ __ mist
9. ex __ ltation	eu __ __ __ ria	e __ __ tion	dyspho __ __ a
10. ex __ __ eric	known p __ __ licly	un __ __ rstandable	e __ oteric
11. ap __ __ ee	h __ __ hest point	c __ __ mination	ab __ ss
12. homog __ __ eous	sim __ __ ar	al __ ke	he __ __ r ogeneous
13. hy __ __ __ hesis	ass __ __ ption	sup __ __ sition	f __ __ t
14. a __ __ __ hy	dis __ __ terest	ind __ __ ference	__ eal
15. s __ __ pathy	c __ __ passion	e __ pathy	rep __ __ nance

REVIEW 16: FILL AND MATCH

Write the letter of the word or set of words best filling each blank and best matching each italicized expression. (Please note: some of the ten contexts below require only filling blanks, some require only matching italicized words, and some require both filling and matching.)

___ 1. Like England, Thomas More's imaginary country of Utopia is an island. However, More situates Utopia remotely indeed—at England's _____. Readers are thus being invited to compare and contrast English and Utopian societies.

    A. perigee

    B. periphery

    C. antipodes

    D. pseudopod

___ 2. Pity poor Gregor Samsa! One of literature's most _____ characters, he awakens to find himself turned into a giant, repulsive bug!

    A. ludicrous

    B. dyslogistic

    C. complex

    D. pathetic

___ 3. This extraordinary *transformation* is apt because Gregor has just become in form what—in his mindset and in his behavior—he has in fact been like!

    A. metamorphosis

    B. regression

    C. commencement

    D. morphology

___ 4. For some time now at home and on the job, hasn't Gregor been grovelling at the bottom of a *pecking order* headed by two absolute masters, his father and his boss? Hasn't Gregor been inviting them to step on him like a bug?

    A. anarchy

    B. matriarchy

    C. sphere of influence

    D. hierarchy

___ 5. Buglike, hasn't Gregor also been scurrying nonstop to and fro _____, putting up with bites of *wretched* food snatched here and there?

    A. hyperactively . . unsavory

    B. exoterically . . unwieldy

    C. outlandishly . . unfathomable

    D. peripherally . . unseasoned

___ **6.** Aldous Huxley's BRAVE NEW WORLD portrays a future *society where values commonly cherished are trampled on.* For example, advances in *the science of improving the species* are misapplied, enabling the State not only to mass produce infants but to "hatch" them with such traits as will guarantee that as adults they will conform to their predestined niches in the rigid social hierarchy.

    A. dystopia . . eugenics

    B. macrocosm . . genetic engineering

    C. hyperopia . . euthenics

    D. nirvana . . technology

___ **7.** Eighteenth-century Venice was governed by a(n) *few dozen nobles* who were *abnormally thin-skinned* about any conceivable threat to public order.

    A. oligarchy . . supercritical

    B. autarchy . . psychopathic

    C. polyarchy . . hypersensitive

    D. hierarchy . . hyperbolic

___ **8.** For example, the open-mouthed marble faces sculpted on many Venetian walls were tools of the rulers' secret police, from whose dreaded _____ no citizen was *secure.*

    A. surveillance . . immune

    B. antipathy . . peripatetic

    C. perusal . . vulnerable

    D. scrutiny . . incognito

___ **9.** Through the marble mouths, not just well-intentioned informants but also those _____ could thrust *unsigned* accusations able to bring even the mightiest low.

    A. maliciously disposed . . anomalous

    B. bent on censure . . posthumous

    C. malignantly inclined . . anonymous

    D. not averse to euphemism . . heteronymous

___ **10.** A fruitful _____ offered in 1913 by the Danish physicist Neils Bohr models the *tiniest elemental particle* of hydrogen as an electron whirling about a nucleus, a *miniature replica* of a solar original—the earth orbiting the sun.

    A. hypothesis . . atom . . microcosm

    B. realization . . neutron . . epitome

    C. discovery . . macron . . duplicate

    D. conjecture . . molecule . . macrocosm

Chapter 5

Words Derived From Latin

When the Latin-speaking Romans ruled Britain, approximately A.D. 75–410, there was no English language. The native Britons spoke Celtic, a language akin to Irish and Welsh. After the Romans withdrew, the Britons were overwhelmed by Germanic invaders, the Angles and Saxons. The English we speak today is a continuation of the language of the Angles and Saxons.

Before invading Britain, the Angles and Saxons had adopted some Latin words from contacts with the vast neighboring Roman Empire. In Britain, they acquired a few more Latin words from the Britons, who had lived so long under Roman domination. And after 597, when the Roman monk St. Augustine introduced Christianity and the Holy Scripture—in Latin—to Britain, the Anglo-Saxons absorbed more words from Latin. But Latin had no major impact on English until 1066, when the Normans conquered England.

The Normans spoke French, a Romance language, i.e., a language developed from the language of the Romans. French, which is 85 percent descended from Latin, was England's official language for two hundred years after the Norman Conquest. The language of the Normans gradually blended with the Anglo-Saxon spoken by the common people. In the process, a considerable number of Latin words were incorporated into English indirectly, by way of French.

Later, a substantial number of other words came into English directly from Latin itself. From the Renaissance, in the sixteenth century, to the present day, as English-speaking authors and scientists have needed new words to express new ideas, they have been able to form them from Latin—or Greek.

It is no wonder, then, that more than 50 percent of the vocabulary of English derives directly or indirectly from Latin.

To boost your word power, study the common Latin prefixes and roots presented in this chapter. Each of them, as the following pages will show, can help you learn a cluster of useful English words.

Latin Prefixes 1–15

PREFIX	MEANING	SAMPLE WORDS
1. **a, ab**	away, from	*a*vert (turn *away*), *ab*duct (lead *from*)
2. **ad**	to	*ad*mit (grant entrance *to*)
3. **ante**	before	*ante*room (room *before* another)
4. **bi**	two	*bi*cycle (vehicle having *two* wheels)
5. **circum**	around	*circum*navigate (sail *around*)
6. **con (col, com, cor)**	together, with	*con*spire (plot *together* or *with*), *col*loquy (talking *together*; conference), *com*pose (put *together*), *cor*respond (agree *with*; communicate *with* by exchange of letters)
7. **contra**	against	*contra*dict (speak *against*; deny)
8. **de**	from, down	*de*duction (conclusion drawn *from* reasoning), *de*mote (move *down* in rank)
9. **dis**	apart, away	*dis*rupt (break *apart*), *dis*miss (send *away*)
10. **e, ex**	out	*e*mit (send *out*; utter), *ex*pel (drive *out*)
11. **extra**	beyond	*extra*ordinary (*beyond* the ordinary)
12. **in (il, im, ir)**	not	*in*significant (*not* significant), *il*legal (*not* legal), *im*moral (*not* moral), *ir*regular (*not* regular)
13. **in (il, im, ir)**	in, into, on	*in*ject (throw or force *in*), *il*luminate (direct light *on*; light up), *im*port (bring *into* one country from another), *ir*rigate (pour water *on*)
14. **inter**	between	*inter*rupt (break *between*; stop)
15. **intra**	within	*intra*mural (*within* the walls; inside)

EXERCISE 5.1

Fill in the prefix in column I and the new word in column III. (The answer to question 1 has been inserted as an example.)

COLUMN I	COLUMN II	COLUMN III
1. __in__ *not*	+ tangible *able to be touched*	= __intangible__ *not able to be touched*
2. _____ *against*	+ vene *come; go*	= _____ *go against or contrary to*
3. _____ *out*	+ hale *breathe*	= _____ *breathe out*
4. _____ *down*	+ mote *move*	= _____ *reduce to lower rank*
5. _____ *to*	+ here *stick*	= _____ *stick to*
6. _____ *together*	+ gregate *gather*	= _____ *gather together; assemble*
7. _____ *from*	+ normal	= _____ *deviating from the normal*
8. _____ *around*	+ scribe *write; draw*	= _____ *write or draw a line around; encircle; limit*
9. _____ *between*	+ cede *go*	= _____ *go between arguing parties; mediate*
10. _____ *two*	+ sect *cut*	= _____ *cut into two parts*
11. _____ *beyond*	+ mural *pertaining to a wall*	= _____ *occurring beyond the walls*
12. _____ *before*	+ diluvian *pertaining to a flood*	= _____ *belonging to the period before the Biblical Flood; therefore, very old*
13. _____ *within*	+ venous *pertaining to a vein*	= _____ *within a vein*
14. _____ *apart*	+ pel *drive*	= _____ *drive apart; scatter*
15. _____ *in*	+ fuse *pour*	= _____ *pour in; fill; instill*

16. _____ + scend = _____
    down   *climb*   *climb down*

17. _____ + sensory = _____
    beyond   *pertaining to the senses*   *beyond the scope of the senses*

18. _____ + sect = _____
    apart   *cut*   *cut apart*

19. _____ + solve = _____
    from   *loose*   *loose from; release from*

20. _____ + pute = _____
    apart   *think*   *think apart (differently from others); argue*

EXERCISE 5.2

In the space before each Latin prefix in column I, write the *letter* of its correct meaning from column II.

COLUMN I	COLUMN II
___ 1. contra	*a.* within
___ 2. ante	*b.* between
___ 3. de	*c.* in; into; on; not
___ 4. extra	*d.* from; down
___ 5. a, ab	*e.* out
___ 6. in (il, im, ir)	*f.* against
___ 7. bi	*g.* around
___ 8. intra	*h.* beyond
___ 9. dis	*i.* apart; away
___ 10. e, ex	*j.* to
___ 11. ad	*k.* together; with
___ 12. inter	*l.* before
___ 13. circum	*m.* two
___ 14. con (col, com, cor)	*n.* away; from

Latin Prefixes 16–30

PREFIX	MEANING	SAMPLE WORDS
16. **ob, op**	against	*ob*loquy (talking *against*; censure), *op*pose (set oneself *against*)
17. **per**	through, thoroughly	*per*ennial (lasting *through* the years; enduring), *per*vert (*thoroughly* turn from the right way; corrupt)
18. **post**	after	*post*war (*after* the war)
19. **pre**	before	*pre*monition (warning *before*; forewarning)
20. **preter**	beyond	*preter*human (*beyond* what is human)
21. **pro**	forward	*pro*gressive (moving *forward*)
22. **re**	again, back	*re*vive (make alive *again*), *re*tort (twist *back*; reply sharply)
23. **retro**	backward	*retro*gression (act of moving *backward*)
24. **se**	apart	*se*cede (move *apart*; withdraw)
25. **semi**	half	*semi*circle (*half* of a circle)
26. **sub, sup**	under	*sub*merge (put *under* or plunge into water), *sup*port (uphold)
27. **super**	above	*super*natural (*above* what is natural; miraculous)
28. **trans**	across, through	*trans*continental (extending *across* a continent), *trans*mit (send *through*)
29. **ultra**	beyond, exceedingly	*ultra*conservative (*exceedingly* conservative)
30. **vice**	in place of	*vice* president (officer acting *in place of* the president)

 **EXERCISE 5.3**

In the space before each Latin prefix in column I, write the *letter* of its correct meaning from column II. (Exercise continues on next page.)

COLUMN I

___ **1.** semi

___ **2.** ob

COLUMN II

a. against

b. beyond; exceedingly

___ **3.** sub   *c.* again; back

___ **4.** trans   *d.* before

___ **5.** vice   *e.* after

___ **6.** ultra   *f.* half

___ **7.** super   *g.* apart

___ **8.** re   *h.* under

___ **9.** pro   *i.* in place of

___ **10.** post   *j.* above

___ **11.** se   *k.* forward

___ **12.** pre   *l.* across; through

 EXERCISE 5.4

Fill in the prefix in column I and the new word in column III.

COLUMN I	COLUMN II	COLUMN III
1. _____ *in place of*	+ chancellor	= _____ *person acting in place of a chancellor*
2. _____ *half*	+ annual	= _____ *occurring every half year*
3. _____ *under*	+ vert *turn*	= _____ *turn under; undermine*
4. _____ *apart*	+ clude *shut*	= _____ *shut or keep apart; isolate*
5. _____ *above*	+ sede *sit*	= _____ *sit above; take the place of; replace*
6. _____ *forward*	+ mote *move*	= _____ *move forward; raise in rank*
7. _____ *against*	+ durate *hardened*	= _____ *hardened against; unyielding; stubborn*
8. _____ *through*	+ ient *going*	= _____ *going through (not staying); short-lived*
9. _____ *against*	+ struct *pile up*	= _____ *pile up (an obstacle) against; hinder*
10. _____ *back*	+ calcitrant *kicking*	= _____ *kicking back; rebellious*

11. _____ + pone = _____
    after   *put*   *put after; defer; delay*

12. _____ + nationalistic = _____
    exceedingly   *exceedingly nationalistic*

13. _____ + requisite = _____
    before   *required*   *required before; necessary as a preliminary*

14. _____ + active = _____
    backward   *acting backward; effective in a prior time*

15. _____ + meate = _____
    through   *pass*   *pass through*

16. _____ + sume = _____
    again   *take*   *take up or begin again*

17. _____ + turb = _____
    thoroughly *disturb*   *disturb thoroughly; agitate*

18. _____ + natural = _____
    beyond   *beyond what is natural*

19. _____ + gregate = _____
    apart   *gather*   *set apart; gather into separate groups*

20. _____ + marine = _____
    under   *pertaining to the sea*   *used or existing under the sea's surface*

 **EXERCISE 5.5**

Using your knowledge of the Latin prefixes and the hints given below, insert the basic meaning of these sixty English words. (The answer to question 1 has been inserted as an example.)

Hint: **-port** means "carry"

1. report   _____carry back_____   4. deport   _____

2. import   _____   5. export   _____

3. transport   _____

Hint: **-ject** means "throw"

6. interject   _____   9. project   _____

7. eject   _____   10. inject   _____

8. object   _____

Hint: **-scribe** means "write"

11. superscribe _____
12. transcribe _____
13. prescribe _____

14. inscribe _____
15. subscribe _____

Hint: **-pel** means "drive"

16. dispel _____
17. propel _____
18. expel _____

19. impel _____
20. repel _____

Hint: **-voke** means "call"

21. evoke _____
22. convoke _____
23. provoke _____

24. revoke _____
25. invoke _____

Hint: **-mit** means "send"

26. permit _____
27. admit _____
28. transmit _____

29. emit _____
30. remit _____

Hint: **-tract** means "drag," "draw"

31. protract _____
32. subtract _____
33. distract _____

34. retract _____
35. detract _____

Hint: **-duce** means "lead," "draw"

36. seduce _____
37. induce _____
38. produce _____

39. deduce _____
40. reduce _____

Hint: **-cede** or **-ceed** means "go"

41. intercede _____
42. proceed _____
43. secede _____

44. exceed _____
45. recede _____

Hint: **-fer** means "carry," "bring," "bear"

46. transfer _____   49. infer _____

47. prefer _____   50. defer _____

48. refer _____

Hint: **-vert** means "turn"

51. avert _____   54. revert _____

52. advert _____   55. subvert _____

53. pervert _____

Hint: **-pose** means "put"

56. compose _____   59. propose _____

57. depose _____   60. transpose _____

58. interpose _____

Latin Roots

1. RUPT: "break," "burst"

WORD	MEANING
abrupt (*adj.*) ə-'brəpt	1. broken off; lacking in continuity; steep (*ant.* **sloping**) 2. sudden; quick and unexpected (*ant.* **leisurely; deliberate; gradual**)
corrupt (*adj.*) kə-'rəpt	changed ("broken to pieces") from good to bad; vicious
corrupt (*v.*)	change ("break to pieces") from good to bad; debase; pervert; falsify
disrupt (*v.*) dis-'rəpt	break apart; cause disorder
erupt (*v.*) i-'rəpt	burst or break out

incorruptible (*adj.*)   inflexibly honest; incapable of being corrupted or bribed
,in-kə-'rəp-tə-bəl

interrupt (*v.*)   break into or between; hinder; stop
,in-tə-'rəpt

rupture (*n.*)   1. break; breaking
'rəp(t)-shər   2. hostility

EXERCISE 5.6

In each blank, insert the most appropriate word from group 1, *rupt.*

1. The simmering antipathy between the rivals may _____ into violence.

2. The star's _____ withdrawal from the cast took the producer by surprise.

3. Both sides had faith in the honesty of a judge known to be _____.

4. Many homes were flooded as a result of a(n) _____ in a water main.

5. Please don't _____ me when I am speaking on the telephone.

2. CIDE: "killing," "killer"

bactericide (*n.*)   substance that kills bacteria
bak-'tir-ə-,sīd

biocide (*n.*)   substance that destroys many different organisms
'bī-ə-,sīd

fratricide (*n.*)   act of killing (or killer of) one's brother
'fra-trə-,sīd

fungicide (*n.*)   substance that kills fungi or inhibits their growth
'fən-jə-,sīd

genocide (*n.*)   deliberate extermination of a racial or cultural group
'je-nə-,sīd

germicide (*n.*)   substance that kills germs
'jər-mə-,sīd

herbicide (*n.*)   substance that kills plants
'(h)ər-bə-,sīd

homicide (*n.*)   killing of one human by another
'hä-mə-,sīd

infanticide (*n.*)   act of killing (or killer of) an infant
in-'fan-tə-,sīd

insecticide (*n.*)   substance that kills insects
in-'sek-tə-,sīd

matricide (*n.*)   act of killing (or killer of) one's mother
'ma-trə-,sīd

patricide (*n.*)   act of killing (or killer of) one's father
'pa-trə-,sīd

pesticide (*n.*)   substance that kills rats, insects, bacteria, etc.
'pes-tə-,sīd

regicide (*n.*)   act of killing (or killer of) a king
're-jə-,sīd

sororicide (*n.*)   act of killing (or killer of) one's sister
sə-'ròr-ə-,sīd

suicide (*n.*)   act of killing (or killer of) one's self
'sü-ə-,sīd

tyrannicide (*n.*)   act of killing (or killer of) a tyrant
tə-'ra-nə-,sīd

 **EXERCISE 5.7**

In each blank, insert the most appropriate word from group 2, *cide*.

1. The murderers planned to escape prosecution by making their deed appear like a(n) _____.

2. The assailant was told that he would be charged with _____ if his victim were to die.

3. To prevent the extermination of minorities, the United Nations voted in 1948 to outlaw _____.

4. In the Bible, when Cain killed his brother Abel, he committed _____.

5. Two _____s meant to further the cause of popular government were the beheadings of Charles I (1649) of England and Louis XVI of France (1793).

6. One way to get rid of weeds is to spray them with a(n) _____.

3. STRING (STRICT): "bind," "draw tight"

astringent (*adj.*)   1. drawing (the tissues) tightly together (e.g., to check bleeding)
ə-'strin-jənt   2. stern; austere

astringent (*n.*)   substance that shrinks the tissues and checks flow of blood

boa constrictor (*n.*)   snake that "constricts" or crushes its prey in its coils
'bō-ə-kən-'strik-tər

constrict (*v.*)   draw together; render narrower; shrink (*ant.* **expand**)
kən-'strikt

restrict (*v.*)   keep within limits (literally, "keep back"); confine
ri-'strikt

stricture (*n.*)   1. adverse criticism (literally, "tightening"); censure
'strik-chər   2. restriction

stringent (*adj.*)   strict (literally, "binding tight"); rigid; severe
'strin-jənt

unrestricted (*adj.*)   1. not confined within bounds; free
ˌən-ri-'strik-təd   2. open to all

 **EXERCISE 5.8**

In each blank, insert the most appropriate word from group 3, *string (strict)*.

1. All residents enjoy _____ use of the pool, except children under 16, who must leave at 5 P.M.

2. Unless you _____ your remarks to the topic on the floor, the chair will rule you "out of order."

3. A styptic pencil or other _____ will check bleeding from razor nicks.

4. Jean Valjean's sentence of five years at hard labor for stealing a loaf of bread seems an unusually _____ punishment.

5. If you interpret a minor suggestion for improvement as a major _____, you are being hypersensitive.

4. VOR: "eat greedily"

carnivore (*n.*)   flesh-eating animal
ˈkär-nə-ˌvȯ(ə)r

carnivorous (*adj.*)   flesh-eating
kär-ˈni-və-rəs

devour (*v.*)   1. eat greedily or ravenously
di-ˈvau̇ə(r)   2. seize upon and destroy

frugivorous (*adj.*)   feeding on fruit
frü-ˈji-və-rəs

herbivore (*n.*)   plant-eating animal
ˈ(h)ər-bə-ˌvȯ(ə)r

herbivorous (*adj.*)   dependent on (literally, "eating") plants as food
ˌ(h)ər-ˈbiv-ə-rəs

insectivorous (*adj.*)   dependent on (literally, "eating") insects as food
ˌin-ˌsek-ˈtiv-ə-rəs

omnivore (*n.*)   person or animal that eats everything (both flesh and plants)
ˈäm-ni-ˌvȯr

omnivorous (*adj.*)   1. eating everything, both plant and animal substances
äm-ˈniv-ə-rəs   2. avidly taking in everything, as an *omnivorous* reader

voracious (*adj.*)   1. greedy in eating
vȯ-ˈrā-shəs   2. insatiable, as a *voracious* appetite

EXERCISE 5.9

In each blank, insert the most appropriate word from group 4, *vor.*

1. Spiders are _____; their principal food is insects.

2. A ravenous eater will _____ a sandwich in two or three gulps.

3. The diet of the _____ lion may include the zebra, antelope, buffalo, and ostrich.

4. Since human beings generally obtain food from both plants and animals, they may be described as _____ organisms.

5. The rabbit is _____; it eats grass, vegetables, and berries.

6. _____ insects damage fruit crops.

5. *VIV: "live," "alive"*

convivial (*adj.*) kən-ʹviv-ē-əl	fond of eating and drinking with friends; sociable; jovial; hospitable (*ant.* **taciturn**, inclined to silence; **stolid**, unemotional)
revive (*v.*) ri-ʹvīv	bring back to life; restore
survive (*v.*) sər-ʹvīv	outlive; remain alive after (*ant.* **perish**)
vivacious (*adj.*) və-ʹvā-shəs	lively in temper or conduct (*ant.* **languid**, lacking in vigor)
vivacity (*n.*) və-ʹva-sə-tē	liveliness of spirit
vivid (*adj.*) ʹvi-vəd	1. (used with things) having the vigor and spirit of life 2. sharp and clear; graphic
vivify (*v.*) ʹvi-və-ˌfī	enliven; make vivid
vivisection (*n.*) ˌvi-və-ʹsek-shən	operation on a living animal for scientific investigation

 **EXERCISE 5.10**

In each blank, insert the most appropriate word from group 5, *viv.*

1. A business must eliminate waste if it is to _____ in a competitive market.

2. When fashion designers can offer no new styles, they usually _____ old ones.

3. By using carefully chosen verbs and adjectives, you can turn a dull description into a _____ one.

4. David Copperfield found a warm welcome in the _____ Peggotty family.

5. A few inexpensive art reproductions, cleverly arranged, can _____ an otherwise drab wall.

6. I admire her _____ and zest for life.

6. TORT (TORS): "twist"

contortionist (*n.*) person who can twist his or her body into odd postures
kən-'tȯr-shə-nist

distort (*v.*) 1. twist out of shape; contort
di-'stȯrt 2. twist out of the true meaning; misrepresent; pervert; falsify

extort (*v.*) wrest (money, promises, etc.) from a person by force (literally, "twist out")
ek-'stȯrt

retort (*v.*) reply quickly or sharply ("twist back")
ri-'tȯrt

retort (*n.*) quick, witty, or cutting reply

torsion (*n.*) act of twisting; stress due to twisting forces exerted on a body
'tȯr-shən

tortuous (*adj.*) 1. full of twists or curves; winding, as a *tortuous* road
'tȯrch-ə-wəs 2. tricky; crooked; circuitous

torture (*v.*) 1. wrench; twist
'tȯr-chər 2. inflict severe pain upon

torture (*n.*) anguish of body or mind; agony

 ## EXERCISE 5.11

In each blank, insert the most appropriate word from group 6, *tort* (*tors*).

1. Captured soldiers worry that the enemy will do its utmost to _____ military secrets from them.

2. It is very easy to _____ another's ideas by quoting them out of context.

3. When children are asked to help with the chores, they often _____ that they have no time.

4. _____s amaze us by their remarkable ability to throw their bodies into extraordinary postures.

5. Near its mouth, the Mississippi winds among numerous swamps in a(n) _____ course to the Gulf of Mexico.

7. VICT (VINC): "conquer," "show conclusively"

convict (*v.*) kən-'vikt	prove guilty; show conclusively to be guilty
convict (*n.*) 'kän-,vikt	person serving a prison sentence
conviction (*n.*) kən-'vik-shən	1. state of having been judged guilty of an offense 2. strong belief
convince (*v.*) kən-'vins	persuade or show conclusively by argument or proof
evict (*v.*) i-'vikt	1. expel by legal process, as to *evict* a tenant 2. oust
evince (*v.*) i-'vins	show clearly; disclose; reveal
invincible (*adj.*) in-'vin-sə-bəl	incapable of being conquered
vanquish (*v.*) 'van-kwish	overcome in battle; conquer; defeat
victor (*n.*) 'vik-tər	winner; conqueror

 **EXERCISE 5.12**

In each blank, insert the most appropriate word from group 7, *vict* (*vinc*).

1. Stadium security officers are empowered to _____ unruly spectators.

2. After the match, the _____ shook hands with the loser.

3. Students who _____ a talent for writing should be encouraged to contribute to the school newspaper and literary magazine.

4. Facts alone will usually not _____ a biased person that he or she is wrong.

5. Our apparently _____ swimming team has been neither beaten nor tied in the past two seasons.

8. *FRACT (FRAG): "break"*

fraction (*n.*) ʼfrak-shən	one or more of the equal parts of a whole; fragment
fractious (*adj.*) ʼfrak-shəs	apt to break out into a passion; cross; irritable (*ant.* **peaceable**)
fracture (*n.*) ʼfrak-chər	1. break or crack 2. breaking of a bone
fragile (*adj.*) ʼfra-jəl	easily broken; frail; delicate (*ant.* **tough; durable**)
fragment (*n.*) ʼfrag-mənt	part broken off
infraction (*n.*) in-ʼfrak-shən	act of breaking; breach; violation, as an *infraction* of a law
refract (*v.*) ri-ʼfrakt	bend (literally, "break back") from a straight path (as when light rays, having traveled through air, change direction when entering water, or as when sunlight—having traveled through a prism—breaks up into the colors of the rainbow)
refractory (*adj.*) ri-ʼfrak-tə-rē	resisting; intractable; hard to manage, as a *refractory* mule (*ant.* **malleable; tractable; adaptable**)

EXERCISE 5.13

In each blank, insert the most appropriate word from group 8, *fract* (*frag*).

1. Glassware and other _____ materials require special packaging to prevent breakage.

2. Failure to stop at a Stop sign is a(n) _____ of the traffic laws.

3. X-rays showed that the child had not sustained a(n) _____.

4. When I find the missing _____, I will restore the broken vase.

5. The _____ ³⁄₁₂ reduces to ¼.

9. *OMNI: "all," "every," "everywhere"*

omnibus (*adj.*)
'äm-ni-bəs

covering many things at once, as an *omnibus* bill

omnibus (*n.*)

1. bus
2. book containing a variety of works by one author, as a Hemingway *omnibus*

omnifarious (*adj.*)
,äm-nə-'far-ē-əs

of all varieties, forms, or kinds

omnific (*adj.*)
äm-'ni-fik

all-creating

omnipotent (*adj.*)
äm-'ni-pə-tənt

unlimited in power; almighty

omnipresent (*adj.*)
,äm-ni-'pre-zᵊnt

present everywhere at the same time; ubiquitous

omniscient (*adj.*)
äm-'ni-shənt

knowing everything

omnivorous (*adj.*)
äm-'niv-ə-rəs

1. eating everything, both plant and animal substances
2. avidly taking in everything, as an *omnivorous* reader

EXERCISE 5.14

In each blank, insert the most appropriate word from group 9, *omni*.

1. I cannot answer all questions, since I am not _____.

2. Aladdin became _____; his magic lamp put no feat beyond his power.

3. The _____ uses of a Swiss Army knife make it indispensable for camping.

4. With several desirable invitations for the same evening, I regretted that I could not be _____.

5. It was a conviction of the ancient Egyptians that their sun god was _____. They believed that he had created everything.

10. FLECT (FLEX): "bend"

deflect (*v.*)　　　　　turn ("bend") aside
di-'flekt

flex (*v.*)　　　　　　bend, as to *flex* a limb
'fleks

flexible (*adj.*)　　　　pliable ("capable of being bent"); not rigid; tractable (*ant.* **inflexible**)
'flek-sə-bəl

flexor (*n.*)　　　　　muscle that serves to bend a limb
'flek-sər

genuflect (*v.*)　　　　bend the knee; touch the right knee to the ground, as in worship
'jen-yə-ˌflekt

inflection (*n.*)　　　　change ("bend") in the pitch or tone of a person's voice
in-'flek-shən

inflexibility (*n.*)　　　rigidity; firmness
in-ˌflek-sə-'bi-lə-tē

reflect (*v.*)　　　　　1. throw ("bend") back light rays, as from a mirror (but *not* from a prism,
ri-'flekt　　　　　　　　　which *refracts* rays)
　　　　　　　　　　　　2. think

reflex (*n.*)　　　　　involuntary response ("bending back") to a stimulus; for example, sneezing
'rē-ˌfleks　　　　　　　is a *reflex*

EXERCISE 5.15

In each blank, insert the most appropriate word from group 10, *flect (flex)*.

1. The secretion of tears, as when a cinder enters the eye, is a(n) _____,
since it is beyond our control.

2. Copper tubing is easy to shape, but it is much less _____ than rubber
hose.

3. Unable to catch the line drive, I managed to _____ the ball toward the
infield, holding the batter to a single.

4. Loyal subjects would _____ before an absolute monarch.

5. The _____ of both sides makes an early settlement unlikely.

11. *TEN (TIN, TENT): "hold," "keep"*

detention (*n.*) di-'ten-shən	act of keeping back or detaining
impertinent (*adj.*) im-'pər-tən-ənt	1. irrelevant; not pertinent; inappropriate (*ant.* **pertinent**) 2. rude
pertinacious (*adj.*) ,pər-t°n-'ā-shəs	adhering ("holding") firmly to a purpose or opinion; very persistent
pertinent (*adj.*) 'pər-tən-ənt	having to do with ("holding to") the matter at hand; relevant (*ant.* **impertinent**)
retentive (*adj.*) ri-'ten-tiv	tenacious; able to retain or remember
retinue (*n.*) 're-t°n-,yü	group of followers or assistants attending a distinguished person
tenacity (*n.*) tə-'na-sə-tē	firmness in holding fast; persistence
tenancy (*n.*) 'te-nən-sē	period of a tenant's temporary holding of real estate
tenet (*n.*) 'te-nət	principle, belief, or doctrine generally held to be true
tenure (*n.*) 'ten-yər	1. period for which an office or position is held, as: "U.S. Supreme Court Justices enjoy life *tenure*." 2. status assuring an employee a permanent position
untenable (*adj.*) ,ən-'te-nə-bəl	incapable of being held or defended (*ant.* **tenable**)

✍ EXERCISE 5.16

In each blank, insert the most appropriate word from group 11, *ten (tin, tent)*.

1. The _____ of a member of the House of Representatives is only two years.

2. The rebels withdrew to their stronghold from a(n) _____ outpost.

3. A remark may be ruled "out of order" if not _____ to the case.

4. Though she can't recall names, Sylvia has a(n) _____ memory for faces.

5. The basketball star was accompanied by a(n) _____ of admirers.

6. Freedom of speech is one of the _____s of democracy.

12. MON (MONIT): "warn"

admonish (*v.*)
ad-'mä-nish
warn of a fault; reprove; rebuke (*ant.* **commend**)

admonition (*n.*)
,ad-mə-'ni-shən
gentle reproof ("warning"); counseling against a fault or error

admonitory (*adj.*)
ad-'mä-nə-,tȯr-ē
conveying a gentle reproof

monitor (*n.*)
'mä-nə-tər
person or device that keeps track of, checks, or warns

monitor (*v.*)
keep track of, regulate, or control the operation of a machine or process

monument (*n.*)
'män-yə-mənt
means of reminding us of a person or event (e.g., a statue or a tomb)

premonition (*n.*)
,prē-mə-'ni-shən
forewarning; intuitive anticipation of a coming event

premonitory (*adj.*)
pri-'mä-nə-,tȯr-ē
conveying a forewarning

 **EXERCISE 5.17**

In each blank, insert the most appropriate word from group 12, *mon* (*monit*).

1. Had they heeded your _____ to fill the gas tank, they would not have been stranded on the road.

2. I must _____ you that you will be unable to vote if you do not register.

3. Some think that an early autumn snowstorm is a(n) _____ of a severe winter, but you really can't tell in advance.

4. A(n) _____ in the town square honors veterans fallen in foreign wars.

5. A _____ rumbling from afar signaled the storm's approach.

6. Intensive care wards _____ their patients' vital signs.

13. MAND (MANDAT): "order," "command," "commit"

countermand (*v.*)   issue a contrary order
'kaůn-tər-,mand

mandate (*n.*)   1. authoritative command
'man-,dāt   2. territory administered by a trustee (supervisory nation)

mandatory (*adj.*)   obligatory; required by command (*ant.* **optional**)
'man-də-,tȯr-ē

remand (*v.*)   send ("order") back; recommit, as to a prison
ri-'mand

writ of mandamus   written order from a court to enforce the performance of some public duty
(*n.*) 'rit-əv-man-'dā-məs

EXERCISE 5.18

In each blank, insert the most appropriate word from group 13,
mand (*mandat*).

1. The reelected candidate regarded her huge popular vote as a _____
from the people to continue the policies of her first term in office.

2. Because the general did not agree with the colonel's order, he decided to
_____ it.

3. Several prominent citizens have applied for a _____ to compel the
Mayor to publish the budget, as required by law.

4. The coach regards attendance at today's practice as _____; no one
is excused.

5. Since the retrial resulted in a verdict of "guilty," the judge was obliged to
_____ the defendant to the state penitentiary.

14. CRED (CREDIT): "believe"

accredited (*adj.*)   officially authorized or recognized; provided with credentials
ə-'kre-dət-id

credence (*n.*)   belief as to the truth of something
'krē-dᵊns

credentials (*n. pl.*)   documents, letters, references, etc., that inspire belief or trust
kri-'den-shəlz

credible (*adj.*)   believable (*ant.* **incredible**)
'kre-də-bəl

credit (*n.*)   belief; faith; trust
'kre-dət

credulous (*adj.*)   too ready to believe; easily deceived (*ant.* **incredulous; skeptical**)
'kre-jə-ləs

creed (*n.*)   summary of principles believed in or adhered to
'krēd

  or **credo**
  'krē-(,)dō

discredit (*v.*)   1. cast doubt on; refuse to believe
dis-'kre-dət   2. take trust or credit away from; disgrace

discredit (*n.*)   loss of belief or trust; damage to one's reputation; disgrace

incredible (*adj.*)   not believable
in-'kre-də-bəl

incredulity (*n.*)   disbelief
,in-kri-'d(y)ü-lə-tē

 EXERCISE 5.19

In each blank, insert the most appropriate word from group 14, *cred* (*credit*).

1. His rudeness brought _____ on his team, as well as himself.

2. I showed _____ negligence in not removing the pot from the burner when the timer rang.

3. When applying for admission to college, you are likely to be asked for such _____ as your high school transcript, standardized test scores, and letters of recommendation.

4. Gerald is too _____; he will believe anything a salesperson says.

5. Olga, learning that she had won the lottery, wore a look of _____.

6. The diplomas and licenses in Dr. Chen's office show that she is _____ in dermatology.

15. FID: "faith," "trust"

affidavit (*n.*) ‚a-fə-'dā-vət	sworn written statement made before an authorized official
bona fide (*adj.*) 'bō-nə-‚fīd	made or carried out in good faith; genuine
confidant (*n.*) 'kän-fə-‚dänt	(*confidante*, if a woman) one to whom secrets are entrusted
confident (*adj.*) 'kän-fə-dənt	having faith in oneself; self-reliant; sure (*ant.* **apprehensive; diffident**)
confidential (*adj.*) ‚kän-fə-'den-shəl	communicated in trust; secret; private
diffident (*adj.*) 'di-fə-dənt	lacking self-confidence (faith in oneself); unduly timid; shy (*ant.* **confident**)
fidelity (*n.*) fə-'de-lə-tē	1. faithfulness to a trust or vow (*ant.* **perfidy; infidelity**) 2. accuracy; faithfulness of sound reproduction
fiduciary (*adj.*) fə-'d(y)ü-shē-‚er-ē	1. held in trust (*fiduciary* property) 2. confidential (*fiduciary* duties of a trustee)
infidel (*n.*) 'in-fə-dᵊl	one who does not accept a particular faith; unbeliever
perfidious (*adj.*) pər-'fi-dē-əs	false to a trust; faithless; treacherous
perfidy (*n.*) 'pər-fə-dē	violation of a trust; treachery; faithlessness; disloyalty (*ant.* **fidelity; fealty**)

 **EXERCISE 5.20**

In each blank, insert the most appropriate word from group 15, *fid*.

1. Benedict Arnold's _____ during the American Revolution was his plan to betray West Point to the British.

2. Marie looks upon her cousin Anderia as a(n) _____ with whom she can freely discuss her personal problems.

3. At first, new drivers are usually nervous, but with experience they become more _____.

4. Our teacher recommends a particular translation of the ODYSSEY because of its _____ to the original.

5. Steve was very _____ as he mounted the platform, even though he knew his speech by heart.

6. The witness signed a(n) _____ and agreed to testify in person.

7. The trustees were sued for having used _____ property for their own benefit.

Review Exercises

REVIEW 1: DEFINING LATIN ROOTS

In the space before each Latin root in column I, write the *letter* of its correct meaning from column II.

COLUMN I

___ 1. CIDE

___ 2. VOR

___ 3. FLECT (FLEX)

___ 4. TORT (TORS)

___ 5. OMNI

___ 6. VICT (VINC)

___ 7. TEN (TIN, TENT)

___ 8. MAND (MANDAT)

___ 9. FID

___ 10. FRACT (FRAG)

___ 11. VIV

___ 12. MON (MONIT)

___ 13. CRED (CREDIT)

___ 14. STRING (STRICT)

COLUMN II

a. live; alive

b. break; burst

c. order; command; commit

d. bind; draw tight

e. faith; trust

f. warn

g. killing; killer

h. believe

i. conquer; show conclusively

j. bend

k. eat greedily

l. twist

m. hold; keep

n. all; every; everywhere

REVIEW 2: USING LATIN ROOTS

Enter the Latin roots needed to complete the partially spelled words below.

DEFINITION

1. break asunder

2. germ-killing substance

WORD

D I S __ __ __ __

G E R M I __ __ __ __

3. part broken off   _ _ _ _ M E N T

4. faithfulness to a trust   _ _ _ E L I T Y

5. one who conquers   _ _ _ _ O R

6. flesh-eating   C A R N I _ _ _ O U S

7. issue a contrary order   C O U N T E R _ _ _ _

8. forewarning   P R E _ _ _ _ _ I O N

9. muscle that serves to bend a limb   _ _ _ _ O R

10. readiness to believe on slight evidence   _ _ _ _ U L I T Y

11. snake that crushes (constricts) its prey   B O A C O N _ _ _ _ _ _ O R

12. bring back to life   R E _ _ _ E

13. adhering firmly to a purpose or opinion   P E R _ _ _ A C I O U S

14. present everywhere at the same time   _ _ _ _ P R E S E N T

15. bend the knee   G E N U _ _ _ _ _

16. greedy in eating   _ _ _ A C I O U S

17. breaking of a bone   _ _ _ _ _ U R E

18. show conclusively by proof   C O N _ _ _ _ E

19. killing of a human by another   H O M I _ _ _ _

20. documents inspiring trust   _ _ _ _ E N T I A L S

REVIEW 3: SENTENCE COMPLETION

In the blank space, write the *letter* of the word or set of words that best completes the sentence.

___ **1.** Circus elephants are usually _____, but occasionally they are refractory.
  a. unmanageable   *b.* stubborn   *c.* tractable   *d.* uncooperative   *e.* resisting

___ **2.** Harvey believes he is omniscient, but we are not particularly impressed by his _____.
  a. power   *b.* knowledge   *c.* manners   *d.* personality   *e.* appearance

___ **3.** The promise had been extorted; like all promises growing out of _____, it was _____.
  a. ignorance . . perfidious   *b.* haste . . untenable   *c.* rumor . . false
  d. compulsion . . unreliable   *e.* friendship . . dependable

___ **4.** An act of regicide always has a _____ as its victim.
  a. rebel   *b.* general   *c.* president   *d.* prime minister   *e.* monarch

___ 5. I usually admonished my brother for distorting facts, but Mom seldom _____ him.

   a. reproved *b.* encouraged *c.* remanded *d.* praised *e.* supported

___ 6. An omnibus bill deals with proposed legislation on _____ problems.

   a. economic *b.* many *c.* minor *d.* transportation *e.* few

___ 7. The rapid withdrawal of your hand from the flame was a reflex, not a(n) _____, reaction.

   a. protective *b.* dangerous *c.* involuntary *d.* natural *e.* voluntary

___ 8. The author read the critics' _____ with incredulity; they were too laudatory to be _____.

   a. censures . . heeded *b.* strictures . . ignored *c.* admonitions . . challenged
   d. encomiums . . believed *e.* rebukes . . answered

___ 9. It is advisable to take along plenty of sandwiches because hungry picnickers are _____ eaters.

   a. admonitory *b.* abstemious *c.* omnifarious *d.* heterogeneous
   e. voracious

___ 10. No one would dare to offer a bribe to an official who is known to be thoroughly _____.

   a. incorruptible *b.* invincible *c.* credulous *d.* retentive *e.* convivial

REVIEW 4: ANTONYMS

Each italicized word in column I has an ANTONYM in column II. Enter the *letter* of that ANTONYM in the space provided.

COLUMN I	COLUMN II
___ 1. *perfidious* adviser	*a.* languid
___ 2. *fragile* structure	*b.* optional
___ 3. probably *survived*	*c.* expanded
___ 4. *credulous* audience	*d.* peaceable
___ 5. *confident* of the outcome	*e.* durable
___ 6. *constricted* passageways	*f.* commended
___ 7. *fractious* neighbors	*g.* faithful
___ 8. *admonished* for their deed	*h.* perished
___ 9. *vivacious* manner	*i.* apprehensive
___ 10. *mandatory* attendance	*j.* skeptical

REVIEW 5: SYNONYMS

In the space provided, write the *letter* of the word that has most nearly the SAME MEANING as the italicized word.

___ 1. *fragile* flower: *a.* fragrant   *b.* broken   *c.* colorful   *d.* frail

___ 2. cling *tenaciously*:   *a.* stubbornly   *b.* dangerously   *c.* hopefully   *d.* timidly

___ 3. beyond *credence*:   *a.* detention   *b.* doubt   *c.* belief   *d.* recall

___ 4. *omnipotent* ruler: *a.* almighty   *b.* wise   *c.* cruel   *d.* greedy

___ 5. *mandatory* increase: *a.* deserved   *b.* required   *c.* temporary   *d.* substantial

___ 6. surprising *impertinence*:   *a.* firmness   *b.* unreliability   *c.* impatience   *d.* rudeness

___ 7. *breach* of trust: *a.* atmosphere   *b.* testing   *c.* breaking   *d.* abundance

___ 8. *unvanquished* foe: *a.* defeated   *b.* exhausted   *c.* treacherous   *d.* unbeaten

___ 9. in a *fiduciary* capacity: *a.* confidential   *b.* special   *c.* professional   *d.* important

___ 10. refused to *genuflect*:   *a.* admit   *b.* kneel   *c.* cooperate   *d.* disclose

REVIEW 6: CONCISE WRITING

Express the thought of each sentence below in no more than four words.

1. Jim twisted the plan that we had presented out of its true meaning.

_____

2. Rosa submitted a sworn statement made before an authorized official.

_____

3. Coughing is an act that is not subject to the control of the will.

_____

4. Do not take roads that are full of twists and turns.

_____

5. What is the reason that you have no faith in yourself?

_____

6. The remark that Patrice made has nothing to do with the matter at hand.

_____

7. Leticia had words of praise for our firmness in holding fast.

_____

8. The position that we found ourselves in could not be defended.

_____

9. George did not have anyone to whom he could entrust secrets.

_____

10. The aim of logic is to show conclusively by means of argument or proof.

_____

REVIEW 7: BRAINTEASERS

Fill in the missing letters.

1. We usually listen to rumors with __ __ __ **r e d** __ __ __ __ __.

2. To everyone's surprise, the __ __ __ **t o r t** __ __ __ __ __ __ squeezed himself into a small metal box.

3. My brother uses a(n) __ __ __ **r i n g** __ __ __ after shaving.

4. The __ __ __ **d e n t** __ __ __ __ of nominees to fill important vacancies are sometimes not checked too carefully.

5. The dictator is suspected of __ **r a t** __ __ __ __ __ __, though some say that he could not have murdered his own brother.

6. Elephants never hunt; they are not **c a r** __ __ __ __ __ __ __ __.

7. Many oppose __ __ __ __ **s e c t** __ __ __ because they feel animals have the same right to live as humans have.

8. Some who claim to be honest turn out to be __ __ __ __ **u p** __.

9. The Pilgrims had to leave their native land because they refused to surrender their __ __ **n e t s** .

10. Foolish humans who may consider themselves __ __ __ __ __ __ **t e n t** will soon learn that they are not gods.

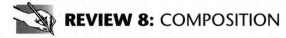

REVIEW 8: COMPOSITION

Answer in two or three sentences.

1. Should the death penalty be mandatory for all persons convicted of homicide? Explain.

   _____

   _____

   _____

2. Why should we not put too much credence in the opinions of those who claim to be omniscient?

   _____

   _____

   _____

3. Discuss two precautions that might help a driver survive a collision with another vehicle.

   _____

   _____

   _____

4. Should an ordinary citizen take it upon himself or herself to admonish someone about to commit an infraction? Explain.

   _____

   _____

   _____

5. Discuss a possible result of the unrestricted use of pesticides.

   _____

   _____

   _____

REVIEW 9: ANALOGIES

Write the *letter* of the word that best completes the analogy.

___ 1. *Matricide* is to *mother* as *genocide* is to _____.
   a. uncle   *b.* country   *c.* race   *d.* tyrant   *e.* general

___ 2. *Flesh* is to *carnivorous* as *fruit* is to _____.
   a. omnivorous   *b.* insectivorous   *c.* vegetarian   *d.* frugivorous
   e. agricultural

___ 3. *Fraction* is to *whole* as *follower* is to _____.
   a. creed   *b.* retinue   *c.* tenure   *d.* fragment   *e.* torsion

___ 4. *Reservation* is to *cancel* as *directive* is to _____.
   a. command   *b.* proclaim   *c.* flex   *d.* demand   *e.* countermand

___ 5. *Orphan* is to *guardian* as *mandate* is to _____.
   a. victor   *b.* monitor   *c.* trustee   *d.* confidant   *e.* commission

16. GRAT: *"pleasant," "thank," "favor"*

congratulate (*v.*) kən-'gra-chə-ˌlāt	express one's pleasure to another person at that person's success
gracious (*adj.*) 'grā-shəs	pleasant; courteous; kindly (*ant.* **ungracious**)
grateful (*adj.*) 'grāt-fəl	feeling or expressing gratitude; thankful; obliged (*ant.* **ungrateful**)
gratify (*v.*) 'gra-tə-ˌfī	give or be a source of pleasure or satisfaction
gratis (*adv.*) 'gra-təs	without charge or payment; free
gratitude (*n.*) 'gra-tə-ˌtüd	thankfulness (*ant.* **ingratitude**)
gratuitous (*adj.*) grə-'tü-ə-təs	1. given freely 2. unwarranted, as a *gratuitous* remark
gratuity (*n.*) grə-'tü-ə-tē	present of money in return for a favor or service; tip

ingrate (*n.*)   ungrateful ("not thankful") person
'in-,grāt

ingratiate (*v.*)   establish (oneself) in the favor or good graces of another
in-'grā-shē-,āt

EXERCISE 5.21

In each blank, insert the most appropriate word from group 16, *grat.*

1. I would consider myself a(n) _____ if I did not express my gratitude to those who have helped me.

2. Some restaurants charge for a second cup of coffee, but most provide it _____.

3. We were so pleased with the service that we left a generous _____.

4. Candidates relish opportunities to _____ themselves with voters.

5. I am sorry I was so discourteous; I will try to be more _____.

6. Compliments are meant to _____.

17. MOR (MORT): "death"

immortal (*adj.*)   1. not subject to death (*ant.* **mortal**)
i-'mȯr-t°l   2. not subject to oblivion (being forgotten); imperishable

immortality (*n.*)   1. eternal life (*ant.* **mortality**)
,i-mȯr-'ta-lə-tē   2. lasting fame

moribund (*adj.*)   dying; near death
'mȯr-ə-,bənd

mortal (*adj.*)   1. destined to die
'mȯr-t°l   2. human
                         3. causing death; fatal, as a *mortal* blow

mortal (*n.*)   human being; person; individual

mortality (*n.*)   1. death rate
mȯr-'ta-lə-tē   2. mortal nature

mortician (*n.*)   undertaker
mȯr-'ti-shən

mortification (*n.*)   shame; humiliation; embarrassment
,mȯr-tə-fə-'kā-shən

mortify (*v.*)   embarrass; shame; humiliate (literally, "make dead," "kill")
'mȯr-tə-ˌfī

mortuary (*n.*)   funeral home
'mȯr-chə-ˌwer-ē

rigor mortis (*n.*)   stiffness of the body that sets in several hours after death (literally,
ˌri-gər-'mȯr-təs   "stiffness of death")

✎ EXERCISE 5.22

In each blank, insert the most appropriate word from group 17, *mor* (*mort*).

1. Patrick Henry's _____ rests on a speech ending "Give me liberty,
   or give me death!"

2. Nations with few physicians and hospitals have a relatively high infant
   _____.

3. The head of the department did not realize what _____ she caused her
   assistant when she scolded him in the presence of the entire staff.

4. Though the mountain climber's injury is critical, it may not be _____;
   he has a chance of recovery.

5. The _____ community has been given a new lease on life since the
   reopening of two large factories that were shut down three years ago.

18. CORP: "body"

corporal (*adj.*)   bodily, as *corporal* punishment
'kȯr-p(ə-)rəl

corporation (*n.*)   body authorized by law to act as a single person and to have rights and
ˌkȯr-pə-'rā-shən   duties

corps (*n.*)   1. organized body of persons
'kȯr   2. branch of the military, as the Marine *Corps*

corpse (*n.*)   dead body
'kȯrps

corpulent (*adj.*)   bulky; obese; very fat
'kȯr-pyə-lənt

corpus (*n.*)   general collection or body of writings, laws, etc.
'kȯr-pəs

corpuscle (*n.*) 'kȯr-pə-səl	1. blood cell (literally, "little body") 2. minute particle
corpus delicti (*n.*) ,kȯr-pəs-di-'lik-,tī	1. facts proving that a crime has been committed 2. body of the victim in a murder case
esprit de corps (*n.*) es-,prē-də-'kȯr	spirit of a body of persons; group spirit
habeas corpus (*n.*) ,hā-bē-əs-'kȯr-pəs	1. writ (order) requiring a detained person to be brought before a court to investigate the legality of that person's detention (the writ begins with the words **habeas corpus**, meaning "you should have the body") 2. right of a citizen to secure court protection against illegal imprisonment
incorporate (*v.*) in-'kȯr-pə-,rāt	combine so as to form one body

 **EXERCISE 5.23**

In each blank, insert the most appropriate word from group 18, *corp.*

1. The executive in charge of administration has a(n) _____ of able assistants.

2. Criminals were flogged or put in the stocks in olden times, but such _____ punishment is rare today.

3. The _____ patient was advised by a physician to try to lose weight.

4. Publishers often _____ several works of an author into one volume.

5. Until the _____ is produced, it cannot be established that a crime has been committed.

6. The residents proudly support their block association; they have a fine _____.

7. In countries where there is no _____, a suspect can be kept in prison without ever being brought to trial.

19. DUC (DUCT): "lead," "conduct," "draw"

aqueduct (*n.*) 'a-kwə-,dəkt	artificial channel for conducting water over a distance
conducive (*adj.*) kən-'dü-siv	tending to lead to; contributive; helpful
conduct (*v.*) kən-'dəkt	lead; guide; escort

deduction (*n.*)
di-'dək-shən
1. taking away; subtraction (*ant.* **addition**)
2. reasoning from the general to the particular

duct (*n.*)
'dəkt
tube or channel for conducting a liquid, air, etc.

ductile (*adj.*)
'dək-t°l
1. able to be drawn out or hammered thin (said of metal)
2. easily led; docile

induce (*v.*)
in-'d(y)üs
lead on; move by persuasion

induct (*v.*)
in-'dəkt
admit ("lead in") as a member; initiate

induction (*n.*)
in-'dək-shən
1. ceremony by which one is made a member; initiation
2. reasoning from the particular to the general

seduction (*n.*)
si-'dək-shən
enticement; leading astray into wrongdoing

traduce (*v.*)
trə-'d(y)üs
(literally, "lead along" as a spectacle to bring into disgrace); malign; slander; vilify; calumniate

viaduct (*n.*)
'vī-ə-,dəkt
bridge for conducting a road or railroad over a valley, river, etc.

 **EXERCISE 5.24**

In each blank, insert the most appropriate word from group 19, *duc* (*duct*).

1. A(n) _____ conducts water from a source of supply to a point of distribution.

2. How much of a(n) _____ is made from your weekly salary for taxes?

3. Though John had said that he wouldn't join, I was able to _____ him to become a member.

4. As our bus crossed the _____, we had a superb view of the valley below.

5. When films that exaggerate the luxury and idleness of American life are shown abroad, they _____ our good name.

20. SECUT (SEQU): "follow"

consecutive (*adj.*)
kən-'se-kyə-tiv
following in regular order; successive

consequence (*n.*)
'kän-sə-,kwens
1. that which follows logically; result
2. importance, as a person of *consequence*

execute (*v.*)
'ek-si-,kyüt
1. follow through to completion; carry out
2. put to death

inconsequential (*adj.*)
in-,kän-sə-'kwen-shəl
of no consequence; trivial; unimportant

non sequitur (*n.*)
nän-'se-kwə-tər
statement that does not follow from previous statements

persecute (*v.*)
'pər-si-,kyüt
oppress; harass; annoy

prosecute (*v.*)
'präs-i-,kyüt
1. follow to the end or until finished
2. conduct legal proceedings against; sue

sequel (*n.*)
'sē-kwəl
something that follows; continuation; consequence; outcome

sequence (*n.*)
'sē-kwəns
the following of one thing after another; succession; orderly series

sequential (*adj.*)
si-'kwen-chəl
arranged in a sequence; serial

EXERCISE 5.25

In each blank, insert the most appropriate word from group 20, *secut* (*sequ*).

1. The town will _____ the vandals if they refuse to pay for the damage.

2. After a string of seven _____ victories, we suffered our first loss.

3. The book about the clever detective proved so popular that the author was induced to write a(n) _____.

4. The volumes were shelved in alphabetical_____ by title.

5. The shortage of water during dry spells is a matter of serious _____.

21. CUR (CURR, CURS): "run"

concur (*v.*)
kən-'kər

1. agree; be of the same opinion (literally, "run together") (*ant.* **contend**)
2. happen together; coincide

concurrent (*adj.*)
kən-'kər-ənt

running together; occurring at the same time; simultaneous

current (*adj.*)
'kər-ənt

now in progress; prevailing

current (*n.*)

flow (as electrical or river *currents*)

curriculum (*n.*)
kə-'ri-kyə-ləm

course of study in a school or college

cursive (*adj.*)
'kər-siv

running or flowing (said of handwriting in which the letters are joined)

cursory (*adj.*)
'kər-sə-rē

running over hastily; superficially done, as a *cursory* glance

discursive (*adj.*)
dis-'kər-siv

wandering ("running") from one topic to another; rambling; digressive

excursion (*n.*)
ik-'skər-zhən

going ("running") out or forth; expedition

incur (*v.*)
in-'kər

1. meet with ("run into") something undesirable
2. bring upon oneself

incursion (*n.*)
in-'kər-zhən

1. rushing into
2. hostile invasion; raid

precursor (*n.*)
pri-'kər-sər

forerunner; predecessor

recur (*v.*)
ri-'kər

happen again (literally, "run again")

 **EXERCISE 5.26**

In each blank, insert the most appropriate word from group 21, *cur* (*curr, curs*).

1. If you are habitually late, you will _____ the displeasure of your employer.

2. Does your school _____ include a course in driver's education?

3. All of the _____ movies showing at the multiplex are comedies, but two suspense films open Friday.

4. A difficult passage requires much more than a(n) _____ reading if it is to be fully understood.

5. Our conversation, as usual, was _____, ranging from the latest in music to the prospects of our favorite teams.

22. GRESS (GRAD): "step," "walk," "go"

aggressive (*adj.*) ə-'gre-siv	disposed to attack (literally, "step toward"); militant; assertive; pushing
egress (*n.*) 'ē-ˌgres	means of going out; exit (*ant.* **access**)
gradation (*n.*) grā-'dā-shən	1. change by steps or stages 2. act of grading
grade (*n.*) 'grād	step; stage; degree; rating
gradient (*n.*) 'grā-dē-ənt	1. rate at which a road, railroad track, temperature, voltage, etc., rises or falls ("steps" up or down) 2. slope; inclination
gradual (*adj.*) 'graj-ə-wəl	step-by-step; proceeding by small stages or degrees (*ant.* **abrupt**)
graduate (*v.*) 'gra-jə-ˌwāt	complete all the steps of a course and receive a diploma or degree
graduated (*adj.*) 'gra-jə-ˌwāt-əd	arranged in regular steps, stages, or degrees
progressive (*adj.*) prə-'gre-siv	going forward to something considered better (*ant.* **reactionary; retrogressive**)
regressive (*adj.*) ri-'gre-siv	disposed to move ("step") backward; retrogressive
retrograde (*adj.*) 're-trə-ˌgrād	1. going backward 2. becoming worse
retrogression (*n.*) ˌre-trə-'gre-shən	act of going from a better to a worse state; deterioration (*ant.* **progress**)
transgress (*v.*) trans-'gres	step beyond the limits or barriers; go beyond; break a law; violate

EXERCISE 5.27

In each blank, insert the most appropriate word from group 22, *gress (grad)*.

1. Learning to play an instrument is a(n) _____ process; it cannot be achieved overnight.

2. The offenders know they will be dealt with severely if they _____ again.

3. When the game ended, hordes of spectators jammed the stadium exits, making _____ painfully slow.

4. The medical report showed _____ rather than progress, for the patient's hypertension had worsened.

5. In a string of _____ pearls, the individual pearls are arranged in the order of increasing size on both halves of the string.

23. PED: *"foot"*

biped (*n.*) 'bī-,ped	two-footed animal
centipede (*n.*) 'sen-tə-,pēd	(literally, "hundred-legged" creature); wormlike animal with one pair of legs on most of its segments
expedite (*v.*) 'ek-spə-,dīt	1. facilitate (literally, "extricate someone caught by the foot") 2. accelerate or speed up (*ant.* **delay**)
impede (*v.*) im-'pēd	hinder (literally, "entangle the feet"); obstruct; block (*ant.* **assist; aid**)
impediment (*n.*) im-'pe-də-mənt	1. hindrance; obstacle (literally, "something entangling the feet") 2. defect
millipede (*n.*) 'mi-lə-,pēd	(literally, "thousand-legged" creature); wormlike animal with two pairs of legs on most of its segments
pedal (*n.*) 'pe-dᵊl	lever acted on by the foot
pedestal (*n.*) 'pe-dəs-tᵊl	1. support or foot of a column or statue 2. foundation
pedestrian (*n.*) pə-'des-trē-ən	person traveling on foot
pedestrian (*adj.*)	commonplace, as a *pedestrian* performance; unimaginative; dull
velocipede (*n.*) və-'lä-sə-,pēd	1. child's tricycle (literally, "swift foot") 2. early form of bicycle

EXERCISE 5.28

In each blank, insert the most appropriate word from group 23, *ped*.

1. A supervisor is expected to _____, not impede, production.

2. Brakes screeched as a foolhardy_____ crossed against the light.

3. For a smooth stop, apply foot pressure to the brake _____ gradually, not abruptly.

4. As a youth, Demosthenes, the famous orator, is said to have suffered from a speech _____.

5. At the age of six, Ana abandoned her _____ and learned to ride a bicycle.

24. TACT (TANG): "touch"

contact (*n.*) 'kän-,takt	touching or meeting; association; connection
contiguous (*adj.*) kən-'ti-gyə-wəs	touching; in physical contact; adjoining
contingent (*adj.*) kən-'tin-jənt	1. dependent on something else (literally, "touching together") 2. accidental
intact (*adj.*) in-'takt	untouched or uninjured; kept or left whole (*ant.* **defective**)
intangible (*adj.*) in-'tan-jə-bəl	1. not capable of being perceived by the sense of touch 2. hard to grasp or define exactly (*ant.* **tangible**)
tact (*n.*) 'takt	sensitive mental perception of what is appropriate on a given occasion (literally, "sense of touch")
tactful (*adj.*) 'takt-fəl	having or showing tact; diplomatic (*ant.* **tactless**)
tactile (*adj.*) 'tak-tᵊl	1. pertaining to the sense of touch 2. tangible
tangent (*adj.*) 'tan-jənt	touching at only one point
tangent (*n.*)	line or surface meeting a curved line or surface at one point, but not intersecting it
tangential (*adj.*) tan-'jen(t)-shəl	merely touching; slightly connected; digressive

 **EXERCISE 5.29**

In each blank, insert the most appropriate word from group 24, *tact* (*tang*).

1. To discuss your admission to college in the presence of someone who has just received a rejection notice is _____.

2. The missing sum was found _____; not a penny had been spent.

3. The Federal grant is _____ on our raising a matching sum; if we fail to raise that sum, we will not qualify.

4. Though _____, a firm's goodwill with its clients is a valuable asset.

5. Alumni associations help classmates maintain _____ after graduation.

25. PREHEND (PREHENS): "seize," "grasp"

apprehend (*v.*) ,a-pri-'hend	1. seize or take into custody 2. understand
apprehensive (*adj.*) ,a-pri-'hen-siv	1. quick to understand or grasp 2. fearful of what may come; anxious (*ant.* **confident**)
comprehensible (*adj.*) ,käm-pri-'hen-sə-bəl	able to be grasped mentally; understandable (*ant.* **incomprehensible**)
comprehensive (*adj.*) ,käm-pri-'hen-siv	including ("seizing") very much; extensive
prehensile (*adj.*) prē-'hen-səl	adapted for seizing, as a *prehensile* tail
reprehend (*v.*) ,re-pri-'hend	find fault with (literally, "hold back"); rebuke; reprimand; censure
reprehensible (*adj.*) ,re-pri-'hen(t)-sə-bəl	deserving of censure; culpable

EXERCISE 5.30

In each blank, insert the most appropriate word from group 25, *prehend* (*prehens*).

1. Unchallenged, bullies become more aggressive and more _____.

2. A helicopter gives a(n) _____ view of the city for the traffic report.

3. Computers excel in making coded messages _____.

4. Before the curtain rose, I was _____ about my performance, even though I had rehearsed my part many times.

5. Law enforcement officials are doing their best to _____ the escaped convict.

6. The instructor is quick to _____ us when we violate safety regulations.

26. JECT: "throw," "cast"

abject (*adj.*) 'ab-ˌjekt	sunk or cast down to a low condition; downtrodden; deserving contempt; wretched
conjecture (*n.*) kən-'jek-chə(r)	guess; supposition; inference
dejected (*adj.*) di-'jek-təd	downcast ("thrown down"); discouraged; depressed
eject (*v.*) ē-'jekt	throw out; expel; evict
inject (*v.*) in-'jekt	force ("throw in"); introduce (as *inject* a liquid or a remark)
interject (*v.*) ˌin-tər-'jekt	throw in between; insert; interpose
object (*v.*) əb-'jekt	protest ("throw against"); disapprove
project (*v.*) prə-'jekt	thrust or "throw forward" (as *projecting* one's ideas for a plan, one's voice to be heard more clearly, or one's slides on a screen); plan
projectile (*n.*) prə-'jek-tᵊl	body (bullet, missile, ball, etc.) to be shot or otherwise "thrown forward"
reject (*v.*) ri-'jekt	discard ("throw back"); refuse to take (*ant.* **accept**)
subject (*v.*) səb-'jekt	force (someone) to undergo something unpleasant or inconvenient; expose; make liable to

 **EXERCISE 5.31**

In each blank, insert the most appropriate word from group 26, *ject*.

1. My friend is _____ over the damage to her new car.

2. A wise policy in buying stocks is to be guided by fact rather than _____.

3. The umpire was obliged to _____ a player who refused to accept his decision.

4. A hypodermic syringe is used to _____ a dose of medicine beneath the skin.

5. The mob hurled bricks, eggs—anything that could serve as a(n) _____.

6. We tend to avoid rude people because we do not wish to _____ ourselves to their insults.

27. VERT (VERS): "turn"

advert (*v.*) ad-ˈvərt	turn attention; refer (as *adverting* to a previous topic)
aversion (*n.*) ə-ˈvər-zhən	feeling of repugnance toward something with a desire to turn away from it; strong dislike; antipathy
avert (*v.*) ə-ˈvərt	prevent ("turn away"); avoid
controversy (*n.*) ˈkän-trə-ˈvər-sē	dispute (literally, a "turning against"); debate; quarrel
convert (*v.*) kən-ˈvərt	transform (e.g., "turn" from one belief to another, one currency into another—as dollars into euros, or one physical state to another—as a liquid to a solid)
diversion (*n.*) də-ˈvər-zhən	entertainment; amusement
divert (*v.*) də-ˈvərt	1. turn aside 2. amuse; entertain
extrovert (*n.*) ˈek-strə-ˌvərt	someone "turned outward" (e.g., social, outgoing, gregarious, focused on outside matters rather than on inner concerns) (*ant.* **introvert**)
inadvertently (*adv.*) ˌi-nəd-ˈvər-tənt-lē	without turning one's mind to the matter at hand; carelessly; unintentionally

incontrovertible (*adj.*) in-,kän-trə-'vər-tə-bəl	not able to be "turned opposite" or disputed; not open to question (*ant.* **controvertible; disputable**)
introvert (*n.*) 'in-trə-,vərt	someone "turned inward" (e.g., shy, diffident, focused on one's own thoughts and feelings rather than on outside matters)
introvert (*v.*)	turn inward
invert (*v.*) in-'vərt	turn upside down
obverse (*n.*) 'äb-,vərs	side turned toward the observer; therefore, the front of a coin, medal, etc. (*ant.* **reverse**)
perverse (*adj.*) pər-'vərs	turned away from what is right or good; corrupt; wrongheaded
pervert (*v.*) pər-'vərt	turn away from right or truth; give a wrong meaning to
revert (*v.*) ri-'vərt	return; go back, as: "The property will *revert* to the owner when the lease is up."
versatile (*adj.*) 'vər-sə-tᵊl	able to turn with ease from one thing to another; adaptable
verse (*n.*) 'vərs	line of poetry (literally, "turning around"; After a fixed number of syllables, the poet has to "turn around" to begin a new line.)
vertigo (*n.*) 'vər-ti-,gō	condition in which one feels that one's surroundings are turning about; dizziness

EXERCISE 5.32

In each blank, insert the most appropriate word from group 27, *vert* (*vers*).

1. Between Thanksgiving and Christmas, most department store employees work overtime; afterward, they _____ to their normal working hours.

2. "In God We Trust" appears above Lincoln's image on the _____ of a cent.

3. No sooner did we settle one quarrel than we became involved in another _____.

4. The first _____ of Katherine Lee Bates' "America, the Beautiful" begins "O beautiful for spacious skies."

5. A(n) _____ musician can play several instruments.

6. The proof of his guilt was so _____ that the defendant confessed to the crime.

28. MIS (MISS, MIT, MITT): *"send"*

commitment (*n.*) kə-'mit-mənt	1. consignment ("sending") to prison or a mental institution 2. pledge
demise (*n.*) di-'mīz	death (literally, "sending or putting down")
emissary (*n.*) 'e-mə-ˌser-ē	person sent out on a mission
emit (*v.*) ē-'mit	send out; give off
intermittent (*adj.*) ˌin-tər-'mi-tᵊnt	coming and going at intervals, as an *intermittent* fever (literally, "sending between")
missile (*n.*) 'mi-səl	weapon (spear, bullet, rocket, etc.) capable of being propelled ("sent") to hit a distant object
missive (*n.*) 'mi-siv	written message sent; letter
remiss (*adj.*) ri-'mis	negligent (literally, "sent back"); careless; lax (*ant.* **scrupulous**)
remission (*n.*) ri-'mi-shən	lessening, relieving, or disappearance (as of disease symptoms); forgiveness, abatement, or cancellation (as of guilt or of a penalty)
remit (*v.*) ri-'mit	1. send money due 2. forgive, as to have one's sins *remitted*
transmit (*v.*) tranz-'mit	convey (literally, "send across or through"); cause something (as knowledge, tradition, wealth, infection, radio waves, or light beams) to go from one person or place to another

✎ EXERCISE 5.33

In each blank, insert the most appropriate word from group 28, *mis* (*miss, mit, mitt*).

1. This morning's rain was _____, starting and stopping several times.

2. It was my fault. I was _____ in not writing sooner.

3. A distinguished veteran diplomat has been chosen as the President's _____ to the international conference.

4. If I don't _____ the full amount by the tenth of the month, the bank will charge me a late fee.

5. My large searchlight can _____ a powerful beam.

6. We gave you our word; we will not go back on our _____.

7. Just when the patient's recovery seemed unlikely, a(n) _____ occurred.

29. *LOCUT (LOQU): "speak," "talk"*

circumlocution (*n.*)
,sər-kəm-lō-'kyü-shən
roundabout way of speaking

colloquial (*adj.*)
kə-'lō-kwē-əl
conversational; informal (as *colloquial* speech or writing)

colloquy (*n.*)
'kä-lə-kwē
talking together; conference; conversation

elocution (*n.*)
'el-ə-'kyü-shən
art of speaking out or reading effectively in public

eloquent (*adj.*)
'e-lə-kwənt
speaking with force and fluency; movingly expressive

grandiloquent (*adj.*)
gran-'di-lə-kwənt
using lofty or pompous words; bombastic

interlocutor (*n.*)
,in-tər-'lä-kyə-tər
1. questioner
2. one who participates in a conversation

loquacious (*adj.*)
lō-'kwā-shəs
talkative; garrulous

obloquy (*n.*)
'ä-blə-kwē
1. speaking against; censure; reproach (*ant.* **praise**)
2. bad repute

EXERCISE 5.34

In each blank, insert the most appropriate word from group 29, *locut (loqu)*.

1. "Your services will be terminated if you persist in disregarding our requirement of punctuality" is a(n) _____. More direct is, "You will be dismissed if you are late again."

2. _____ students who carry on noisy conversations in the library prevent others from concentrating

3. A course in _____ can help one to become an effective public speaker.

4. The referee held a short _____ with the judges before announcing the winner.

5. Witnesses appearing before the investigating committee found that its chief counsel was the principal _____; the committee members asked very few questions.

30. FER(ous): "bearing," "producing," "yielding"

auriferous (*adj.*)
ȯ-'ri-fə-rəs
bearing or yielding gold

coniferous (*adj.*)
kō-'ni-fə-rəs
bearing cones, as the pine tree

odoriferous (*adj.*)
ˌō-də-'ri-fə-rəs
yielding an odor, usually fragrant

pestiferous (*adj.*)
pes-'ti-fə-rəs
1. infected with or bearing disease; pestilential
2. evil

proliferous (*adj.*)
prə-'li-fə-rəs
producing new growth rapidly and extensively

somniferous (*adj.*)
säm-'ni-fə-rəs
bearing or inducing sleep

vociferous (*adj.*)
vō-'si-fə-rəs
producing a loud outcry; clamorous; noisy

 **EXERCISE 5.35**

In each blank, insert the most appropriate word from group 30, *fer(ous)*.

1. The infant emitted so _____ a protest when placed in the crib that his mother picked him up at once.

2. A vase of _____ lilacs gave the room an inviting fragrance.

3. Mild insomnia may yield to the _____ effect of a glass of warm milk.

4. Swarms of _____ locusts devastated the cornfields.

5. The cones of pines, firs, and other _____ trees contain their seeds.

6. _____ weeds are a serious problem for gardeners.

7. The lucky miner struck a(n) _____ vein.

Review Exercises

REVIEW 10: DEFINING LATIN ROOTS

In the space before each Latin root in column I, write the *letter* of its correct meaning from column II.

COLUMN I	COLUMN II
___ 1. MOR (MORT)	*a.* body
___ 2. TACT (TANG)	*b.* step; walk; go
___ 3. LOCUT (LOQU)	*c.* run
___ 4. GRAT	*d.* bearing; producing; yielding
___ 5. SECUT (SEQU)	*e.* speak; talk
___ 6. CORP	*f.* throw
___ 7. CUR (CURR, CURS)	*g.* touch
___ 8. PED	*h.* pleasant; thank; favor
___ 9. PREHEND (PREHENS)	*i.* lead; conduct; draw
___ 10. JECT	*j.* death
___ 11. VERT(VERS)	*k.* send
___ 12. FER (ous)	*l.* turn
___ 13. GRESS (GRAD)	*m.* seize; grasp
___ 14. MIS (MISS, MIT, MITT)	*n.* foot
___ 15. DUC (DUCT)	*o.* follow

REVIEW 11: USING LATIN ROOTS

Enter the Latin roots needed to complete the partially spelled words below.

DEFINITION	WORD
1. going forward to something better	P R O __ __ __ __ __ I V E
2. person traveling on foot	__ __ __ E S T R I A N
3. combine so as to form one body	I N __ __ __ __ O R A T E
4. something that follows; continuation	__ __ __ __ E L
5. artificial channel for conducting water	A Q U E __ __ __ __

6. undertaker   __ __ __ __ I C I A N

7. gift of money in return for a favor   __ __ __ __ U I T Y

8. producing a loud outcry   V O C I __ __ __ __ __ __

9. turning away; repugnance   A __ __ __ __ I O N

10. pertaining to the sense of touch   __ __ __ __ I L E

11. speaking against; censure   O B __ __ __ __ Y

12. running or flowing (handwriting)   __ __ __ __ I V E

13. by steps or degrees   __ __ __ __ U A L

14. written message sent; letter   __ __ __ __ I V E

15. talkative   __ __ __ __ A C I O U S

16. throw in between; interpose   I N T E R __ __ __ __

17. tending to lead to; contributive   C O N __ __ __ I V E

18. person sent on a mission   E __ __ __ __ A R Y

19. running together; occurring simultaneously   C O N __ __ __ __ E N T

20. turning easily from one thing to another   __ __ __ __ A T I L E

✍ **REVIEW 12:** SENTENCE COMPLETION

Which of the two terms makes the sentence correct? Write the *letter* of your answer in the space provided.

___ 1. The _____ speaker moved the audience deeply in her brief address.
      a. loquacious   *b.* eloquent

___ 2. Andres is an _____; he shows little interest in what is going on around him.
      a. extrovert   *b.* introvert

___ 3. The authorities know the identity of the _____ and expect to apprehend him soon.
      a. transgressor   *b.* precursor

___ 4. Larry's diverting account of his experiment _____ the class.
      a. confused   *b.* amused

___ 5. The entire foreign diplomatic _____ attended the funeral rites for the eminent leader.
      a. corpse   *b.* corps

___ 6. For all the kindness you have shown us, we are extremely _____.
      a. grateful   *b.* gratuitous

— 7. Emily's motion was adopted by a 12-to-2 vote, showing that most of the members
_____.

     a. incurred   *b.* concurred

— 8. If you had used fewer technical terms, your explanation would have been more
_____.

     a. comprehensible   *b.* comprehensive

— 9. The employer explained that salary increases are not automatic but _____ on satisfactory service.

     a. contiguous   *b.* contingent

— 10. The following is an example of _____: "Swimmers come to the surface within seconds after a dive; when Dee didn't come up immediately, we knew she was in trouble."

     a. induction   *b.* deduction

REVIEW 13: OPPOSITES

Write the word that means the OPPOSITE of the defined word by adding, dropping, or changing a prefix or a suffix. (The first answer has been filled in as an example.)

DEFINITION	WORD	OPPOSITE
1. important	consequential	*inconsequential*
2. unbelievable	incredible	_____
3. having no tact	tactless	_____
4. discourteous; rude	ungracious	_____
5. disposed to move backward	regressive	_____
6. thrown in	injected	_____
7. yielding no odor	odorless	_____
8. indefensible	untenable	_____
9. having faith in oneself	confident	_____
10. unrelated to the matter at hand	impertinent	_____
11. front of a coin	obverse	_____
12. capable of being corrupted	corruptible	_____
13. a going ("running") out	excursion	_____
14. touchable	tangible	_____
15. reasoning from particular to general	induction	_____

16. understandable   comprehensible   _____

17. trust in the truth of   credit   _____

18. faithfulness to a trust   fidelity   _____

19. unconquered   unvanquished   _____

20. person more interested in own thoughts   introvert   _____
    than in outside matters

REVIEW 14: MEANINGS

In the space before each word or expression in column I, write the *letter* of its correct meaning from column II.

COLUMN I	COLUMN II
___ 1. death rate	*a.* invert
___ 2. turn upside down	*b.* grandiloquent
___ 3. felicitate	*c.* retrograde
___ 4. adapted for seizing	*d.* congratulate
___ 5. give a wrong meaning to	*e.* mortality
___ 6. bombastic	*f.* pervert
___ 7. interpose	*g.* ductile
___ 8. going backward	*h.* corpuscle
___ 9. minute particle	*i.* interject
___ 10. able to be hammered thin	*j.* prehensile

REVIEW 15: CONCISE WRITING

Express the thought of each sentence below in no more than four words.

1. He never appreciates a favor, and he never says "thank you."

   _____

2. Is it possible for the process of growth to be speeded up?

   _____

3. The talk that you gave kept wandering from one topic to another.

   _____

4. It is important for us to have a sensitive mental perception of what is appropriate on a given occasion.

_____

5. There are few individuals who can speak with force and fluency.

_____

6. We drove by several people who were traveling on foot.

_____

7. No evidence exists to prove that a crime has been committed.

_____

8. The opinion that she has expressed is open to question.

_____

9. You are so absorbed with your own thoughts and feelings that you pay little attention to what is going on in the world around you.

_____

10. Some of the artificial channels that the Romans built for conducting water over a distance survive to this day.

_____

REVIEW 16: BRAINTEASERS

Fill in the missing letters.

1. The firm's purchase of a computer network is __ __ __ **t i n g e** __ __ on getting a bank loan.

2. The horse-drawn carriage was a(n) __ __ __ **c u r** __ __ __ of the automobile.

3. After his defeat by an unknown young newcomer, the ex-champion could not conceal his __ __ __ __ __ __ __ **c a t** __ __ __.

4. A United Nations __ **m i s s** __ __ __ is being sent to help mediate the dispute between the two nations.

5. As a result of the six __ __ __ __ __ **c u t** __ __ __ days of rain, we have had severe flooding.

6. My neighbor is a(n) __ __ __ **r a t e**. I washed his car, and he didn't even thank me.

7. Because of the legislator's __ __ __ __ __ **h e n s** __ __ __ __ conduct, the voters overwhelmingly rejected his bid for a second term.

8. Benjamin Franklin—printer, author, scientist, inventor, philosopher, and diplomat—was one of the most __ __ __ s a t __ __ __ people of his time.

9. Charges against the defendant were dropped when her defense attorney presented __ __ __ __ __ __ r o v e r __ __ __ __ __ evidence of her innocence.

10. Some department stores have posted signs stating that all shoplifters who are apprehended will be __ __ __ __ __ c u t e __.

REVIEW 17: COMPOSITION

Answer in two or three sentences.

1. If you were mayor, how might you expedite the settlement of a labor-management controversy in your town?

2. Would you be remiss if you made an important decision on the basis of conjecture? Explain.

3. Must the gradual loss of population to the suburbs be a mortal blow to a city? Why, or why not?

4. Explain how a gratuitous remark incurred someone's displeasure.

5. Would it be a sign of retrogression or of progress for a nation to abolish the death penalty? Explain.

REVIEW 18: ANALOGIES

Write the *letter* of the word that best completes the analogy.

___ **1.** *River* is to *bridge* as *valley* is to _____.
   a. viaduct   *b.* mountain   *c.* pontoon   *d.* projectile   *e.* road

___ **2.** *Olfactory* is to *smell* as *tactile* is to _____.
   a. see   *b.* grasp   *c.* touch   *d.* hear   *e.* taste

___ **3.** *Birth* is to *demise* as *preface* is to _____.
   a. foreword   *b.* conclusion   *c.* footnote   *d.* introduction   *e.* outline

___ **4.** *Corpse* is to *life* as *ingrate* is to _____.
   a. fear   *b.* ingratitude   *c.* unkindness   *d.* dejection   *e.* gratitude

___ **5.** *Plan* is to *execution* as *outline* is to _____.
   a. summary   *b.* organization   *c.* killing   *d.* composition   *e.* topic

REVIEW 19: SIMILAR AND CONTRARY

Fill in the missing letters so that each line contains three words or phrases with similar meanings and one with a contrary meaning.

Similar Meaning	Similar Meaning	Similar Meaning	Contrary Meaning
1. perf __ __ y	fa __ __ hlessness	tre __ __ hery	f __ delilty
2. convi __ __ al	j __ vial	soci __ __	in __ __ __ pitable
3. vict __ __	c __ __ queror	v __ __ quisher	__ oser
4. fr __ __ __ ious	cr __ ss	irr __ __ able	pe __ __ eable
5. t __ __ ctable	fle __ ible	p __ iable	refr __ __ __ ory
6. per __ __ nent	rele __ __ nt	fit __ __ ng	in __ ppropriate
7. admon __ __ __	repr __ __ e	reb __ __ e	com __ __ __ __
8. mon __ __ or	reg __ __ ate	che __ k	ig __ ore
9. __ __ __ datory	r __ quired	ob __ __ __ atory	op __ __ onal
10. cr __ dible	be __ __ __ vable	t __ __ __ __ worthy	incr __ __ ible
11. con __ __ dent	self-r __ liant	su __ __	appre __ __ __ sive

12. cre __ __ __ ous	easily decei __ __ d	g __ lible	s __ eptical
13. feal __ __	lo __ __ lty	fa __ __ hfulness	infi __ __ __ ity
14. confi __ __ __ tial	s __ cret	priv __ __ e	pub __ __ __
15. __ __ pede	hin __ __ __	obst __ __ ct	a __ d
16. g __ __ cious	co __ __ teous	plea __ __ __ t	un __ __ __ cious
17. in __ __ rsion	inv __ __ ion	ra __ d	__ __ __ hdrawal
18. imm __ __ __ al	im __ __ rishable	de __ __ hless	mort __ __
19. cal __ mniate	trad __ __ e	vil __ __ y	eulo __ __ __ e
20. pre __ __ rsor	pr __ __ ecessor	f __ __ __ __ runner	fol __ __ wer
21. abr __ __ t	s __ __ den	stee __	g __ __ dual
22. ex __ __ __ ite	acce __ __ __ ate	fac __ __ itate	dela __
23. cont __ __ uous	ad __ __ __ __ __ ing	cont __ __ ting	rem __ te
24. in __ __ ct	unto __ __ hed	un __ __ jured	defe __ tive
25. abj __ __ __	con __ __ __ ptible	d __ __ __ trodden	__ __ alted
26. dejec __ __ __	down __ __ __ __	d __ __ couraged	e __ static
27. c __ __ jecture	sup __ __ sition	gu __ __ s	fa __ t
28. in __ __ vertently	unin __ __ ntionally	c __ __ elessly	d __ liberately
29. re __ __ ss	neg __ __ __ ent	la __	sc __ __ __ ulous
30. pest __ __ erous	pesti __ __ ntial	in __ __ ctious	sal __ brious

REVIEW 20: FILL AND MATCH

Write the letter of the word or set of words best filling each blank and best matching each italicized expression.

___ 1. King Hamlet's unexpected _____ (officially attributed to the sting of a serpent) has prompted the return to Denmark of his son, Prince Hamlet, for the funeral.

   A. departure

   B. hospitalization

   C. incapacitation

   D. demise

___ **2.** From his closest friend, Horatio, Hamlet learns of an extraordinary visitation that took place the night before. Horatio witnessed the marching by of a fearsome apparition—surely no *flesh-and-blood* creature—but rather some spirit or ghost in the very image of the late king arrayed in battle armor.

    A. immortal

    B. mortal

    C. benevolent

    D. misanthropic

___ **3.** Hamlet, suspecting his father may have met with "foul play," asks Horatio to keep his strange report *to himself* and determines to seek a _____ with the spirit.

    A. tangential . . confrontation

    B. fiduciary . . premonition

    C. confidential . . colloquy

    D. restricted . . circumlocution

___ **4.** That night, when Hamlet has placed himself where Horatio saw the royal apparition, it returns, draws the prince apart from his companions, and—*casting doubt upon* the official version of the king's death—recounts instead a tale of *fantastic disloyalty*.

    A. invalidating . . unbelievable fealty

    B. confirming . . anomalous treachery

    C. discrediting . . incredible perfidy

    D. accrediting . . surpassing infidelity

___ **5.** The ghost reports that King Hamlet was deliberately poisoned, making his death _____; the murderer is his own brother, Claudius (Denmark's new king), making the murder _____ as well; and Claudius had subverted the marital *fealty* of Queen Gertrude, the old king's wife and young Hamlet's mother, making Claudius an "incestuous, . . . adulterate beast."

    A. regicide . . fratricide . . fidelity

    B. regicide . . patricide . . concord

    C. patricide . . fratricide . . exogamy

    D. tyrannicide . . regicide . . loyalty

___ **6.** If the spirit's tale is *true*, revenge for this "foul and most unnatural murder" would be *obligatory*. It would be Hamlet's *obligation as a son* to avenge his murdered father by killing Claudius.

    A. counterfeit . . required . . filial mandate

    B. genuine . . impertinent . . paternal commitment

    C. bona fide . . mandatory . . filial duty

    D. authentic . . optional . . familial responsibility

___ 7. However, as Hamlet acknowledges, the tale may be false because the "spirit may be . . . the Devil" scheming to make a *too trusting* Hamlet damn his _____ soul by killing an innocent Claudius.

    A. gullible . . flesh-and-blood

    B. credulous . . immortal

    C. foolishly believing . . mortal

    D. apprehensive . . spiritual

___ 8. To test if his uncle is guilty, Hamlet puts on before Claudius a play mirroring his alleged crime. Hamlet and his _____, Horatio, scrutinize the king's reactions to the unfolding plot, the poisoning of a Duke Gonzago by his _____ nephew, Lucianus.

    A. confederate . . ungracious

    B. accomplice . . fiduciary

    C. confidant . . perfidious

    D. extrovert . . treacherous

___ 9. The moment Lucianus administers the _____ drug, Claudius—distraught— rises *all of a sudden* from the throne and rushes wildly out.

    A. fatal . . abruptly

    B. deadly . . impertinently

    C. mortal . . gradually

    D. somniferous . . cursorily

___ 10. Hamlet and Horatio _____: Claudius has *condemned* himself by _____ a guilty conscience. His guilt is *indubitable*.

    A. are incredulous . . censured . . rejecting . . indisputable

    B. agree . . exculpated . . revealing . . incontestable

    C. are no longer diffident . . betrayed . . displaying . . indeterminate

    D. concur . . convicted . . evincing . . incontrovertible

Words From Classical Mythology and History

This chapter will teach you to use important words taken from classical (ancient Greek and Roman) mythology. The beautiful and profoundly significant myths created by the Greeks and adopted by the Romans have contributed words that an educated person is expected to know. All the words discussed below originate from myths, except the following which are based on historical fact: *Draconian, forum, laconic, Lucullan, Marathon, philippic, Pyrrhic, solon, Spartan*, and *thespian*.

Study Your New Words

WORD	MEANING	TYPICAL USE
Adonis (*n.*) ə-'dä-nəs	very handsome young man (from *Adonis,* handsome youth loved by Aphrodite, goddess of love)	Joanna's former boyfriend was not exactly handsome, but her new one is quite an *Adonis.*
aegis (*n.*) 'ē-jəs	shield or protection; auspices; sponsorship (from *aegis,* protective shield of Zeus, king of the Greek gods)	An international force under the *aegis* of the United Nations was dispatched to the troubled area.
amazon (*n.*) 'am-ə-ˌzän	tall, strong, bold woman (from the *Amazons,* mythological race of women warriors)	The laborious work that pioneer women had to do would have challenged an *amazon.*
ambrosial (*adj.*) am-'brō-zhəl	exceptionally pleasing to taste or smell; extremely delicious; excellent (from *ambrosia,* the literally "not mortal" food of the gods)	The *ambrosial* aroma of the roast whetted our appetites.

atlas (*n.*) 'at-ləs	book of maps (from *Atlas,* giant who supported the heavens on his shoulders. The figure of Atlas supporting the world was prefaced to early map collections—hence the name *atlas.*)	For reliable information about present national boundaries, consult an up-to-date *atlas.*
auroral (*adj.*) ə-'ròr-əl	pertaining to or resembling the dawn; rosy; radiant (from *Aurora,* Roman goddess of the dawn)	The darkness waned, and a faint *auroral* glow began to appear in the east.
bacchanalian (*adj.*) ,ba-kə-'nāl-yən (or **bacchic**)	jovial or wild with drunkenness (from *Bacchus,* Roman god of wine)	Some fans celebrated the Rose Bowl win with *bacchanalian* revelry.
Cassandra (*n.*) kə-'san-drə	one who prophesies doom or disaster; pessimist (from *Cassandra,* given the power of prophecy by Apollo. When she spurned his love, he could not take back his gift, but stipulated that no one would ever believe her.) (*ant.* **Pollyanna**)	Many say we will lose, but the coach is urging us to pay no attention to those *Cassandras.*
chimerical (*adj.*) kī-'mer-i-kəl (or **chimeric**)	fantastic; unreal; impossible; absurd (from the *Chimera,* fire-breathing monster with a lion's head, goat's body, and serpent's tail)	At first, Robert Fulton's plans for his steamboat were derided as *chimerical* nonsense.
Draconian (*adj.*) drə-'kō-nē-ən (or **draconian**)	cruel; harsh; severe; ironhanded (from *Draco,* Athenian lawmaker who drew up a harsh code of laws)	The victors in the civil war imposed *Draconian* restrictions on the vanquished.
echolalia (*n.*) ,e-kō-'lā-lē-ə	automatic and immediate repetition (echoing) of what others say (from *Echo,* maiden who loved Narcissus. When he rejected her, she pined away until nothing was left of her but her voice.)	The *echolalia* of infants is part of the process by which they learn to speak.
Elysian (*adj.*) i-'li-zhən	delightful; blissful; heavenly (from *Elysium,* mythological paradise where after death the blessed, mortals especially favored by the gods, dwell)	Students yearn for the *Elysian* leisure of the summer vacation.
eristic (*adj.*) i-'ris-tik	prone to controversy; disputatious; argumentative (from *Eris,* goddess of discord)	It is extremely difficult to reach an agreement with anyone who has an *eristic* temperament.
fauna (*n.*) 'fò-nə	animal life; animals of a particular region or period (from *Faunus,* Roman god of animals)	The careless use of pesticides threatened to remove the bald eagle from our nation's *fauna.*

flora (*n.*) ˈflȯr-ə	plant life; plants of a particular region or period (from *Flora*, Roman goddess of flowers)	Pollution is harming not only the residents of the area, but also its *fauna* and *flora*.
forum (*n.*) ˈfȯr-əm	medium or place for open discussion and expression of ideas—a public meeting, radio or TV discussion, editorial page, etc. (from *forum*, marketplace or other place of assembly for judicial or public business in an ancient Roman city)	A dictatorship permits no *forum* where ideas can be freely and openly discussed.
hector (*v.*) ˈhek-tər	bully; intimidate with threats; bluster (from *Hector*, bravest of the Trojans)	The sheriff refused to turn the suspect over to the *hectoring* mob.
herculean (*adj.*) ˌhər-kyə-ˈlē-ən (or **Herculean**)	very difficult; requiring the strength of *Hercules* (a hero of superhuman strength)	Among the *herculean* tasks confronting our nation is the rebuilding of roads, bridges, and tunnels.
hermetic (*adj.*) hər-ˈme-tik	airtight; secret; obscure; magical; mysterious (from *Hermes* —Zeus's swift messenger; god of eloquence and commerce; patron of travelers, rogues, and thieves; Greek name for Thoth, Egyptian god linked with the occult and the reputed inventor of a magic seal to keep a vessel airtight)	To get a vitamin pill from a new bottle, you must unscrew the cap and break the *hermetic* seal.
iridescent (*adj.*) ˌir-ə-ˈde-sᵊnt	having colors like the rainbow (from *Iris*, goddess of the rainbow)	Children enjoy blowing *iridescent* soap bubbles.
jovial (*adj.*) ˈjō-vē-əl	jolly; merry; good-humored (from *Jove*, or *Jupiter*, king of the Roman gods. The planet Jupiter was believed to make people born under its influence cheerful or *jovial*.)	Our *jovial* hostess entertained us with some amusing anecdotes about her family.
labyrinthine (*adj.*) ˌla-bə-ˈrin-thən	full of confusing passageways; intricate; complicated, like the *Labyrinth* (a fabled maze in Crete)	Out-of-towners may easily lose their way in New York City's *labyrinthine* subway passages.
laconic (*adj.*) lə-ˈkä-nik	using words sparingly; terse; concise (from *Lakonikos,* meaning "Spartan." The citizens of the Greek city-state of Sparta made terseness a virtue. See *Spartan*, below.)	All I received in response to my request was the *laconic* reply "Wait."
lethargic (*adj.*) lə-ˈthär-jik	unnaturally drowsy; sluggish; dull (from *Lethe*, river in Hades—Hell—whose water, when drunk, caused forgetfulness of the past)	For several hours after the operation, the patient was *lethargic* because of the anesthetic.

Lucullan (*adj.*)
lü-'kə-lən

sumptuous; luxurious (from *Lucullus,* Roman host who gave lavish banquets)

Many a Thanksgiving dinner is a *Lucullan* feast.

marathon (*n.*)
'mar-ə-,thän

1. long-distance footrace of 26 miles 385 yards (from *Marathon,* where the Greeks defeated the Persian invaders in 490 B.C. The fleet-footed Pheidippides raced to Athens with the joyous news, but fell dead after announcing the victory.)

Runners from all over the world compete in the annual Boston and New York City *marathons.*

2. endurance contest, as a dance *marathon*

martial (*adj.*)
'mär-shəl

pertaining to war; warlike (from *Mars,* god of war)

The Helvetians were a *martial* people who tried to conquer southern Gaul.

mentor (*n.*)
'men-,tȯr

1. wise and trusted adviser (from *Mentor,* to whom Odysseus entrusted the education of his son)

The retiring supervisor was persuaded to stay on for a month as *mentor* to her successor.

2. tutor; coach

The basketball *mentor* says that our team is the best he has ever coached.

mercurial (*adj.*)
mər-'kyur-ē-əl

1. quick; vivacious; active; lively (*ant.* saturnine) (from *Mercury,* the Roman *Hermes;* see *hermetic,* above. A planet and a chemical element, of course, are named *Mercury.*)

The older partner is rather dull and morose, but the younger has a *mercurial* temperament that appeals to customers.

2. inconstant; unstable; capricious; subject to rapid and unpredictable mood changes

Someone with a *mercurial* disposition may at any moment turn from contentment to dissatisfaction, or from friendliness to hostility.

myrmidon (*n.*)
'mər-mə-,dän

obedient and unquestioning follower (from the *Myrmidons,* martial tribe that accompanied Achilles to the Trojan War)

Adolf Hitler's *myrmidons* were the SS, who would execute all his orders loyally and pitilessly.

narcissistic (*adj.*)
,när-sə-'sis-tik

in love with oneself; excessively fascinated and gratified by one's own physical and mental qualities; egocentric (from *Narcissus,* a handsome youth who didn't even look at any of the many maidens who loved him. However, looking in a pool, he fell madly in love with his own image, and this futile longing soon led to his death.)

Narcissistic individuals tend to overevaluate their own merits and to see no desirable qualities in others.

nectar (*n.*)
ˈnek-tər

something exceptionally delicious to drink (from *nectar,* the literally "death-overcoming" drink that made the gods immortal)

The juice of those mangoes is like *nectar.*

nemesis (*n.*)
ˈne-mə-səs

1. due punishment for evil deeds (from *Nemesis,* goddess of vengeance)

A conviction for tax evasion has been the *nemesis* of many a criminal who had previously escaped justice.

2. one who inflicts such punishment

Napoleon crushed many opponents, but Wellington was his *nemesis.*

odyssey (*n.*)
ˈä-də-sē

long series of wanderings or travels (from the *Odyssey,* epic poem dealing with Odysseus' ten years of wandering on his way home from the Trojan War)

A travel agent will gladly plan a year's *odyssey* to places of interest around the world.

Olympian (*adj.*)
ə-ˈlim-pē-ən

1. Majestic; godlike; lofty (from *Mt. Olympus,* highest mountain in Greece. Its summit, obscured by clouds from human view, was home to Zeus and other gods.)

Chief executive officers are usually given offices and staffs that are commensurate with their *Olympian* responsibilities.

2. having to do with the *Olympic Games,* international athletic competitions held every four years

paean (*n.*)
ˈpē-ən

song or hymn of praise, joy, or triumph (from *paean,* hymn in praise of Apollo, god of deliverance)

When the crisis was resolved, people danced in the streets and sang *paeans* of joy.

palladium (*n.*)
pə-ˈlā-dē-əm

safeguard; protection (from *Palladium,* statue of the goddess *Pallas Athena* preventing the fall of Troy—but giving no protection if stolen from the city)

The little girl habitually fell asleep clutching a battered doll, her *palladium.*

panic (*n.*)
ˈpa-nik

sudden, overpowering terror, sometimes causing mass flight (from *Pan,* rural god whose unexpected shout would terrify)

A *panic* ensued when someone in the crowded auditorium yelled "Fire!"

philippic (*n.*)
fə-ˈli-pik

bitter denunciation; tirade (from the *Philippics,* orations by Demosthenes denouncing King Philip of Macedon)

In an hour-long *philippic,* the legislator denounced the lobbyists opposing her bill.

plutocratic (*adj.*)
ˌplü-tə-ˈkra-tik

having great influence because of one's wealth (from *Plutus,* god of wealth)

Owning 51% of the billion-dollar firm, three *plutocratic* investors determine its policies.

procrustean (*adj.*)
prə-'krəs-tē-ən
(or **Procrustean**)

cruel or inflexible in enforcing conformity (from *Procrustes,* villain who made travelers fit the length of his bed, either stretching them if they were too short, or cutting off their legs if they were too tall)

The magistrate dispensed a *procrustean* kind of justice, imposing a fine of $500 on everyone who had received a summons, regardless of the circumstances.

protean (*adj.*)
'prō-tē-ən

exceedingly variable; readily assuming different forms or shapes (from *Proteus,* sea god who could readily change his shape to elude capture)

The microscopic ameba, a *protean* organism, is continually changing its shape.

Pyrrhic (*adj.*)
'pir-ik

ruinous; gained at too great a cost (from *Pyrrhus,* who suffered enormous losses in a "victory" over the Romans)

We won, but it was a *Pyrrhic* victory, as our leading scorer was injured and put out of action for the balance of the season.

saturnine (*adj.*)
'sa-tər-,nīn

heavy; dull; sullen; gloomy; morose (*ant.* **mercurial**) (from *Saturn,* father of Jupiter. Though Saturn's reign was supposedly a golden age, he has become a symbol of heaviness and dullness because the alchemists and astrologers associated his name with the metal lead.)

The research assistant was a *saturnine* scholar who said very little and smiled rarely.

siren (*n.*)
'sī-rən

1. dangerous, attractive woman (from the *Sirens,* creatures half woman and half bird whose sweet singing lured mariners to destruction on the rocks)

The enemy employed a vivacious polyglot *siren* as a spy.

2. woman who sings with bewitching sweetness

The nightclub *siren's* final number brought down the house.

3. apparatus for sounding loud warnings

Emergency vehicles raced to the scene with *sirens* screaming.

solon (*n.*)
'sō-lən

legislator; wise lawgiver (from *Solon,* noted Athenian lawgiver)

The *solons* are back for the opening of the legislative session.

Spartan (*adj.*)
'spär-tᵊn

marked by simplicity and avoidance of comfort; marked by self-discipline, bravery, and ability to endure pain (from *Sparta,* whose citizens pursued those traits; see *laconic,* above)

We were offered *Spartan* accommodations; the rooms had neither rugs nor sofas nor easy chairs.

stentorian (*adj.*)
sten-'tȯr-ē-ən

very loud (from *Stentor,* legendary herald whose voice was as loud as fifty voices)

Speak softly; you don't need a *stentorian* voice to be heard in this small room.

Stygian (*adj.*) 'sti-jē-ən	infernal; especially dark; gloomy (from *Styx*, river of the lower world leading into Hades—Hell)	A power failure at 11:30 P.M. plunged the city into *Stygian* blackness.
tantalize (*v.*) 'tan-t³l-,iz	excite a hope but prevent its fulfillment; tease (from *Tantalus*, kept hungry and thirsty in Hades with food and water very near but just beyond his reach)	We removed the strawberry shortcake from the table so as not to *tantalize* our cholesterol-conscious guest.
terpsichorean (*adj.* or *n.*) ,tərp-si-kə-'rē-ən	pertaining to dancing (from *Terpsichore*, muse of dancing); dancer	The reviewers lauded the ballet troupe for its *terpsichorean* artistry.
thespian (*adj.* or *n.*) 'thes-pē-ən (or **Thespian**)	pertaining to the drama or acting (from *Thespis*, reputed father of Greek drama); actor	Shakespeare was not only a playwright but a *thespian* and a producer as well.
titanic (*adj.*) tī-'tan-ik	of enormous strength, size, or power (from the *Titans*, lawless, powerful giants defeated by Zeus)	By a *titanic* effort, our football team halted an onrush at our one-yard line.

Apply What You Have Learned

EXERCISE 6.1: MEANINGS

In the blank space, enter the *letter* of the best definition of the italicized word.

_d_ 1. *ambrosial* fare: *a.* expensive *b.* cut-rate *c.* railroad *d.* delicious

_b_ 2. unemployed *thespians*: *a.* musicians *b.* actors *c.* dancers *d.* loafers

_c_ 3. *martial* airs: *a.* matrimonial *b.* tuneful *c.* military *d.* soothing

_d_ 4. impassioned *philippic*: *a.* plea *b.* message *c.* praise *d.* tirade

_d_ 5. *plutocratic* associates: *a.* loyal and wealthy *b.* jovial *c.* carefree *d.* rich and influential

_b_ 6. *Draconian* laws: *a.* democratic *b.* ironhanded *c.* unpopular *d.* unenforced

_c_ 7. *hermetic* compartments: *a.* rigid *b.* tiny *c.* airtight *d.* iridescent

_b_ 8. road *atlas*: *a.* traveler *b.* map collection *c.* network *d.* surface

_b_ 9. endless *odyssey*: *a.* story *b.* wanderings *c.* sufferings *d.* errands

_d_ 10. new *Adonis*: *a.* lover *b.* movie actor *c.* myrmidon *d.* handsome youth

EXERCISE 6.2: SENTENCE COMPLETION

In the blank space, enter the *letter* of the choice that best completes the sentence.

e 1. Photographs of _____ celebrities decorated the walls of the dance studio.
  a. operatic   *b.* Olympic   *c.* thespian   *d.* eristic   *e.* terpsichorean

b 2. The wrestler's _____ maneuvers made it difficult for an opponent to obtain a hold.
  a. hermetic   *b.* protean   *c.* titanic   *d.* procrustean   *e.* philippic

a 3. In a locker-room speech between halves, the _____ reaffirmed his confidence in his _____.
  a. conductor . . myrmidons   *b.* amazon . . team   *c.* myrmidon . . adherents
  d. mentor . . squad   *e.* conductor . . mentors

e 4. Many literatures describe a paradise where the _____ dwell in _____ repose.
  a. heroic . . Stygian   *b.* unvanquished . . bacchanalian   *c.* sirens . . abject
  d. perfidious . . ambrosial   *e.* blessed . . Elysian

a 5. When people become _____, their ability to reason gives way to fear.
  a. lethargic   *b.* saturnine   *c.* panicky   *d.* Draconian   *e.* plutocratic

d 6. The audience laughed to see the burly actor _____ by his puny companion's hectoring.
  a. convinced   *b.* betrayed   *c.* tripped   *d.* intimidated   *e.* encouraged

D 7. The Pyrrhic victory was cause for widespread _____.
  a. dejection   *b.* optimism   *c.* paeans   *d.* satisfaction   *e.* promotions

e 8. Only a person with a _____ voice could have been heard above the din of the angry crowd.
  a. herculean   *b.* stentorian   *c.* jovial   *d.* laconic   *e.* titanic

d 9. Our _____ host always enjoys having friends to share his Lucullan suppers.
  a. cursive   *b.* martial   *c.* fractious   *d.* convivial   *e.* sanguine

a 10. Psychoanalysis can help patients recall long-forgotten experiences from the _____ recesses of their minds.
  a. labyrinthine   *b.* chimerical   *c.* iridescent   *d.* auroral   *e.* mercurial

EXERCISE 6.3: CONCISE WRITING

Express the thought of each sentence below in no more than four words.

1. Those who make predictions of doom and disaster are not popular.

   Cassandra

2. Some people are inclined to be too much in love with themselves.

   Narsisism

3. You aroused their hopes while you made it impossible for them to realize those hopes.

   tantalize

4. This is not an ordinary beverage; it is exceptionally delicious.

   nectar

5. People should avoid the practice of automatically and instantly repeating what others say.

   echolalia

6. We attended a meeting at which there was open discussion and audience participation.

7. Make an effort to be sparing in your use of words.

8. Her cousin is the sort of person who likes to engage in disputes.

9. Tell us about the long series of wanderings that you were involved in.

10. Rumors can be the cause of sudden and overpowering terror.

EXERCISE 6.4: BRAINTEASERS

Fill in the missing letters.

1. Feeling **l e t** _h a r g i c_ , the driver stopped for a short nap.

2. To lift the heavy weight trapping the victim would have required _h u r c u_ **l e a n** strength.

3. Sometimes, after a summer shower, a(n) i r i d e s c e n t arc appears in the sky.

4. __ __ __ m e t __ __ seals help to make some products tamperproof.

5. A home run in the nineteenth inning won the game, a six-hour __ __ r a t __ __ __.

6. Our __ t e n t __ __ __ __ __ instructor needs no microphone to be heard in our gym.

7. No one expects a(n) l u c u l l a n dinner to be served in a fast-food restaurant.

8. Long before the first a u r o r a l light, the farmer is up and ready for the day's chores.

9. The audience cheered when—at last—the evildoers met their n e m e s i s.

10. We spent an hour finding our way back through the l a b y r i n thine corridors

EXERCISE 6.5: COMPOSITION

Answer in two or three sentences.

1. Would you be in a jovial mood after achieving a victory? Why, or why not?

Yes, because jovial means jolly, and after
a victory, I would feel jolly.

2. Why is it normal for someone exploring a labyrinthine cave to be gripped with panic?

It is normal because it'd be really
confusing and scary, with all the confusing
passageways.

3. Of all the foods you have tasted, name one that was ambrosial, and another that was like nectar. Give reasons for your choices.

Of all the foods I've tasted, steak was ambrosial
because it is delicious, and mango juice tastes
like nectar because it is a sweet, good, juice-

4. Are Draconian penalties an effective palladium against crime? Why, or why not?

cruel   protection

Yes, because in order to have an
effective palladium against crimes, cruel
punishments are required.

5. Would you withdraw from an election campaign if your rival's myrmidons hectored you at every place you tried to speak? Explain.

worships w/o 2 *bully*

No, because being bullied into something by someone's worshippers is not right.

EXERCISE 6.6: ANALOGIES

Write the *letter* of the word-pair that best expresses a relationship similar to that existing between the capitalized word-pair.

c 1. SOLON : LAWS

a. atlas : maps   d. artisan : trade

b. ruler : subjects   e. composer : operas

c. philosopher : credentials

d 2. SIREN : BEAUTY

a. victim : trap   d. alarm : confidence

b. temptress : prey   e. worm : fish

c. hunter : bait

d 3. CASSANDRA : POLLYANNA

a. amazon : myrmidon   d. pessimist : optimist

b. Spartan : laconic   e. titanic : herculean

c. Olympian : majestic

b 4. NEMESIS : EVILDOER

a. avenger : victim   d. justice : misdeed

b. retribution : culprit   e. penalty : evil

c. punishment : benefactor

b 5. AMAZON : STRENGTH

a. comedienne : humor   d. warrior : civilian

b. river : jungle   e. servant : indifference

c. nurse : invalid

e 6. PALLADIUM : DANGER

a. rumor : panic   d. experience : skill

b. arena : excitement   e. vaccination : smallpox

c. investigation : truth

a   7. MERCURIAL : CAPRICIOUS
- *a.* procrustean : rigid
- *b.* protean : uniform
- *c.* ethereal : earthly
- *d.* saturnine : hilarious
- *e.* narcissistic : unselfish

e   8. PAEAN : ECSTASY
- *a.* anthem : nation
- *b.* suffering : rejoicing
- *c.* lament : sorrow
- *d.* sadness : joy
- *e.* hymn : congregation

d   9. THESPIAN : TERPSICHOREAN
- *a.* painter : dancer
- *b.* orator : musician
- *c.* comedian : sculptor
- *d.* actress : ballerina
- *e.* composer : singer

b   10. AURORAL : DAWN
- *a.* fragile : care
- *b.* autumnal : fall
- *c.* visual : ear
- *d.* annual : season
- *e.* juvenile : delinquency

Chapter 7

Anglo-Saxon Vocabulary

About 25 percent of our modern English vocabulary comes from the language of the Angles and Saxons, Germanic tribes who invaded Britain beginning about the year 450. The Anglo-Saxons ruled until 1066, when Harold, their last king, was defeated at the Battle of Hastings by an army from France led by William, Duke of Normandy. For the next two centuries, French was England's official language, but the common people continued to use Anglo-Saxon. The basic words of English today are of Anglo-Saxon origin. They include the articles (*a, an, the*), the words for numbers, the verb *to be,* prepositions (*at, by, from, in, out, with,* etc.), conjunctions (*and, but, as, when,* etc.), many commonly used verbs (*to go, to fight, to sleep, to eat,* etc.), many commonly used nouns (*father, mother, land, house, water,* etc.), and most pronouns.

After 1066, a wealth of Latin-derived parallels for Anglo-Saxon words came into our language through French. These borrowings, and others directly from Latin, endowed English with a rich supply of synonyms and near-synonyms. For example, for the Anglo-Saxon verb *lighten,* we have (1) the synonym *relieve,* borrowed from French, which had earlier gotten it from Latin, and (2) the synonym *alleviate,* borrowed directly from Latin.

This brief chapter deals with (1) Anglo-Saxon elements selected to help you increase your store of words and (2) Latin-derived synonyms and near-synonyms for Anglo-Saxon words.

Anglo-Saxon Prefixes

1. *A-: "on," "in," "in a state of"*

WORD	MEANING
aboard (*adv.*) ə-'bȯrd	on a ship, train, bus, etc. (Come *aboard*!)
aboard (*prep.*)	on (A stowaway was *aboard* the freighter.)

Also: **ashore, afoot**

WORD	MEANING
afoul (*adj.*) ə-'fau̇l	in a state of entanglement (fishermen with their lines *afoul*)
afoul of (prep.)	in or into collision or entanglement with (They ran *afoul* of the law.)
aloof (*adv.*) ə-'lüf	in the state of being at a distance (I stood *aloof*.)
aloof (*adj.*)	withdrawn (Join us. Don't be *aloof*.)
amiss (*adv.*) ə-'mis	in a missing-the-mark manner; wrong (Something went *amiss*.)
amiss (*adj.*)	wrong; imperfect; faulty (Is anything *amiss*?)
asunder (*adv.*) ə-'sən-dər	in an apart position; apart (Friends were torn *asunder*.)

Also: **abed, adrift, afield, afire, afloat, aloft,** etc.

2. WITH-: "against," "back"

withdraw (*v.*)   draw back; take back
wi<u>th</u>-'drȯ

withhold (*v.*)   hold back
wi<u>th</u>-'hōld

withstand (*v.*)   stand up against; resist
wi<u>th</u>-'stand

notwithstanding   despite (*Notwithstanding* her inexperience, she was hired.)
(*prep.*)
‚nät-wi<u>th</u>-'stan-diŋ

3. BE- has these meanings:

a. "all around," "on all sides," "thoroughly"

beset (*v.*)   attack on all sides; surround
bi-'set

   Also: **begrudge, belabor, bemuddle, besiege, besmirch**, etc.

b. "affect with," "cover with"

begrime (*v.*)   cover with grime; make dirty
bi-'grīm

benighted (*adj.*)   overtaken by darkness of night; unenlightened; intellectually or morally
bi-'nī-təd   ignorant

   Also: **becloud, bedevil, befog, belie, bewitch**, etc.

c. "cause to be"

belittle (*v.*)   cause to be or seem little or unimportant; disparage
bi-'li-tᵊl

   Also: **becalm, bedim, bewilder**, etc.

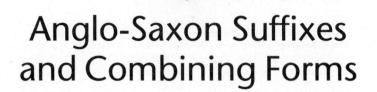

Anglo-Saxon Suffixes and Combining Forms

1. *-WISE: "way," "manner"*

contrariwise (*adv.*)   on the contrary (*ant.* **likewise**)
ˈkän-ˌtrer-ē-ˌwīz

nowise (*adv.*)   in no way; not at all
ˈnō-ˌwīz

    Also: **breadthwise, lengthwise, otherwise,** etc.

2. *-DOM: "dignity," "office," "realm," "state of being," "those having the character of"*

earldom (*n.*)   realm or dignity of an earl
ˈərl-dəm

martyrdom (*n.*)   state of being a martyr
ˈmär-tər-dəm

officialdom (*n.*)   those having the authority of officials; officials collectively
ə-ˈfi-shəl-dəm

    Also: **dukedom, fiefdom, kingdom, serfdom, sheikdom, stardom,** etc.

3. *-SOME has these meanings:*

a. **"full of the thing or quality denoted in the first part of the *-SOME* word"**

cumbersome (*adj.*)   full of encumbrances; burdensome
ˈkəm-bər-səm

fulsome (*adj.*)   offensive because of excessive display or obvious insincerity (literally, "full
ˈfül-səm   of fullness")

lissom(e) (*adj.*) 'li-səm	lithesome (literally, "full of a lithe or supple quality"); limber; nimble
meddlesome (*adj.*) 'me-dᵊl-səm	intrusive; impertinent; interfering (literally, "full of meddling—mixing in the business of others")
mettlesome (*adj.*) 'me-tᵊl-səm	full of mettle (courage); spirited
noisome (*adj.*) 'nȯi-səm	offensive to the sense of smell (literally, "full of an annoying quality"); unwholesome
winsome (*adj.*) 'win-səm	full of a winning quality (literally, "full of wynn," the Anglo-Saxon word for joy); winning; cheerful; merry

Also: **awesome, bothersome, fearsome, frolicsome, gruesome, irksome, loathsome, lonesome, nettlesome, quarrelsome, toothsome, troublesome**, etc.

b. **"group of"**

twosome (*n.*) tü-səm	group of two

Also: **threesome, foursome**, etc.

4. -LING *has these meanings:*

a. **"one pertaining to or concerned with whatever is denoted in the first part of the -LING word"**

hireling (*n.*) 'hīr-liŋ	one whose only interest in his or her work is the *hire* (pay)
starveling (*n.*) 'stärv-liŋ	one who is thin from lack of food
suckling (*n.*) 'sə-kliŋ	child or animal that is nursed
yearling (*n.*) 'yir-liŋ	one who is a year old

b. **"little," "young"**

changeling (*n.*) 'chānj-liŋ	child secretly ex*changed* for another in infancy
duckling (*n.*) 'dək-liŋ	little duck

foundling (*n.*)   infant found after being deserted by its unknown parents
ˈfau̇nd-liŋ

gosling (*n.*)   young goose
ˈgäz-liŋ

sibling (*n.*)   brother or sister (literally, "little *sib*"—i.e., "little *blood relative*")
ˈsi-bliŋ

stripling (*n.*)   lad (literally, "little strip" from the main stem)
ˈstri-pliŋ

Also: **fledgling, princeling, sapling, underling,** etc.

Miscellaneous Anglo-Saxon Words

anent (prep.)   about; concerning; in respect to
ə-ˈnent

anon (*adv.*)   soon; presently
ə-ˈnän

behest (*n.*)   command; order
bi-ˈhest

beholden (*adj.*)   bound in gratitude; indebted
bi-ˈhōl-dən

behoove (*v.*)   be necessary for; be proper for
bi-ˈhüv

betimes (*adv.*)   early
bi-ˈtīmz

heath (*n.*)   tract of wasteland
ˈhēth

wane (*v.*)   decrease; dwindle
ˈwān

warlock (*n.*)   sorcerer; wizard
ˈwȯr-ˌläk

warp (*n.*) 'wȯrp	threads running lengthwise in the loom, crossed by the woof
wax (*v.*) 'waks	grow; increase (e.g., "the moon *waxes*, then wanes")
withal (*adv.*) wi<u>th</u>-'ȯl	with it all; in addition; despite that (e.g., "firm but *withal* kind")
woof (*n.*) 'wu̇f	threads running from side to side in a woven fabric
yclept (*adj.*) or **ycleped** i-'klept	named; called

EXERCISE 7.1: WORD COMPLETION

In each sentence, fill in the missing letters of the incomplete word. Each dash stands for one missing letter.

1. Do not **b** __ __ __ __ __ __ (*obscure, as with clouds*) the issue.

2. A **n** __ __ __ __ __ __ (*offensive to the sense of smell*) odor filled the chemistry laboratory.

3. Jim is friendly, but his uncle holds himself **a** __ __ __ __ (*at a distance*).

4. Try as I might, I could not **b** __ __ __ __ __ (*cause to be calm*) the anxious mother.

5. In the fog, we ran **a** __ __ __ __ of (*came in collision with*) a stalled car.

6. Officials refuse gifts so as not to be **b** __ __ __ __ __ __ __ (*bound in gratitude*) to anyone.

7. Don't you agree they make an attractive **t** __ __ __ __ __ __ (*group of two*)?

8. I **w** __ __ __ __ __ __ __ (*take back*) about twice the cash in December as I do in other months.

9. The emperor basked in the **f** __ __ __ __ __ __ (*offensively insincere*) praise of his toadies.

10. Her talent and drive destined her for **s** __ __ __ __ __ __ (*the state of being a star*).

11. She is an only child; she has no **s** __ __ __ __ __ __ (*brother or sister*).

EXERCISE 7.2: ANGLO-SAXON SYNONYMS

In the space provided, write an Anglo-Saxon synonym for the word or expression in italics. The letters of each synonym appear in scrambled form in the parentheses. (The first answer has been filled in as an example.)

1. It *is necessary for* (VESHOOBE) students to be attentive.   *behooves*

2. She rose before dawn and retired *early* (MESBETI).   _____

3. Much was said *concerning* (TENNA) the grant of a pardon. _____

4. The witches first met Macbeth on the *wasteland* (TEHAH). _____

5. We are *indebted* (HODNEBLE) to no one. _____

6. Hope for world peace *grows* (XESWA) and wanes. _____

7. With a small stone, the *lad* (GRINPLITS) David slew the giant Goliath. _____

8. Richard I, *called* (PLETCY) the Lion-Hearted, was a twelfth-century king of England. _____

9. I'll be there *soon* (NANO). _____

10. The fleet set sail at the queen's *command* (SETHEB). _____

11. Let us help those who are *in a state of ignorance* (THINGBEED). _____

EXERCISE 7.3: COMPOSITION

Answer in two or three sentences.

1. Why would it belittle someone to be called a hireling?

_____

_____

2. Is it likely that a person can achieve stardom without being beholden to anyone? Explain.

_____

_____

3. Suggest a possible solution for a particularly noisome problem that besets us today.

_____

_____

4. Would you be able to withstand the flatteries of fulsome admirers? Why, or why not?

_____

_____

5. Briefly describe a situation that resulted in tearing siblings asunder.

_____

_____

Latin-Derived Synonyms and Near-Synonyms for Anglo-Saxon Words

Because English has incorporated so many Latin words into its vocabulary, it often has two or more words for an idea: one from Anglo-Saxon (for example, *brotherly*) and another from Latin (for example, *fraternal*). The two words, however, are seldom exactly synonymous.

To illustrate, both *brotherly* and *fraternal* have the general meaning "pertaining to brothers." Yet, *brotherly* conveys a greater warmth of feeling than *fraternal*, which is less intimate and more formal. Thus, we speak of "brotherly love," but "fraternal organizations." This abundance of synonyms enables us to express varying shades of meaning.

In the pages that follow, Anglo-Saxon-derived adjectives, verbs, and nouns will be presented side by side with similar, but not exactly synonymous, Latin-derived adjectives, verbs, and nouns.

1. Adjectives

FROM ANGLO-SAXON

fatherly
pertaining to a father (warmer than *paternal*)

motherly
pertaining to a mother (warmer than *maternal*)

brotherly
pertaining to a brother (more affectionate than *fraternal*)

daughterly
pertaining to a daughter (less formal than *filial*)

FROM LATIN

paternal pə-'tər-nᵊl
1. fatherly
2. inherited from or related to the father's side

maternal mə-'tər-nᵊl
1. motherly
2. inherited from or related to the mother's side

fraternal frə-'tər-nᵊl
1. brotherly
2. having to do with a *fraternal* society (group organized to pursue a common goal in brotherlike union)

filial 'fi-lē-əl
of or befitting a daughter or son, as *filial* respect

childlike
of or like a child in a good sense, as *childlike* innocence

childish
of or like child in a bad sense, as *childish* mentality

manly
having qualities characteristic of or usually attributed to a man, as a *manly* voice

womanly
having qualities characteristic of or usually attributed to a woman, as a *womanly* intuition

devilish
like a devil; mischievous

bearish
1. like a bear; rough
2. tending to depress stock prices
3. expecting a fall in stock prices

bullish
1. like a bull; obstinate
2. tending to cause rises in stock prices
3. expecting a rise in stock prices

catlike
like a cat; stealthy

cowlike
resembling a cow
oxlike
resembling an ox

doggish
doglike

donkeyish
like a donkey

infantile 'in-fən-,tīl
of or like a very young child; babyish

puerile 'pyür-əl
foolish for an adult to say or do, as a *puerile* remark

masculine 'mas-kyə-lən
1. denoting the opposite gender of feminine
2. having qualities appropriate to a man

virile 'vir-əl
having the physical capabilities of a male (stronger word than *masculine*)

feminine 'fe-mə-nən
1. denoting the opposite gender of masculine
2. having the features, qualities, and characteristics belonging to women

diabolic(al) ,dī-ə-'bä-lik (li-kəl)
very cruel; wicked; fiendish (stronger word than *devilish*)

ursine ər-,sīn
of or like a bear

taurine 'tȯ-,rīn
1. of or like a bull
2. relating to Taurus (a sign of the zodiac)

feline 'fē-,līn
of or pertaining to the cat family (cat, lion, tiger, leopard, etc.); sly; stealthy

bovine 'bō-,vīn
1. of or like the cow or ox
2. sluggish and patient, as a *bovine* disposition

canine 'kā-,nīn
1. of or pertaining to the dog family (dog, wolf, jackal, etc.)
2. designating one of the four pointed teeth next to the incisors

asinine 'as-ə-,nīn
like an ass or donkey (thought to be the most stupid beast of burden); stupid; silly

fishy
like a fish in smell or taste

piscine 'pi-,sīn
of or like a fish

foxy
foxlike; wily; sly

vulpine 'vəl-,pīn
of or like a fox; crafty; cunning

goatish
goatlike; coarse; lustful

hircine 'hər-,sīn
goatlike, especially in smell

horsy
having to do with horses or horse racing, as
horsy talk

equine 'ē-,kwīn
of or like a horse

piggish
hoggish; swinish

porcine 'pȯr-,sīn
of or like a pig

sheepish
1. like a sheep in timidity or stupidity
2. awkwardly bashful or embarrassed

ovine 'ō-,vīn
of or like a sheep

wolfish
characteristic of a wolf; ferocious

lupine 'lü-,pīn
of or like a wolf; ravenous

bloody
smeared with blood; involving bloodshed

sanguine 'saŋ-gwən
1. red; ruddy, as a *sanguine* complexion
2. confident, as *sanguine* of success

sanguinary 'saŋ-gwə-,ner-ē
bloodthirsty; murderous; bloody, as a
sanguinary battle

 ## EXERCISE 7.4: ANALOGIES

Write the *letter* of the word or set of words that best completes the analogy.

___ **1.** *Canine* is to *dog* as *feline* is to _____.
   a. ox   *b.* wolf   *c.* bull   *d.* tiger   *e.* donkey

___ **2.** *Fraternal* is to *brother* as *filial* is to _____.
   a. son   *b.* son-in-law   *c.* daughter   *d.* son or daughter   *e.* daughter-in-law

___ **3.** *Neigh* is to *equine* as *bleat* is to _____.
   a. horsy   *b.* bashful   *c.* sanguinary   *d.* zodiacal   *e.* ovine

___ **4.** *Mature* is to *puerile* as *intelligent* is to _____.
   a. paternal   *b.* asinine   *c.* cunning   *d.* porcine   *e.* infantile

___ **5.** *Courageous* is to *mettle* as *sanguine* is to _____.
   a. success   *b.* despair   *c.* battle   *d.* complexion   *e.* hope

___ **6.** *Bullish* is to *bearish* as *up* is to _____.
   a. above   *b.* under   *c.* down   *d.* over   *e.* beyond

___ **7.** *Devilish* is to *diabolical* as *interested* is to _____.
   a. spoiled   *b.* enthusiastic   *c.* ruddy   *d.* cherubic   *e.* clever

___ **8.** *Cow* is to *bull* as *feminine* is to _____.
   a. masculine   *b.* ferocity   *c.* bovine   *d.* manly   *e.* virile

___ **9.** *Bear* is to *ursine* as *fox* is to _____.
   a. vulpine   *b.* taurine   *c.* lupine   *d.* wily   *e.* stealthy

___ **10.** *Hircine* is to *goat* as *piscine* is to _____.
   a. leopard   *b.* speed   *c.* lion   *d.* fish   *e.* swine

EXERCISE 7.5: SENTENCE COMPLETION

Fill each blank with the most appropriate word from the vocabulary list at the end of the exercise.

1. Realizing my blunder, I managed a _____ (*awkwardly bashful*) grin.

2. The name "Fido" may remind one of _____ (*of the dog family*) fidelity.

3. My _____ (*expecting a rise in stock prices*) cousin keeps buying shares.

4. The archvillain devised a _____ (*fiendish*) extortion scheme.

5. How should parents handle _____ (*of a son or daughter*) disobedience?

6. Rarely have we witnessed such _____ (*foolish*) behavior from a mature person.

7. The _____ (*used to denote a female*) form of "confidant" is "confidante."

8. My _____ (*on my mother's side*) grandfather was a Senator.

9. At the close of THE CALL OF THE WILD, the dog Buck gradually lapses into _____ (*wolfish*) characteristics.

10. The fratricidal Battle of Gettysburg was one of the world's most _____ (*bloody*) conflicts.

VOCABULARY LIST

sanguinary	canine	puerile
diabolical	bearish	feminine
lupine	filial	bullish
fraternal	vulpine	feline
sheepish	masculine	maternal

2. Verbs

FROM ANGLO-SAXON	FROM LATIN		FROM LATIN	
beget	procreate	'prō-krē-,āt	generate	'je-nə-,rāt
begin	originate	ə-'ri-jə-,nāt	initiate	in-'ish-ē-,āt
behead	decapitate	di-'ka-pə-,tāt		
bless	consecrate	'kän-sə-,krāt		
bow, stoop	condescend	,kän-di-'send	prostrate	'präs-,trāt
break	disintegrate	di-'sin-tə-,grāt	invalidate	in-'va-lə-,dāt
chew	masticate	'mas-tə-,kāt		
curse	execrate	'ek-sə-,krāt		
drink	imbibe	im-'bīb		
eat	devour	di-'vau̇r	consume	kən-'süm
flay, fleece, skin	excoriate	ek-'skȯr-ē-,āt		
free	emancipate	i-'man-sə-,pāt	liberate	'li-bə-,rāt
frighten	intimidate	in-'ti-mə-,dāt		
lie	prevaricate	pri-'var-ə-,kāt		
lighten	relieve	ri-'lēv	alleviate	ə-'lē-vē-,āt
sail	navigate	'na-və-,gāt		
shorten	abridge	ə-'brij	abbreviate	ə-'brē-vē-,āt
show	demonstrate	'de-mən-,strāt		
soothe	assuage	ə-'swāj	pacify	'pa-sə-,fī
spit	expectorate	ek-'spek-tə-,rāt		
steal	peculate	'pek-yə-,lāt		
strengthen	corroborate	kə-'rä-bə-,rāt	invigorate	in-'vi-gə-,rāt
sweat	perspire	pər-'spīr		
take (for oneself)	appropriate	ə-'prō-prē-,āt		
think	cogitate	'kä-jə-,tāt	ratiocinate	,ra-tē-'ō-sᵊn-,āt
twinkle, sparkle	scintillate	'sin-tᵊl-,āt		
understand	comprehend	,käm-pri-'hend		
withstand	resist	ri-'zist	oppose	ə-'pōz
worship	venerate	've-nə-,rāt	revere	ri-'vir
yield	capitulate	kə-'pich-ə-,lāt	succumb	sə-'kəm

EXERCISE 7.6: LATIN-DERIVED SYNONYMS

Replace the italicized Anglo-Saxon word with a Latin-derived synonym from the verb list just presented.

1. Tell the truth. Don't *lie*. _____

2. The young acrobat gave a *sparkling* performance. _____

3. Your opponents will *flay* you if you accuse them without proof. _____

4. We cannot *understand* how such a small dog can intimidate him. _____

5. Don't gulp down your food; take the time to *chew* it. _____

6. At the end of the play, Macbeth is *beheaded* by Macduff. _____

7. *Spitting* in a public place is an offense punishable by a fine. _____

8. I am not afraid of you; you can't *frighten* me. _____

9. Sir Toby Belch's excessive *drinking* got him into trouble with his niece. _____

10. The vanquished have been evicted, their homes *taken*. _____

3. Nouns

FROM ANGLO-SAXON	FROM LATIN		FROM LATIN	
blessing	benediction	ˌbe-nə-'dik-shən		
breach	infraction	in-'frak-shən	rupture	'rəp-chər
burden	obligation	ˌäb-lə-'gā-shən		
curse	execration	ˌek-sə-'krā-shən	malediction	ˌma-lə-'dik-shən
fire	conflagration	ˌkän-flə-'grā-shən		
food	nutriment	'nü-trə-mənt		
greed	avarice	'a-və-rəs		
heaven	firmament	'fər-mə-mənt		
home	domicile	'dä-mə-ˌsīl	residence	're-zə-dəns
mirth	hilarity	hi-'lar-ə-tē		
name	appellation	ˌa-pə-'lā-shən		
oath	affirmation	ˌa-fər-'mā-shən		
shame	ignominy	'ig-nə-ˌmi-nē		
shard	fragment	'frag-mənt		
smear	vilification	ˌvi-lə-fə-'kā-shən		
snake	serpent	'sər-pənt	reptile	'rep-t°l

sorrow	contrition	kən-'trish-ən	remorse	ri-'mȯrs
speed	velocity	və-'lä-sə-tē	celerity	sə-'ler-ə-tē
strength	impregnability	im-,preg-nə-'bi-lə-tē		
theft	larceny	'lär-sə-nē	peculation	pek-yə-'lā-shən
thread	filament	'fi-lə-mənt		
threat	menace	'me-nəs		
truth	verity (of things)	'ver-ə-tē		
truthfulness	veracity (of persons)	və-'ra-sə-tē		
wedding	nuptials	'nəp-shəlz		

EXERCISE 7.7: SENTENCE COMPLETION

Which of the two terms makes the sentence correct? Write the *letter* of your answer in the space provided.

___ 1. It is a well-known _____ that the early bird catches the worm.
   a. verity   *b.* veracity

___ 2. The guillotine was an instrument of _____.
   a. capitulation   *b.* decapitation

___ 3. It was difficult to carry the _____ crowbar.
   a. lissome   *b.* cumbersome

___ 4. Cats, leopards, and tigers belong to the _____ family.
   a. feline   *b.* canine

___ 5. Dan's brawl with the umpire was a serious _____ of the rules of the game.
   a. fragment   *b.* breach

___ 6. Shares of stock are relatively cheap in a _____ market.
   a. bullish   *b.* bearish

___ 7. Your fine attendance and homework record should make you _____ about passing.
   a. sanguinary   *b.* sanguine

___ 8. A _____ question risks a rude reply: "Mind your own business!"
   a. meddlesome   *b.* mettlesome

___ 9. The hungry hiker _____ her sandwiches quickly.
   a. consumed   *b.* imbibed

___ 10. The drowning man was saved by a _____ of 14.
   a. yearling   *b.* stripling

EXERCISE 7.8: BRAINTEASERS

Fill in the missing letters.

1. The Rock of Gibraltar is a symbol of __ __ __ __ __ __ **n a b** __ __ __ __ __.

2. How can we forgive those who feel no __ __ __ **o r** __ __ for their misdeeds?

3. The hunger striker drank some water but refused __ __ **t r i m** __ __ __.

4. We have no faith in the __ **e r a** __ __ __ __ of a prevaricator.

5. There was not a cloud in the **f i r** __ __ __ __ __ __.

6. How could anyone who looks so innocent be capable of __ **a r c** __ __ __?

7. Light travels at a much higher __ __ __ __ **c i t y** than sound.

8. There is no __ __ **n o** __ __ __ __ in defeat if one has done one's best.

9. "The Father of His Country" is an __ __ __ **e l l** __ __ __ __ __ conferred on George Washington by his fellow Americans.

10. The vase fell and shattered into a hundred __ **h a r d** __.

EXERCISE 7.9: CONCISE WRITING

Express the thought of each sentence below in no more than four words.

1. She paid no attention to her brothers and her sisters.

   _____

2. Many of those who invest are expecting a fall in the price of stocks.

   _____

3. Your friend had an awkwardly bashful grin on his face.

   _____

4. Their praise was offensive because it obviously was not sincere.

   _____

5. Don't do or say things that are foolish for an adult to do or say.

   _____

6. The ones who had been digging were covered with grime.

   _____

7. The plan that you are presenting is full of encumbrances.

   _____

8. Who are the individuals who took our bicycles for their own personal use?

_____

9. The remarks that they made caused us to seem little and unimportant.

_____

10. Those who have the authority of officials often move at a slow pace.

_____

EXERCISE 7.10: COMPOSITION

Answer in two or three sentences.

1. How serious a menace are drivers who imbibe? Why?

_____

_____

_____

2. Under what circumstances, if any, might it be forgivable for an individual to appropriate a vacant domicile? Explain.

_____

_____

_____

3. Why do some candidates stoop to vilification in the closing hours of a political campaign?

_____

_____

_____

4. Should the shortage of jail space influence judges in sentencing those who have committed larceny but no other infractions? Explain.

_____

_____

_____

5. Under what circumstances would it be ignominy to capitulate? Explain.

_____

_____

_____

French Words in English

English has never hesitated to adopt useful French words. Any French expression that describes an idea better than the corresponding English expression may sooner or later be incorporated into English. The process has been going on for centuries.

This chapter will teach you how to use some of the more important French words and expressions that are today part of an educated person's English vocabulary.

1. Terms Describing Persons

WORD	MEANING	TYPICAL USE
au courant (*adj.*) ˌō-ˌku̇-ʹrän	well-informed; up-to-date	By reading reviews, you can keep *au courant* with the latest in literature, films, television, and the theater.
blasé (*adj.*) blä-ʹzā	tired of pleasures; bored	After a while, Carmela had had her fill of mountain scenery, and when the guide pointed out some additional peaks, she reacted in a *blasé* manner.
bourgeois (*adj.*) ʹbu̇rzh-ˌwä	1. having to do with the middle class 2. concerned with petty, materialistic interests; lacking in culture or refinement	At first, the aristocrat firmly opposed his daughter's prospective marriage into a *bourgeois* family.
chic (*adj.*) ʹshēk	stylish	You looked very *chic* in your new outfit.

clairvoyant (*adj.*) kler-'vȯi-ənt	1. clear-sighted; unusually perceptive; discerning 2. able to perceive matters beyond the ordinary senses	If General Braddock had listened to George Washington, his *clairvoyant* young subordinate, he would not have been caught in an ambush.
complaisant (*adj.*) kəm-'plā-sᵊnt	willing to please; obliging; amiable	We were sorry to hear that the Reeds were moving because they had been very *complaisant* neighbors.
debonair (*adj.*) ‚de-bə-'nar	gracious; courteous; charming; suave	The headwaiter was *debonair* with the guests but haughty with the waiters.
gauche (*adj.*) 'gōsh	lacking social grace; crude; tactless; awkward	For a host or hostess to begin eating before the guests have been served would be *gauche*.
maladroit (*adj.*) ‚ma-lə-'drȯit	unskillful; clumsy (*ant.* **adroit**)	Our new supervisor is expert in many matters in which his predecessor was *maladroit*.
naive (*adj.*) nä-'ēv	simple in nature; artless; ingenuous	You are *naive* if you believe implacable foes can be reconciled easily.
nonchalant (*adj.*) ‚nän-shə-'länt	without concern or enthusiasm; indifferent	I am amazed that you can be so *nonchalant* about the coming test when everyone else is so worried.

EXERCISE 8.1

In each blank, insert the most appropriate word or expression from group 1.

1. Some advertising is so exaggerated that only a(n) _____ person would believe it.

2. If every meal were a banquet, we should soon greet even the most delicious food with a(n) _____ expression.

3. Read a good daily newspaper to keep _____ with what is going on in the world.

4. The cuts on Ralph's face show that he is _____ in the use of his razor.

5. Unlike her discourteous predecessor, the new office manager is quite _____.

2. Terms for Persons

attaché (*n.*)
,at-ə-'shā
member of the diplomatic staff of an ambassador or minister
Unable to see the ambassador, we spoke to one of her *attachés*.

bourgeoisie (*n.*)
,bùrzh-wä-'zē
the middle class
A strong *bourgeoisie* contributes to a nation's prosperity.

chargé d'affaires (*n.*)
'shär-,zhā-də-'far
temporary substitute for an ambassador
A career diplomat was named the *chargé d'affaires* when the ambassador resigned.

concierge (*n.*)
kōⁿ-'syerzh
1. doorkeeper; custodian; janitor
2. hotel employee who handles mail, arranges for theater reservations, etc.
We gave the *concierge* the names of the guests we would like him to admit.

confrere (*n.*)
'kän-,frer
colleague; co-worker; comrade
Our attorney shares an office with her *confrere*, Mr. Quinones.

connoisseur (*n.*)
,kä-nə-'sər
expert; critical judge
A *connoisseur* of rare diamonds has verified the gem's value.

coterie (*n.*)
'kō-tə-rē
set or circle of acquaintances; clique
Helen won't bowl with us; she has her own *coterie* of bowling friends.

debutante (*n.*)
'de-byù-,tänt
young woman who has just had her *debut* (introduction into society)
The *debutante's* photograph was at the head of the society page.

devotee (*n.*)
,de-və-'tē
zealous follower; ardent adherent of something or someone; fan
Eva is a *devotee* of the guitar.

elite (*n.*)
ā-'lēt
group of individuals thought to be superior; aristocracy; choice part
Nobel Prize winners are members of the intellectual *elite*.

émigré, *masc.* (*n.*)
'em-i-,grā
(**émigrée**, *fem.*)
refugee; person who has fled (*emigrated*) from his or her native land because of political conditions
A committee was formed to find housing and employment for the anxious *émigrés*.

entourage (*n.*)
,än-tù-'räzh
group of attendants, assistants, or associates accompanying a person
Our vice president was at the airport to welcome the prime minister and his *entourage*.

entrepreneur (*n.*)
,än-trə-prə-'nər
one who assumes the risks and management of a business
What *entrepreneur* invests capital without some prospect of a profit?

envoy (*n.*)
'en-,voi
diplomatic agent or messenger
The president's *envoy* to the conference has not yet been chosen.

fiancé, *masc.* (*n.*)
,fē-än-'sā
(**fiancée**, *fem.*)

person engaged to be married

Madeline introduced Mr. Cole as her *fiancé*.

gendarme (*n.*)
'zhän-,därm

armed police officer, especially in France and other European countries

The chargé d'affaires requested that extra *gendarmes* be posted outside the embassy.

gourmand (*n.*)
'gur-,mänd

person excessively fond of eating and drinking; glutton

The food was so good that I ate like a *gourmand*.

gourmet (*n.*)
,gur-'mā

connoisseur in eating and drinking

Valerie can recommend a good restaurant; she is a *gourmet*.

ingenue (*n.*)
'an-jə-,nü

actress playing the role of a naive young woman; naive young woman

The same actress plays not only the film's *ingenue* but also its siren!

maître d'hôtel (*n.*)
,mā-trə-dō-'tel or
maître d'
,mā-trə-'dē

headwaiter

Knowing the *maître d'hôtel* often assures being seated at a choice table.

martinet (*n.*)
,mär-tə-'net

person who enforces very strict discipline

Our dean is an understanding counselor, not a *martinet*.

nonpareil (*n.*)
,nän-pə-'rel

person of unequalled excellence; paragon

Don Quixote regards Lady Dulcinea as the *nonpareil*.

nouveaux riches
(*n. pl.*) ,nü-vō-'rēsh

persons newly rich

An unexpected inheritance lifted him into the ranks of the *nouveaux riches*.

parvenu, *masc.* (*n.*)
'pär-və-,nü
(**parvenue**, *fem.*)

person suddenly risen to wealth or power who lacks the proper social qualifications; upstart

A few of the social elite stigmatized the entrepreneur as a *parvenu* for his loud ties.

protégé, *masc.* (*n.*)
'prō-tə-,zhā
(**protégée**, *fem.*)

someone taught, protected, or advanced by a person of experience or influence

The veteran infielder passed on numerous fielding hints to his young *protégé*.

raconteur (*n.*)
,ra-kän-'tər

person who excels in telling stories, anecdotes, etc.

Mark Twain was an excellent *raconteur*.

valet (*n.*)
'va-lət

manservant who attends to the personal needs of his employer, as by taking care of his clothes

That morning, the old gentleman got dressed without the help of his *valet*.

EXERCISE 8.2

In each blank, insert the most appropriate word or expression from group 2.

1. After a particularly unpleasant quarrel with her _____, Rita considered breaking their engagement.

2. Between the nobles on one extreme and the peasants on the other, a middle class known as the _____ emerged.

3. The _____ brushed the duke's formal clothes.

4. Sherlock Holmes collaborated on the case with his _____, Dr. Watson.

5. Louise can relate an anecdote better than I; she is a fine _____.

6. Though the food was delicious, Ed refused a second helping; he is no _____.

7. If I were a(n) _____, I would be able to tell whether the cheese in this salad is imported or domestic.

8. When the young attorney was elected to a seat on the board of directors, some of the veteran members considered her a(n) _____.

9. A man who flees his native land to escape political oppression is a(n) _____.

10. Though the Allens are friendly with everyone, they have rarely visited with anyone outside their tightly knit _____.

3. Terms for Traits or Feelings of Persons

aplomb (*n.*) ə-'pläm	absolute confidence in oneself; poise; self-possession	As usual, the mayor met all challenges at the hearing with *aplomb*.
éclat (*n.*) ā-'klä	brilliancy of achievement	The violinist performed with rare *éclat*.
élan (*n.*) ā-'läⁿ	enthusiasm; eagerness for action	Because the cast had rehearsed with such *élan*, the director was sanguine about opening night.
ennui (*n.*) än-'wē	feeling of weariness and discontent; boredom; tedium	Even a few days in a hospital bed is likely to cause *ennui*.
esprit de corps (*n.*) is-,prē-də-'kȯr	feeling of union and common interest pervading a group; devotion to a group or to its ideals	The volunteers showed extraordinary *esprit de corps*, working round the clock to quell the fires.

finesse (*n.*) fə-'nes	skill and adroitness in handling a difficult situation	The prosecutor conducted the cross-examination with admirable *finesse*.
legerdemain (*n.*) ˌle-jər-də-'mān	sleight of hand; artful trick	By a feat of *legerdemain,* the magician produced a rabbit from her hat.
malaise (*n.*) mə-'lāz	vague feeling of bodily discomfort or illness	The gourmand's late Lucullan supper brought on *malaise*.
noblesse oblige (*n.*) nō-'bles-ə-'blēzh	principle that persons of high rank or birth are obliged to act nobly	Kings and other nobles were observing *noblesse oblige* when they fought at the head of their troops.
rapport (*n.*) ra-'pȯr	relationship characterized by harmony, conformity, or affinity	A common love of gardening drew May and Lori into closer *rapport*.
sangfroid (*n.*) 'säⁿ- 'f(r)wä	coolness of mind in difficult circumstances; composure; equanimity	The quarterback's *sangfroid* during the tense last moments of the game enabled him to call the winning play.
savoir faire (*n.*) ˌsav-ˌwär-'far	knowledge of just what to say or do; tact	You need both capital and *savoir faire* to be a successful entrepreneur.

 **EXERCISE 8.3**

In each blank, insert the most appropriate word or expression from group 3.

1. The attaché certainly is tactful; he has plenty of _____.

2. Your physician may help you obtain some relief from the _____ that accompanies a severe cold.

3. Instead of reducing their subordinates' salaries, the executives cut their own compensation substantially, in accordance with _____.

4. Some card tricks require complex _____.

5. If you are bored, try reading detective stories; they help to overcome _____.

4. Terms Dealing With Conversation and Writing

adieu (*n.*) ə-'d(y)ü	good-bye; farewell	On commencement day, we shall bid *adieu* to our alma mater.
au revoir (*n.*) ˌō-rə-'vwär	good-bye; till we meet again	Our next party is in a month. *Au revoir!*

billet-doux (*n.*) ˌbi-lē-ʼdü	love letter	A timely *billet-doux* patched up the lovers' quarrel.
bon mot (*n.*) bōⁿ-ʼmō	clever saying; witty remark; witticism	Hamlet recalls the hilarity of jester Yorick's *bon mots.*
brochure (*n.*) brō-ʼshu̇r	pamphlet; booklet	This helpful *brochure* explains how to obtain a driver's license.
canard (*n.*) kə-ʼnärd	false rumor; absurd story; hoax	It took a public appearance by the monarch to disprove the *canard* that he had been assassinated.
cliché (*n.*) klē-ʼshā	worn-out expression; trite phrase	Vivid writing shuns *clichés,* such as "first and foremost" and "last but not least."
entre nous (*adv.*) ˌän-trə-ʼnü	between us; confidentially	The Wildcats expect to win, but *entre nous* their chances are not too good.
mot juste (*n.*) mō-ʼzhūest	exactly right word; most suitable expression	To improve your writing, try to find the *mot juste* for each idea.
nom de plume (*n.*) ˌnäm-də-ʼplüm	pen name; pseudonym	Benjamin Franklin used the *nom de plume* "Silence Dogood" when he submitted essays to his brother's newspaper.
précis (*n.*) ʼprā-sē	brief summary	Include only the essential points when you write a *précis.*
repartee (*n.*) ˌre-pər-ʼtē	skill of replying quickly, cleverly, and humorously; witty reply	Author and critic Dorothy Parker was renowned for her *repartee.*
résumé (*n.*) ʼre-zə-ˌmā	1. brief account of experience and qualifications submitted by an applicant for a position; curriculum vitae	Stacy sent copies of her *résumé* to fourteen prospective employers.
	2. summary	The teacher asked us to write a *résumé* of the last act.
riposte (*n.*) ri-ʼpōst	1. retort; repartee	When Dan was criticized for his error, his *riposte* was "*You* usually don't catch mistakes!"
	2. in fencing, a quick return thrust after a parry	The fencing instructor showed us how to defend ourselves against *ripostes.*
tête-à-tête (*n.*) ˌtet-ə-ʼtet	private conversation between two persons	Before answering, the witness had a *tête-à-tête* with his attorney.

![Exercise icon] **EXERCISE 8.4**

In each blank, insert the most appropriate word or expression from group 4.

1. There are valuable hints on safe driving in this sixteen-page _____.

2. Avoid the expression "old as the hills"; it is a(n) _____.

3. Investigation proved the story was unfounded; it was just a(n) _____.

4. The manager went out to the mound for a brief _____ with his faltering pitcher.

5. Everyone supposes this diamond is genuine, but _____ it's only an imitation.

5. Terms Dealing With Situations

bête noire (*n.*) ,bet-'nwär	dreaded object or person; bugbear	He enjoyed all his subjects except mathematics, his *bête noire*.
carte blanche (*n.*) 'kärt-'bläⁿsh	full discretionary power; freedom to use one's own judgment	Ms. Mauro gave her assistant *carte blanche* in managing the office while she was away.
cause célèbre (*n.*) ,kȯz-sə-'leb	famous case in law that arouses considerable interest; issue, person, incident, or situation attracting much attention	The trial of John Peter Zenger, a *cause célèbre* in the eighteenth century, helped to establish freedom of the press in America.
contretemps (*n.*) 'kän-trə-,täⁿ	inopportune occurrence; embarrassing situation; mishap	The proctor arrived late, but that wasn't the only *contretemps*; the examination sent to our room was not the one we were supposed to take.
cul-de-sac (*n.*) 'kəl-di-,sak	blind alley; dead end	Painting proved to be a *cul-de-sac* for Philip Carey, as he had no real talent.
debacle (*n.*) di-'bä-kəl	collapse; disaster; overthrow; rout; fiasco	The *debacle* at Waterloo signaled the end of Napoleon's power.
fait accompli (*n.*) ,fā-tə-käm-'plē	thing already done	A reconciliation between the bitter foes, once thought an impossibility, may soon become a *fait accompli*.
faux pas (*n.*) 'fō-,pä	misstep; blunder in conduct, manners, speech, etc.	One guest got no dessert because another had committed the *faux pas* of taking too generous a helping.

impasse (*n.*) ′im-,pas	deadlock; predicament with no obvious way out; stalemate	Having reached an *impasse,* the jury could deliberate no further.
liaison (*n.*) ′lē-ə-,zän	1. bond; linking up; coordination of activities 2. person who establishes and maintains this connection	The alumni association fosters the graduates' *liaison* with the school.
mélange (*n.*) mā-′läⁿzh	mixture; medley; potpourri	The amateur show was a *mélange* of skits, acrobatics, ballet, hit songs, and classical music.
mirage (*n.*) mə-′räzh	optical illusion	The sheet of water we thought we saw on the road ahead turned out to be only a *mirage.*

 **EXERCISE 8.5**

In each blank, insert the most appropriate word or expression from group 5.

1. That flippant remark to Mrs. Lee about her ailing son was a(n) _____.

2. The inhabitants of the remote Eskimo village had practically no _____ with the outside world.

3. Mr. Briggs never concerned himself with hiring or dismissing employees, having given his plant manager _____ in these matters.

4. Despite seventeen hours of continuous deliberations, the weary negotiators still faced a(n) _____ over wages.

5. Alice's position turned out to be a(n) _____, since it offered no opportunity for advancement.

Review Exercises

REVIEW 1: MEANINGS

In the space before each word or expression in column I, write the *letter* of its correct meaning from column II. (Exercise continues on next page.)

COLUMN I	COLUMN II
___ 1. refugee	*a.* devotee
___ 2. till we meet again	*b.* debacle
___ 3. well-informed	*c.* bête noire
___ 4. partisan	*d.* concierge
___ 5. brief summary	*e.* sangfroid

___ **6.** hoax   *f.* nom de plume

___ **7.** bugbear   *g.* émigré

___ **8.** rout   *h.* précis

___ **9.** love letter   *i.* au revoir

___ **10.** equanimity   *j.* canard

___ **11.** doorkeeper   *k.* au courant

___ **12.** pen name   *l.* billet-doux

REVIEW 2: SENTENCE COMPLETION

In the space provided, enter the *letter* of the choice that best completes the sentence.

___ **1.** In serving the soup, the _____ waitress spilled some of it on the guest of honor.

   a. chic   *b.* maladroit   *c.* debonair

___ **2.** Monotonous repetition usually brings on _____.

   a. ennui   *b.* éclat   *c.* savoir faire

___ **3.** I'll be glad to give my opinion, but you must realize I am no _____.

   a. raconteur   *b.* martinet   *c.* connoisseur

___ **4.** A bibliophile is usually a _____ of good literature.

   a. protégée   *b.* devotee   *c.* repartee

___ **5.** We made a right turn into the next street, but it proved to be a _____.

   a. mélange   *b.* cul-de-sac   *c.* canard

___ **6.** The president was represented at the state funeral in Paris by a special _____.

   a. ingenue   *b.* bourgeoisie   *c.* envoy

___ **7.** We had a _____ over a couple of ice-cream sodas.

   a. bête noire   *b.* tête-à-tête   *c.* mirage

___ **8.** To seat Frank next to Maria would be a _____; they are not on speaking terms.

   a. faux pas   *b.* impasse   *c.* riposte

___ **9.** Today, my biology teacher began with a _____ of yesterday's lesson.

   a. rapport   *b.* résumé   *c.* brochure

___ **10.** Because of her excellent training, she has developed remarkable _____ at the piano.

   a. sangfroid   *b.* élan   *c.* finesse

___   11. The launch of the space shuttle was delayed by one _____ after another.
       a. mirage   *b.* contretemps   *c.* brochure

___   12. It would be _____ to come to an employment interview in a jogging suit.
       a. chic   *b.* complaisant   *c.* gauche

REVIEW 3: BRAINTEASERS

Fill in the missing letters.

1. The celebrity was surrounded by a **c o t** ___ ___ ___ ___ of admirers.

2. She was as nervous as a(n) ___ ___ ___ ___ **t a n** ___ ___ at a coming-out party.

3. You don't have to be so strict. Don't be a(n) ___ ___ ___ ___ ___ **n e t**.

4. No further progress is possible. The situation is a(n) ___ ___ **p a s s** ___.

5. They get along poorly. There is little **r a p** ___ ___ ___ ___ between them.

6. A(n) ___ **l a i r** ___ ___ ___ ___ ___ ___ person could have seen that trouble was coming.

7. A conceited person with no talent may still think that he or she is
the ___ ___ ___ **p a r** ___ ___ ___.

8. To be a food columnist, you should be a writer and a(n) ___ ___ ___ ___ **m e t**.

9. Most of our school's intellectual ___ **l i t** ___ is in the Honor Society.

10. She enjoys opera, and she is also a(n) ___ ___ **v o t e** ___ of the ballet.

REVIEW 4: COMPOSITION

Answer in two or three sentences.

1. Can a naive entrepreneur succeed in business? Why, or why not?

_____

_____

_____

2. Describe a situation in which it might not be a faux pas to give someone else carte blanche
to make decisions for you.

_____

_____

_____

3. Is it normal for employees who consider themselves in a cul-de-sac to show ennui? Explain.

_____

_____

_____

4. How would a club's esprit de corps be affected if its president were a martinet?

_____

_____

_____

5. Why must you have rapport with your audience to succeed as a raconteur?

_____

_____

_____

6. Terms Dealing With History and Government

coup d'etat (*n.*)
,kü-,dā-'tä or
coup 'kü

sudden violent overthrow of a government

Napoleon seized power by a *coup d'etat.*

demarche (*n.*)
dā-'märsh

course of action (e.g., one involving a change of policy); maneuver

Hitler's attack on Russia, shortly after his pact with Stalin, was a stunning *demarche.*

détente (*n.*)
dā-'tänt

relaxing, as of strained relations between nations

A *détente* in international tensions followed the disarmament treaty.

entente (*n.*)
än-'tänt

understanding or agreement between governments

Canada and the United States have a long-standing *entente* on border problems.

laissez-faire (*n.*)
,le-,sā-'far

doctrine opposing interference by governments in economic affairs; noninterference

Adam Smith believed a policy of *laissez-faire* toward business would benefit a nation.

lettre de cachet (*n.*)
,le-trə-də-,ka-'shā

letter bearing a seal (e.g., of a French king before the Revolution) ordering the imprisonment without trial of a person the letter names

Dr. Manette was imprisoned through a *lettre de cachet.*

premier (*n.*)
pri-'mir

prime minister

A vote of no confidence forced the *premier* out of office.

| **rapprochement** (*n.*)
ˌra-ˌprōsh-'mäⁿ | establishment or state of cordial relations; coming together | The gradual *rapprochement* between the two nations, longtime enemies, cheered their neighbors. |
| **regime** (*n.*)
rā-'zhēm | system of government or rule | The coup d'etat brought to power a *regime* that restored civil liberties. |

 **EXERCISE 8.6**

In each blank, insert the most appropriate word or expression from group 6.

1. Do you favor strict regulation of business or a policy of _____?

2. The tyrannical ruler was eventually overthrown by a(n) _____.

3. The newly elected officials will face many problems left by the outgoing _____.

4. Before 1789, a French nobleman could have an enemy imprisoned without trial by obtaining a(n) _____.

5. The agreement ended the war, and both nations welcomed the _____ that followed.

7. Terms Dealing With the Arts

avant-garde (*n.*) ˌä-ˌvän-'gärd	experimentalists or innovators in any art	Wait Whitman was no conservative; his daring innovations in poetry place him in the *avant-garde* of nineteenth-century writers.
bas-relief (*n.*) ˌbä-ri-'lēf	sculpture in which the figures project only slightly from the background	The ancient Greek Parthenon is famed for its beautiful sculpture in *bas-relief.*
baton (*n.*) bə-'tän	rod a conductor uses to direct an orchestra or band	A downbeat—the downward stroke of the conductor's *baton*—denotes the first beat of a measure.
chef d'oeuvre (*n.*) shā-'doəvrᵉ	chief work; masterpiece in art, literature, etc.	Many connoisseurs regard HAMLET as Shakespeare's *chef d'oeuvre.*
denouement (*n.*) ˌdā-nü-'mäⁿ	solution ("untying") of the plot in a play, story, or complex situation; outcome; end	In the *denouement* of GREAT EXPECTATIONS, Pip's benefactor is identified as the escaped convict whom Pip had once befriended.

encore (*n.*)
'än-,kòr

audience's demand for an additional performance; repetition or additional performance in response to applause

In appreciation of the enthusiastic applause, the vocalist sang an *encore*.

genre (*n.*)
'zhän-rə

1. kind; sort; category

The literary genre to which Virginia Woolf contributed most is the novel.

2. style of painting depicting scenes from everyday life

Painters of genre choose scenes from everyday life as their subject matter.

musicale (*n.*)
,myü-zi-'kal

social gathering with music as the featured entertainment

Last night's *musicale* at the White House featured a popular folk singer.

palette (*n.*)
'pa-lət

thin board (with a thumb hole at one end) on which an artist lays and mixes colors

After a few strokes on the canvas, an artist reapplies the brush to the *palette* for more paint.

repertoire (*n.*)
're-pə(r)-,twär

1. stock of plays, operas, roles, compositions, etc., that a company or individual is prepared to perform

The guitarist apologized for not playing the requested number, explaining that it was not in his *repertoire*.

2. collection

Whenever I hear a good joke, I add it to my *repertoire*.

vignette (*n.*)
vin-'yet

short verbal description; small, graceful literary sketch

James Joyce's DUBLINERS offers some unforgettable *vignettes* of life in Dublin a century ago.

 **EXERCISE 8.7**

In each blank, insert the most appropriate word or expression from group 7.

1. After studying poetry, we took up another _____, short stories.

2. A novel with a suspenseful plot makes the reader impatient to get to the _____.

3. If audience reaction is favorable, Selma is prepared to play a(n) _____.

4. Beethoven's NINTH SYMPHONY is regarded by many as his _____.

5. By diligent study, the young singer added several new numbers to his _____.

8. *Terms Dealing With Food*

a la carte (*adv.*)
,ä-lə-'kärt
according to the menu (bill of fare); dish by dish, from a menu stating the price for each dish
You can get the salad *a la carte* for $6 or as part of the 5-course-$15 dinner special.

a la mode (*adj.*)
,ä-lə-'mōd
1. according to fashion; stylish
Most shoppers buy only the latest fashions because they want their clothes to be *a la mode.*

2. with ice cream
We enjoy apple pie *a la mode.*

aperitif (*n.*)
ə-,per-ə-'tēf
alcoholic drink taken before a meal as an appetizer
The 5-course special includes a nonalcoholic appetizer, such as tomato juice, but not an *aperitif.*

bonbon (*n.*)
'bän-,bän
piece of candy
For St. Valentine's Day, we gave our grandmother a heart-shaped box of delicious *bonbons.*

consommé (*n.*)
,kän-sə-'mā
clear soup; broth
The *consommé* better suits a queasy stomach than the onion soup.

croissant (*n.*)
,kwä-'sänt
rich, flaky crescent-shaped roll
Croissants go well with coffee or tea at breakfast.

cuisine (*n.*)
kwi-'zēn
style of cooking or preparing food
Each of the mall's restaurants specializes in a different one of America's favorite *cuisines.*

demitasse (*n.*)
'de-mē-,tas
small cup for, or of, strong black coffee
Yves shuffled in, downed two *demitasses*, then shot off for work.

entrée (*n.*)
'än-,trā
main dish at lunch or dinner
The menu's *entrées* included roast beef, fried chicken, and lasagna.

filet (*n.*)
fi-'lā or **fillet**
slice of meat or fish without bones
Because *filets* are boneless, they cost more than ordinary cuts.

hors d'oeuvres
(*n. pl.*) òr-'dərv(z)
light foods served as appetizers before the regular courses of a meal
Terry's *hors d'oeuvres* were olives, celery, tortilla chips, and salsa.

pièce de résistance
(*n.*)
pē-,es-də-rə-,zē-'stäns
1. main dish
Saving room for the *pièce de résistance,* I only nibbled at the hors d'oeuvres.

2. main item of any collection, series, program, etc.; showpiece
The preliminaries were followed by the *pièce de résistance,* the title bout.

soup du jour (*n.*)
,süp-də-'zhür
soup served in a restaurant on a particular day
Often, the only soup a restaurant offers is the soup *du jour.*

table d'hôte (*n.*)	complete meal of several courses offered in a hotel or restaurant at a fixed price	If you order the *table d'hôte,* you pay the fixed price for the full meal, even if you pass up some of the dishes.
,tä-bəl-'dōt		

EXERCISE 8.8

In each blank, insert the most appropriate word or expression from group 8.

1. Before dinner, our hostess brought in a large tray of appetizing _____.

2. This chef's style of cooking owes much to traditional Creole _____.

3. When I do not care to have a complete dinner, I order a couple of dishes _____.

4. My little sister has such a sweet tooth that our parents had to restrict her to one _____ after each meal.

5. If you like flounder without fishbones, order _____ of flounder.

6. We would have had some split-pea soup, but unfortunately it was not the _____.

9. *Terms Dealing With Dress*

bouffant (*adj.*)	puffed out; full	The *bouffant* hairdo became a la mode once more after being worn by an Oscar winner.
bü-'fȧnt		
boutique (*n.*)	small shop specializing in fashionable clothes	Rhoda found her outfit in a midtown *boutique*.
bü-'tēk		
chemise (*n.*)	loose-fitting, sacklike dress	Though more comfortable than most other dresses, the *chemise* has often been ridiculed for its shapelessness.
shə-'mēz		
coiffure (*n.*)	style of arranging the hair	Melanie's *coiffure* was created for her by my sister's hair stylist.
kwä-'fyu̇r		
corsage (*n.*)	small bouquet worn by a woman	Holly *corsages* are often worn at Christmas.
kȯr-'säzh		
cravat (*n.*)	necktie; neckband; scarf	He wore a light-blue shirt and a navy-blue *cravat*.
krə-'vat		
ensemble (*n.*)	complete costume of harmonious clothing and accessories	Her red blouse, black skirt, and matching red pumps made an attractive *ensemble*.
än-'säm-bəl		

flamboyant (*adj.*) flam-'bȯi-ənt	flamelike; ornate; showy; vivid	To add a touch of bright color to his outfit, Jack wore a *flamboyant* scarf.
toupee (*n.*) tü-'pā	wig; hairpiece to cover baldness	The actor's blond hair was concealed by a gray *toupee*.
vogue (*n.*) 'vōg	fashion; accepted style	Fashions change rapidly; today's style may be out of *vogue* tomorrow.

EXERCISE 8.9

In each blank, insert the most appropriate word from group 9.

1. The sweltering heat made Hector untie his _____ and unbutton his collar.

2. After trying several elaborate hair styles, Marie has returned to a simple _____ .

3. On your visit to Mount Vernon in Virginia, you will see furniture styles that were in _____ in George and Martha Washington's time.

4. The guest of honor wore a beautiful _____ on her gown.

5. The boutique's cocktail dresses range from sedate blacks to _____ reds and golds.

10. Miscellaneous Terms

ambience (*n.*) 'äm-bē-äns	surroundings; atmosphere; environment	The restaurant merits kudos not only for its food but its *ambience*; never had we dined in pleasanter surroundings.
apropos (*adv.*) ,a-prə-'pō	by the way; incidentally	We'll meet you at the station. *Apropos*, when does your train arrive?
apropos (*adj.*)	appropriate; relevant; pertinent	None of the comments is *apropos*; they are all off the topic.
avoirdupois (*n.*) ,a-vər-də-'pȯiz	weight; heaviness	Dieters constantly check their *avoirdupois*.
bagatelle (*n.*) ,ba-gə-'tel	trifle	Pay attention to important matters; don't waste time on *bagatelles*.

coup de grace (*n.*)
ˌkü-də-ˈgräs

decisive finishing blow

We won, 5–1, thanks to Pat, who administered the *coup de grace*—a grand slam.

en route (*adj.* or *adv.*)
äⁿ-ˈrüt

1. on the way

My friends are *en route*.

2. along the way

They will stop for lunch *en route*.

etiquette (*n.*)
ˈe-ti-kət

required social or official usages; code of behavior

To crash a party is to disregard *etiquette*.

facade (*n.*)
fə-ˈsäd

face or front of a building, or of anything; false front

The convalescent's jovial smile was just a *facade* to hide his ennui.

fete (*n.*)
ˈfāt or ˈfet

festival; entertainment; party

Our block party last year was a memorable *fete*.

fete (*v.*)

honor with a fete

Retiring employees are often *feted* at a special dinner.

foyer (*n.*)
ˈfȯi-(ə)r

entrance hall; lobby; anteroom; vestibule

Let's meet in the *foyer* of the public library.

milieu (*n.*)
mēl-ˈyə

environment; setting; surroundings

Ismael found his new *milieu* more conducive to making friendships.

parasol (*n.*)
ˈpar-ə-ˌsȯl

umbrella for protection against the sun

In French painting of the 19th century, the *parasol* is a common accessory of ladies out for a stroll.

par excellence (*adj.*)
ˌpär-ˌek-sə-ˈläⁿs

above all others of the same sort (follows the word it modifies)

Emily Post's writings on etiquette were the authority *par excellence*.

passé (*adj.*)
pa-ˈsā

old-fashioned; behind the times; outmoded

Rapid advances in technology often make recently bought equipment *passé*.

pince-nez (*n.*)
paⁿs-ˈnā

eyeglasses clipped to the nose by a spring

Because they are held in place by a spring that pinches the nose, *pince nez* may be less comfortable than ordinary eyeglasses.

premiere (*n.*)
pri-ˈmyer

first performance

The second performance was even better than the *premiere*.

queue (*n.*)
ˈkyü

line of persons or vehicles waiting their turn

Buy the tickets now to avoid wasting time on the *queue* later.

raison d'être (*n.*)
ˌrā-ˌzōⁿ-ˈdetrᵊ

reason or justification for existing

Alicia lives for dancing; it is her *raison d'être*.

rendezvous (*n.*) 'rän-di-ˌvü	1. prearranged meeting place; popular gathering place	Our *rendezvous* after the test is to be the cafeteria.
	2. prearranged meeting	Our *rendezvous* with the visiting team's coaches is set for 2 P.M.
silhouette (*n.*) ˌsi-lə-'wet	shadow; outline	I knew Jonah was coming to let me in because I recognized his *silhouette* behind the curtained door.
sobriquet (*n.*) or **soubriquet** 'sō-bri-ˌkā	nickname	Andrew Jackson was known by the *sobriquet* "Old Hickory."
souvenir (*n.*) 'sü-və-ˌnir	reminder; keepsake; memento	The Yearbook will come to be a valued *souvenir* of high-school days.
tour de force (*n.*) ˌtür-də-'fórs	feat of strength, skill, or ingenuity	The sixty-yard run was the *tour de force* that won the game for us.
vis-à-vis (*prep.*) ˌvēz-ə-'vē	1. face-to-face with; opposite	At the banquet table, I had the good fortune to sit *vis-à-vis* an old friend.
	2. in relation to; as compared with	We argued about today's sluggers *vis-à-vis* Babe Ruth.

 **EXERCISE 8.10**

In each blank, insert the most appropriate word or expression from group 10.

1. Carmela brought me a print of the Lincoln Memorial as a(n) _____ of her visit to Washington.

2. Paul mounts the scale morning and night to check his _____.

3. After class, my friends gather at our _____ outside the pizzeria.

4. April is a mimic _____; none of us can outdo her impersonations.

5. Harvey's flaming hair accounts for his _____: "Red."

6. The small merchants in our area are fearful that the opening of another shopping mall will be the _____ for them.

7. Our club is planning a(n) _____ in honor of the outgoing president.

8. On the first day in a new school, arriving students find themselves in a bewildering _____.

9. I did not recognize the hotel because its _____ and foyer had been modernized since I was last there.

10. Winning the league pennant is an outstanding achievement, but going on to capture the World Series in four straight victories is an even greater _____.

11. When the film had its premiere at our local theater, the _____ stretched halfway around the block.

12. Blanche, we're glad to see you. _____, how is your brother?

Review Exercises

REVIEW 5: MEANINGS

In the space before each word or expression in column I, write the *letter* of its correct meaning from column II.

COLUMN I	COLUMN II
___ 1. piece of candy	*a.* silhouette
___ 2. nickname	*b.* coup d'etat
___ 3. relaxing of strained relations	*c.* consommé
___ 4. full; puffed out	*d.* coup de grace
___ 5. style of cooking	*e.* apropos
___ 6. masterpiece	*f.* bonbon
___ 7. shadow	*g.* chef d'oeuvre
___ 8. weight	*h.* cuisine
___ 9. decisive finishing blow	*i.* avoirdupois
___ 10. sudden overthrow of a regime	*j.* sobriquet
___ 11. relevant	*k.* détente
___ 12. broth	*l.* bouffant

REVIEW 6: MORE MEANINGS

In the space provided, write the *letter* of the choice that correctly defines the italicized word or expression.

___ 1. prosperous *bourgeoisie*   *a.* elite   *b.* entrepreneur   *c.* middle class   *d.* citizenry   *e.* officialdom

___ 2. *flamboyant* jacket   *a.* debonair   *b.* warm   *c.* sanguinary   *d.* showy   *e.* stylish

___ 3. happy *denouement*   *a.* ending   *b.* vignette   *c.* milieu   *d.* event   *e.* episode

___ 4. sudden *demarche*   *a.* détente   *b.* reversal   *c.* entrée   *d.* discovery   *e.* aggression

___ 5. attitude of *laissez-faire* *a.* boredom *b.* equanimity *c.* eagerness *d.* cordiality
    e. noninterference

___ 6. enduring *entente* *a.* influence *b.* understanding *c.* bitterness
    d. cause célèbre *e.* entrance

___ 7. serve *hors d'oeuvres* *a.* entrées *b.* appetizers *c.* desserts
    d. pièces de résistance *e.* tables d'hôte

___ 8. join the *avant-garde* *a.* gendarmes *b.* protégés *c.* devotees *d.* underground
    e. innovators

___ 9. welcome *encore* *a.* cancellation *b.* delay *c.* repetition *d.* refund *e.* debut

___ 10. flavor *par excellence* *a.* new *b.* unsurpassed *c.* spicy *d.* mild *e.* inferior

___ 11. has become *passé* *a.* popular *b.* fashionable *c.* outmoded *d.* unnecessary
    e. acceptable

___ 12. delayed *en route* *a.* for a short time *b.* before departure *c.* somewhere
    d. on arrival *e.* on the way

REVIEW 7: SENTENCE COMPLETION

Complete the sentence by inserting the correct word or expression from the vocabulary list below.

VOCABULARY LIST

coiffure	chargé d'affaires	regime
au courant	pièce de résistance	raison d'être
envoy	éclat	avant-garde
genre	bagatelle	nouveaux riches
laissez-faire	facade	souvenir

1. At one time or another, some interest may become so important to us that it is practically our _____ (*reason for existence*).

2. This piece of driftwood is a(n) _____ (*something that serves as a reminder*) of last summer's camping trip.

3. The reason you were not ready is that you spent too much time on a mere _____ (*unimportant, trifling matter*).

4. What _____ (*style of arranging the hair*) is most in vogue today?

5. The _____ (*persons who had newly become rich*) felt ill at ease in their new social milieu.

6. E-mails kept me _____ (*up-to-date*) about homework when I was sick.

7. The _____ (*main number on the program*) of the musicale was a medley of Gilbert and Sullivan airs.

8. In bringing up children, some parents are martinets, others devotees of _____ (*noninterference*).

9. The success of the United States has encouraged many peoples to install a democratic _____ (*system of government or rule*).

10. The _____ (*ambassador's substitute*) has had years of experience in the diplomatic service.

REVIEW 8: BRAINTEASERS

Fill in the missing letters.

1. Don't change your hair style. We like your present __ __ __ __ **f u r** __.

2. Is __ __ **l e t** of sole on today's menu?

3. The matter is of little importance. It is just a **b a g** __ __ __ __ __ __.

4. They enjoy simple cooking; they don't care for fancy __ __ __ **s i n** __.

5. Only the __ __ **c a d** __ has been renovated. The interior is unchanged.

6. We didn't stick to the topic. Little that was said was __ **p r o p** __ __.

7. Residents complain that the park has become a **r e n d** __ __ __ __ __ __ for drug dealers.

8. A(n) __ __ __ __ **b o y** __ __ __ ensemble is not for a conservative dresser.

9. The **r a p** __ __ __ __ __ __ __ __ __ between the rivals ushered in an era of harmony.

10. The song we had asked for was, regrettably, not in the band's __ __ **p e r t** __ __ __ __.

REVIEW 9: CONCISE WRITING

Express the thought of each sentence below in no more than four words.

1. We went into a small shop that specializes in fashionable clothes.

   _____

2. The line of persons waiting their turn kept getting longer and longer.

   _____

3. People who travel on foot sometimes carry umbrellas for protection against the sun.

   _____

4. We arranged an appointment to meet at a fixed time and place.

   _____

5. The loose-fitting, sacklike dress that she wore is not expensive.

   _____

6. What is the time at which the first performance will be presented?

_____

7. Sometimes, people who assume the risks and management of a business go bankrupt.

_____

8. Give us full discretionary power to use our own judgment.

_____

9. The vague feeling of illness that I was having is gone.

_____

10. Do you know anyone who is fond of eating and drinking to excess?

_____

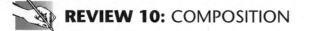 **REVIEW 10:** COMPOSITION

Answer in two or three sentences.

1. Who are more likely to have trouble with their avoirdupois, gourmands or gourmets? Explain.

_____

_____

_____

2. Though the hazards of overexposure to the sun have been widely publicized, parasols do not seem to be in vogue. Why?

_____

_____

_____

3. Suppose you are eager to attend a premiere, but when you get there you find a queue stretching around the block. Would you stay or leave? Explain.

_____

_____

_____

4. Why do so many émigrés from totalitarian regimes seek to settle in our country? Give two important reasons.

_____

_____

_____

5. Why is it advisable to know what the pièce de résistance is going to be before having any of the hors d'oeuvres?

_____

_____

_____

REVIEW 11: ANALOGIES

Write the *letter* of the expression that best completes the analogy.

___ **1.** *Parasol* is to *sun* as *variety* is to _____.
   a. queue   *b.* fete   *c.* ennui   *d.* sky   *e.* souvenir

___ **2.** *Regime* is to *revolutionists* as *custom* is to _____.
   a. elite   *b.* connoisseurs   *c.* devotees   *d.* avant-garde   *e.* conservatives

___ **3.** *Scene I* is to *climax* as *hors d'oeuvres* is to _____.
   a. entrée   *b.* cuisine   *c.* bonbon   *d.* chef d'oeuvre   *e.* bagatelle

___ **4.** *Passé* is to *a la mode* as *apropos* is to _____.
   a. appropriate   *b.* stylish   *c.* outmoded   *d.* irrelevant   *e.* pertinent

___ **5.** *Bottle* is to *neck* as *hotel* is to _____.
   a. facade   *b.* cul-de-sac   *c.* foyer   *d.* suburb   *e.* table d'hôte

___ **6.** *Nourished* is to *food* as *au courant* is to _____.
   a. exercise   *b.* drink   *c.* news   *d.* rest   *e.* rumor

___ **7.** *Star* is to *understudy* as *ambassador* is to _____.
   a. coterie   *b.* valet   *c.* entrepreneur   *d.* chargé d'affaires   *e.* protégé

___ **8.** *Bas-relief* is to *sculpture* as *genre* is to _____.
   a. palette   *b.* painter   *c.* sculptor   *d.* baton   *e.* painting

___ **9.** *Faux pas* is to *embarrassment* as *détente* is to _____.
   a. rapprochement   *b.* impasse   *c.* cul-de-sac   *d.* pièce de résistance   *e.* encore

___ **10.** *Ice* is to *thaw* as *hostility* is to _____.
   a. coup de grace   *b.* détente   *c.* coup d'etat   *d.* tour de force   *e.* denouement

Chapter 9

Italian Words in English

The Italian impact on English is especially important because Italy's rich contributions to the arts have profoundly influenced our cultural life. It is no wonder, then, that many English words that deal with music, painting, architecture, sculpture, and other arts are Italian loanwords.

1. Words for Singing Voices and Singers (arranged in order of increasing pitch)

WORD	MEANING
basso (*n.*) ˈba-sō	lowest male voice; bass (ˈbās)
baritone (*n.*) ˈbar-ə-ˌtōn	male voice between bass and tenor
tenor (*n.*) ˈten-ər	adult male voice between baritone and alto
alto (*n.*) ˈal-tō	1. highest male voice; countertenor 2. lowest female voice; contralto
falsetto (*n.*) fȯl-ˈse-tō	artificially ("falsely") high voice
contralto (*n.*) kən-ˈtral-tō	lowest female voice

mezzo-soprano (*n.*)   female voice between contralto and soprano
,met-sō-sə-'pra-nō

soprano (*n.*)   highest voice in women and boys
sə-'pra-nō

coloratura (*n.*)   1. vocal music ornamented with runs and trills
,kə-lə-rə-'tür-ə   2. soprano specializing in such music

EXERCISE 9.1

In each blank, insert the most appropriate word from group 1.

1. For her superb rendering of ornamental passages, the _____ was wildly acclaimed.

2. The lowest singing voice is contralto for women and _____ for men.

3. Yodeling requires changes from the natural singing voice to a(n) _____.

4. A _____ voice is between baritone and alto.

5. Falsetto enabled the tenor to sing the higher _____ part.

2. Words for Tempos (Rates of Speed) of Musical Compositions (arranged in order of increasing speed)

grave (*adv.* or *adj.*)   slow (the slowest tempo in music)
'grä-vā

largo (*adv.* or *adj.*)   slow and dignified; stately
'lär-gō

adagio (*adv.* or *adj.*)   slow; in an easy, graceful manner
ə-'dä-j(ē-)ō

lento (*adv.* or *adj.*)   slow
'len-,tō

andante (*adv.* or *adj.*)   moderately slow, but flowing
än-'dän-,tā

moderato (*adv.* or   in moderate time
adj.) ,mä-də-'rä-tō

allegro (*adv.* or *adj.*)   brisk; quick; lively
ə-'leg-rō

vivace (*adv.* or *adj.*)   brisk; spirited
vē-'vä-chā

presto (*adv.* or *adj.*)   quick
'pres-tō

prestissimo (*adv.* or   at a very rapid pace
adj.) pre-'sti-sə-,mō

EXERCISE 9.2

In each blank, insert the most appropriate word from group 2.

1. A piece of music marked _____ moves more rapidly than one marked presto.

2. Beethoven's SONATE PATHÉTIQUE opens in the slowest tempo, _____.

3. A ballad with a(n) _____ tempo has to be sung at a moderately slow but flowing pace.

4. The _____ movement of Dvorák's NEW WORLD SYMPHONY is played in a slow and dignified manner.

5. The term _____ over the opening notes of SWEET GEORGIA BROWN indicates that this tune should be played neither rapidly nor slowly, but in moderate time.

3. Words for Dynamics (Degrees of Loudness)

crescendo (*adv., adj.,*   gradually increasing (or a gradual increase) in force or loudness (*ant.*
or *n.*) krə-'shen-dō   **decrescendo**)

decrescendo (*adv.,*   gradually decreasing (or a gradual decrease) in force or loudness;
adj., or *n.*)   diminuendo (*ant.* **crescendo**)
,dā-krə-'shen-dō

dolce (*adv.* or *adj.*)   soft; sweet
'dōl-chā

forte (*adv.* or *adj.*)   loud (*ant.* **piano**)
'for-,tā

fortissimo (*adv.* or   very loud (*ant.* **pianissimo**)
adj.) for-'ti-sə-,mō

pianissimo (*adv.* or   very soft (*ant.* **fortissimo**)
adj.) ,pē-ə-'ni-sə-,mō

piano (*adv.* or *adj.*)   soft (*ant.* **forte**)
pē-'ä-nō

sforzando (*adv.* or   accented; stressed
adj.) sfȯrt-'sän-dō

EXERCISE 9.3

In each blank, insert the most appropriate word from group 3.

1. The word _____ designates a familiar musical instrument, as well as a musical direction meaning "soft."

2. Ravel's BOLERO rises to a dramatic climax by a gradual increase in loudness; few pieces have such an electrifying _____.

3. A chord marked _____ is to be played with a strong accent.

4. The ending of Mendelssohn's SCHERZO is played very softly— _____.

5. A degree of loudness higher than forte is _____.

4. Words for Musical Effects

a cappella (*adv.* or   (literally, "in chapel or church style") without musical accompaniment, as
adj.) ,ä-kə-'pe-lə   to sing *a cappella,* or to sing in an *a cappella* choir

arpeggio (*n.*)   1. playing of the tones of a chord in rapid succession (rather than at the
är-'pe-jē-ō   same time—the normal method)
    2. chord thus played

legato (*adv.* or *adj.*)   smooth and connected
li-'gä-tō

pizzicato (*adv.* or   by means of plucking the strings instead of using the bow
adj.) ,pit-si-'kä-tō

staccato (*adv.* or *adj.*)   with breaks between successive notes; disconnected; abrupt
stə-'kä-tō

tremolo (*n.*)   rapid ("trembling") repetition of a tone or chord, without apparent breaks,
'tre-mə-,lō   to express emotion

vibrato (*n.*)   slightly throbbing or pulsating effect, adding warmth and beauty to the
vi-'brä-tō   tone

EXERCISE 9.4

In each blank, insert the most appropriate word or expression from group 4.

1. By plucking the strings with the fingers, a violinist achieves a(n) _____ effect.

2. In Tchaikovsky's 1812 OVERTURE, the rapid and prolonged repetition of two tones produces a "trembling," emotion-stirring effect known as _____.

3. Jacqueline Du Pré's flawless _____ style made each note of the cello suite flow smoothly into the next.

4. To play a chord's tones simultaneously is far easier than to play them as a(n) _____.

5. In Schubert's AVE MARIA, the notes are smoothly connected, but in his MARCHE MILITAIRE they are mainly _____.

5. *Words Dealing With Musical Compositions*

aria (*n.*)
'är-ē-ə
air, melody, or tune; especially, an elaborate, accompanied melody for a single voice in an opera

bravura (*n.*)
brə-'vyùr-ə
1. piece of music requiring skill and spirit in the performer
2. display of daring or brilliance

cantata (*n.*)
kən-'tä-tə
composite vocal and instrumental work, as one for soloists and chorus accompanied by a small orchestra

concerto (*n.*)
kən-'cher-tō
long musical composition for one or more principal instruments with orchestral accompaniment

duet (*n.*)
dü-'et
1. piece of music for two voices or instruments
2. two singers or players performing together; duo

finale (*n.*)
fə-'na-lē
close or termination, as the last section of a musical composition

intermezzo (*n.*)
,in-tər-'met-sō
1. short musical or dramatic entertainment between the acts of a play
2. short musical piece either standing as an independent work or coming between the main parts of an extended musical composition

libretto (*n.*)
lə-'bre-tō
text or words of an opera or other long musical composition

opera (*n.*)
'ä-p(ə-)rə
play mostly sung, with costumes, scenery, action, and music

oratorio (*n.*) ˌȯr-ə-'tȯr-ē-ˌō	musical composition, usually on a religious theme, for solo voices, chorus, and orchestra
scherzo (*n.*) 'skert-sō	light or playful part of a sonata or symphony
solo (*n.*) 'sō-lō	1. piece of music for one voice or instrument 2. anything done without a partner
sonata (*n.*) sə-'nä-tə	piece of music (for one or two instruments) having three or four movements in contrasted rhythms but related tonality
trio (*n.*) 'trē-ō	1. piece of music for three voices or instruments 2. three singers or players performing together
tutti (*adv.*) 'tü-tē	all (a direction for all the instruments or voices to perform together)
tutti (*n.*)	section of a musical composition played by all the performers

 **EXERCISE 9.5**

In each blank, insert the most appropriate word from group 5.

1. To excel in _____, one should be gifted both as a singer and as an actor.

2. I'm diffident about doing a solo, but willing to join Ava in a(n) _____.

3. From the opening selection to the _____, we enjoyed the concert thoroughly.

4. Beethoven's EMPEROR is a _____ for piano and orchestra.

5. The trio's encore was a light and playful piece, a(n) _____.

6. Not a single instrument in the orchestra is silent in a passage marked
_____.

6. *Words Dealing With Arts Other Than Music*

cameo (*n.*) 'ka-mē-ˌō	1. gem or medallion cut in relief, the carved figure projecting (standing out) from its background (*ant.* **intaglio**) 2. brief role played by a prominent actor 3. brief piece of brilliant film or writing
campanile (*n.*) ˌkam-pə-'nē-lē	bell tower
canto (*n.*) 'kan-ˌtō	one of the chief divisions of a long poem

chiaroscuro (*n.*)
kē-,är-ə-'skyůr-ō

1. distribution and treatment of light and shade in painting or sketching
2. painting or drawing that uses only light and shade

cupola (*n.*)
'kyü-pə-lə

1. rounded roof; dome
2. small dome or tower on a roof

fresco (*n.*)
'fres-,kō

1. art of painting with watercolors on damp fresh plaster
2. picture or design so painted

intaglio (*n.*)
in-'tal-yō

design engraved by making cuts in a surface, into which the incised figure is sunk (*ant.* **cameo**)

majolica (*n.*)
mə-'jä-li-kə

enameled Italian pottery richly decorated in colors

mezzanine (*n.*)
'me-zᵊn-,ēn

intermediate story in a theater between the main floor and the first balcony

mezzotint (*n.*)
'met-sō-,tint

picture engraved on copper or steel by polishing or scraping away parts of a roughened surface

patina (*n.*)
pə-'tē-nə

film or incrustation, usually green, on the surface of old bronze or copper; any such coating on something old

portico (*n.*)
'pȯr-ti-,kō

roof supported by columns, forming a porch or a covered walk

rialto (*n.*)
rē-'al-tō

1. marketplace
2. theater district

rotunda (*n.*)
rō-'tən-də

1. round building, especially one with a dome or cupola
2. large round room

stucco (*n.*)
'stə-kō

plaster made of cement, sand, and lime for covering exterior walls of buildings

tempera (*n.*)
'tem-pə-rə

method of painting in which the colors are mixed with egg yolk or other substances, instead of oil

terra-cotta (*n.*)
,ter-ə-'kä-tə

1. hard clay used for vases, roofing, statuettes, etc.
2. reddish-brown or brownish-orange color

torso (*n.*)
,tȯr-sō

1. trunk or body of a statue without head, arms, or legs
2. human trunk

 **EXERCISE 9.6**

In each blank, insert the most appropriate word from group 6.

1. The scholars were honored in the library's _____, a large round room.

2. The pin's _____ is a carved dove raised above its gem's surface.

3. Centuries of dampness imperiled the plastered wall and its _____.

4. Only the statue's _____ was unearthed, not its head or limbs.

5. A fine natural _____ encrusted the bronze armor's surface.

6. Painters in _____ commonly mix colors with egg yolk.

7. Read the fifth _____ of Dante's INFERNO for a stirring account of the lovers Paolo and Francesca.

8. A fresh coat of _____ revivified the restaurant's outside walls.

9. The sound of bells came from the _____, the tower next to the church.

10. A welcome _____ kept the rain off us as we went from store to store.

11. Just before curtain time, theatergoers pack the sidewalks of the _____.

7. Words Dealing With Persons

buffo (*n.*)
ʹbü-fō
male singer who plays a comic role in an opera; buffoon; clown

cognoscente (*n.*)
ˌkän-yə-ʹshen-tē
person having a superior knowledge of a field; expert; connoisseur

dilettante (*n.*)
ˌdi-lə-ʹtänt
1. dabbler in an art or other field
2. art lover

diva (*n.*)
ʹdē-və
principal female singer in an opera; prima donna

impresario (*n.*)
ˌim-prə-ʹsär-ē-ˌō
organizer or director of an opera or ballet company or a concert series; manager; promoter

inamorata (*n.*)
i-ˌna-mə-ʹrä-tə
woman that one loves

inamorato (*n.*)
i-ˌna-mə-ʹrä-tō
man that one loves

maestro (*n.*) 'mī-strō	1. eminent conductor, composer, or teacher of music 2. master in an art
mountebank (*n.*) 'maùn-ti-,baŋk	boastful pretender; charlatan; quack
politico (*n.*) pə-'li-ti-,kō	politician
prima donna (*n.*) ,pri-mə-'dä-nə	1. principal female singer in an opera 2. extremely high-strung, vain, or sensitive person
simpatico, m. (*adj.*) sim-'pä-ti-,kō (**simpatica**, f.)	possessing attractive qualities; appealing; likable; congenial
virtuoso (*n.*) ,vər-chü-'ō-sō	one who exhibits great technical skill in an art, especially in playing a musical instrument

 **EXERCISE 9.7**

In each blank, insert the most appropriate word or expression from group 7.

1. The _____ ascended the podium to tumultuous applause, then faced the orchestra.

2. She hopes one day to take up the cello as a serious student rather than as a(n) _____.

3. Bach was famed both as a composer and as a _____ at the organ.

4. Count Flavio sent a St. Valentine's greeting to his _____.

5. The owner is unpleasant to deal with, but the manager is very _____.

6. The concert sold out, thanks to the managerial skills of its _____.

7. The _____ in tonight's opera has won acclaim for his portrayal of comic roles.

8. Words for Situations Involving Persons

dolce far niente (*n.*) 'dōl-chē-,fär-nē-'en-tē	delightful idleness (literally, "sweet doing nothing")
fiasco (*n.*) fē-'as-kō	crash; complete or ridiculous failure
imbroglio (*n.*) im-'brōl-yō	1. difficult situation 2. complicated disagreement

incognito (*adv.*) with one's identity concealed
,in-,käg-'nē-tō

incognito (*n.*) disguised state

vendetta (*n.*) feud for blood revenge
ven-'de-tə

9. Words Dealing With Food

antipasto (*n.*) appetizer consisting of fish, meats, etc.; hors d'oeuvres
,än-tē-'päs-tō

Chianti (*n.*) dry, red Italian wine
kē-'än-tē

gusto (*n.*) liking or taste; hearty enjoyment
'gəs-,tō

pasta (*n.*) 1. paste or dough—used dried, as in macaroni, or fresh, as in ravioli
'päs-tə 2. dish of cooked pasta

pizza (*n.*) pie of flattened dough topped with tomatoes, cheese, etc., and then baked
'pēt-sə

10. Miscellaneous Common Words

alfresco (*adv.* or *adj.*) in the open air; outdoor
al-'fres-kō

bravo (*n.* or *interj.*) shout applauding an excellent performance (The trio won *bravos*. The
'brä-vō (**brava**, f.) actress won *bravas*. The guitarist's fans exclaimed, "*Bravo!*")

gondola (*n.*) 1. boat used in the canals of Venice
'gän-də-lə 2. cabin attached to the underpart of a lighter-than-air aircraft

grotto (*n.*) cave
'grä-tō

piazza (*n.*) 1. town square or open market, esp. in Italy
pē-'ä-zə 2. veranda; porch

portfolio (*n.*) 1. briefcase
pȯrt-'fō-lē-,ō 2. position or duties of a cabinet member or minister of state
  3. collection, as of one's artwork, schoolwork, stocks, or bonds

salvo (*n.*)　　　　1. simultaneous discharge of shots
'sal-vō　　　　　　　2. burst of cheers, as a *salvo* of applause

sotto voce (*adv.* or　　under the breath; in an undertone; privately, as a *sotto voce* remark
adj.) ˌsä-tō-'vō-chē

EXERCISE 9.8

In each blank, insert the most appropriate word or expression from groups 8–10.

1. I updated my _____ to include my best papers from last term.

2. The wineglasses were filled with a _____ from the host's own vineyard.

3. Rumors made a trivial difference of opinion seem a(n) _____.

4. Philip's cold prevented him from eating his dinner with his usual _____.

5. Averse to publicity, the royal couple tried to attend the premiere _____.

6. Cues were missed, and lines were flubbed: the play was a _____.

7. After many sanguinary years, the feuding parties ended their _____.

8. I did not hear what the mother said to the daughter, for they conferred
_____.

9. The inamorata anticipated a nighttime tour of Venice by _____.

10. While in prison, Edmond Dantès learned of an immense fortune concealed in an underground _____ on the island of Monte Cristo.

11. The diva's aria completed, her audience sprang to its feet and shouted,
"_____."

12. We had a delightful _____ lunch at a sidewalk café near the piazza.

Review Exercises

REVIEW 1: MEANINGS

In the space before each word or expression in column I, write the *letter* of its correct meaning from column II. (Exercise continues on next page.)

COLUMN I	COLUMN II
___ **1.** rialto	*a.* trunk
___ **2.** canto	*b.* diva
___ **3.** cognoscente	*c.* promoter

— **4.** grotto   *d.* division

— **5.** buffo   *e.* hors d'oeuvres

— **6.** sforzando   *f.* cave

— **7.** torso   *g.* square

— **8.** antipasto   *h.* connoisseur

— **9.** piazza   *i.* dough

— **10.** impresario   *j.* theater district

— **11.** prima donna   *k.* stressed

— **12.** pasta   *l.* clown

REVIEW 2: SENTENCE COMPLETION

In the space provided, enter the *letter* of the choice that correctly completes the sentence.

— **1.** A(n) _____ choir performs without accompaniment.
   a. a cappella   *b.* cantata

— **2.** Requiring an orchestra, a _____ features a solo instrument such as the piano or violin.
   a. sonata   *b.* concerto

— **3.** When Ulysses returned _____ to his palace, he was recognized by his dog, Argus.
   a. incognito   *b.* falsetto

— **4.** The anchored fleet welcomed the chief of state with a thunderous _____.
   a. salvo   *b.* staccato

— **5.** An impression made from an _____ results in a raised image.
   a. imbroglio   *b.* intaglio

— **6.** The overworked executive longed for the _____ of a Caribbean cruise.
   a. sotto voce   *b.* dolce far niente

— **7.** The orchestra and balcony seats are sold out, but a few _____ tickets are available.
   a. mezzanine   *b.* mezzotint

— **8.** To achieve a smooth and flowing effect, I was advised to play the first two measures _____.
   a. tremolo   *b.* legato

___ 9. For an example of a crescendo from pianissimo all the way to _____, listen to Grieg's IN THE HALL OF THE MOUNTAIN KING.

     a. prestissimo   *b.* fortissimo

___ 10. A _____ sketch achieves its effects principally by its treatment of light and shade.

     a. chiaroscuro   *b.* terra-cotta

REVIEW 3: BRAINTEASERS

Fill in the missing letters.

1. While the spaghetti was boiling, our hostess served a delicious ___ ___ ___ ___ **p a s t** ___.

2. The ___ **r o t** ___ ___ had once been used to store stolen treasure.

3. Have you ever heard of the **v e n d** ___ ___ ___ ___ between the Hatfields and the McCoys?

4. Over the years, a(n) ___ ___ **t i n** ___ had formed on the surface of the copper vessel.

5. Responding to the ___ ___ ___ ___ ___ **e n d** ___ of applause, the violinist returned for an encore.

6. Though exhausted from crying, the child continued to punctuate the silence with occasional ___ ___ ___ ___ **c a t** ___ sobs.

7. The ill-matched challenger's bid ended in a(n) ___ ___ **a s** ___ ___ in the opening seconds of the first round.

8. The **m o u n t** ___ ___ ___ ___ ___ convinced gullible customers that his snake oil would cure their aches and pains.

9. My uncle paints as a(n) ___ ___ ___ ___ ___ **t a n** ___ ___, not as a serious artist.

10. The ___ ___ **h e r** ___ ___ movement of that symphony is light and playful.

REVIEW 4: CONCISE WRITING

Express the thought of each sentence below in no more than four words.

1. The plotters arrived wearing disguises so that they would not be recognized.

_____

2. This is a painting in watercolors that was done on damp fresh plaster.

_____

3. Is the section of the theater between the main floor and the first balcony crowded?

_____

4. They met the person who is doing the organizing and the promoting.

_____

5. We sang without the accompaniment of any musical instrument whatsoever.

_____

6. People respect someone who has a superior knowledge and understanding of a particular field.

_____

7. Play these notes by plucking the strings, instead of using the bow.

_____

8. This is the district in which the theaters of the city are concentrated.

_____

9. Here is a piece of music for two voices or instruments.

_____

10. The conversation that we took part in was conducted in an undertone.

_____

REVIEW 5: COMPOSITION

Answer in two or three sentences.

1. Explain why most people usually eat pizza with gusto.

_____

_____

2. Would a virtuoso enjoy being called a dilettante by a music critic? Explain.

_____

_____

3. Who contributes more to the success of an opera, the composer of the music or the author of the libretto? Explain.

_____

_____

4. Why is an action taken on the advice of a mountebank likely to end in a fiasco?

_____

_____

5. What does a salvo of applause for the prima donna—even before she has sung a single note—tell us about the audience?

_____

_____

REVIEW 6: ANALOGIES

Write the *letter* of the word-pair that best expresses a relationship similar to that existing between the capitalized word-pair.

____   **1.** DESSERT : ANTIPASTO

      a. grave : prestissimo   *d.* play : denouement

      b. basso : soprano   *e.* finale : overture

      c. entrée : hors d'oeuvres

____   **2.** STAR : FILM

      a. composer : sonata   *d.* drama : protagonist

      b. soloist : concerto   *e.* actor : cast

      c. aria : vocalist

____   **3.** COGNOSCENTE : DILETTANTE

      a. uncle : aunt   *d.* ignoramus : connoisseur

      b. professional : amateur   *e.* artist : patron

      c. odor : aroma

____   **4.** INCOGNITO : IDENTITY

      a. novel : pen name   d. fiction : real

      b. masquerade : disguise   *e.* anonymous : known

      c. pseudonym : authorship

____   **5.** TORSO : STATUE

      a. trunk : tree   *d.* atom : nucleus

      b. dismember : intact   *e.* violinist : orchestra

      c. shard : vase

____   **6.** PATINA : AGE

      a. film : camera   *d.* mold : cheese

      b. hair : baldness   *e.* tarnish : silver

      c. blush : embarrassment

___ **7.** LENTO : TEMPO

  a. gondola : canal   *d.* piano : volume

  b. papers : portfolio   *e.* allegro : loudness

  c. Chianti : meal

___ **8.** ROTUNDA : EDIFICE

  a. gondola : canal   *d.* stucco : wall

  b. pizza : dough   *e.* portico : columns

  c. sole : fish

___ **9.** BUFFO : ZANY

  a. entrepreneur : risky   *d.* prevaricator : truthful

  b. mediator : partial   *e.* diplomat : tactless

  c. mentor : knowledgeable

___ **10.** PASTA : NOURISHMENT

  a. uncertainty : rumor   *d.* beverage : thirst

  b. instruction : enlightenment   *e.* ignorance : superstition

  c. shelter : domicile

10

Spanish Words in English

It should not surprise you that English has adopted many Spanish words. For centuries, Spain governed many areas of this continent, including Florida and our vast Southwest. Despite the disintegration of the Spanish Empire, Spanish today is spoken in Mexico, virtually all of Central and South America (except Brazil), the Caribbean, the Philippines, and numerous other regions. As one of the world's principal languages, Spanish continues to exert its influence on English.

1. *Words for Persons*

WORD	MEANING
aficionado (*n.*) ə-,fi-shē-ə-'nä-dō	devoted follower of some sport or art; fan; devotee
caballero (*n.*) ,ka-bə-'ler-ō	1. gentleman; gallant; cavalier 2. horseman
caudillo (*n.*) kaù-'<u>th</u>ē-yō	military dictator in Spanish-speaking countries
Chicano (*n.*) chi-'kä-nō	American of Mexican descent
conquistador (*n.*) kän-'kēs-tə-,dòr	conqueror
desperado (*n.*) ,des-pə-'rä-dō	bold, dangerous criminal

duenna (*n.*)
dü-'e-nə

elderly woman chaperon of a young lady; governess

dulcinea (*n.*)
,dəl-sə-'nē-ə

sweetheart; inamorata (from Dulcinea, Don Quixote's beloved)

gaucho (*n.*)
'gau̇-chō

South American cowboy

grandee (*n.*)
gran-'dē

1. nobleman of the highest rank
2. person of eminence

guerilla (*n.*)
gə-'ri-lə

fighter in an irregular military unit engaging in sabotage and harassment

hidalgo (*n.*)
hi-'dal-gō

member of the minor nobility (well below a *grandee*)

junta (*n.*)
'hu̇n-tə

1. council for legislation or administration
2. group of military officers controlling a government after a coup d'etat
3. junto

junto (*n.*)
'jən-tō

group of persons joined for a common purpose; clique; group of plotters; faction; cabal

Latino, m. (*n.* or *adj.*)
lə-'tē-nō
(**Latina**, f.)

Latin American

macho (*n.* or *adj.*)
'mä-,chō

man exhibiting **machismo** (strong sense of masculinity stressing assertiveness, aggressiveness, physical might, domineering behavior, etc.)

matador (*n.*)
'ma-tə-,dȯr

bullfighter assigned to kill the bull

mestizo (*n.*)
me-'stē-zō

person of mixed American Indian and European ancestry

peon (*n.*)
'pē-,än

1. unskilled worker; landless laborer
2. worker kept in servitude to repay a debt

picador (*n.*)
'pi-kə-,dȯr

rider on horseback in a bullfight who lances the bull to weaken its neck and shoulder muscles

picaro (*n.*)
'pē-kä-,rō
picaresque (*adj.*)

adventurer; rogue; vagabond; wanderer

renegade (*n.*)
're-ni-,gād

traitor; turncoat; deserter; defector; apostate (*ant.* **adherent**)

señor (*n.*)
sān-'yȯr

Spanish or Spanish-speaking man; gentleman; Mr.; Sir

señora (*n.*)   married Spanish or Spanish-speaking woman; lady; Mrs.; Madam
sān-'yȯr-ə

señorita (*n.*)   unmarried Spanish or Spanish-speaking woman; young lady; girl; Miss
ˌsän-yə-'rē-tə

stevedore (*n.*)   one who loads or unloads ships
'stē-və-ˌdȯr

toreador (*n.*)   bullfighter; **torero** (tə-'rer-ō)
'tȯr-ē-ə-ˌdȯr

vaquero (*n.*)   herdsman; cowboy; **buckaroo** (variant of *vaquero*)
vä-'ker-ō

 **EXERCISE 10.1**

In each blank, insert the most appropriate word from group 1.

1. Some Democrats snub their former ally, now a Republican, because they consider him a _____.

2. The payroll on the stagecoach made it likely to be robbed by a(n) _____.

3. A(n) _____ ranks much higher on the scale of nobility than a hidalgo.

4. Unskilled, the newcomer could earn only the wages of a(n) _____.

5. The average fan attends a few games a season, but the _____ goes to many more.

6. Hernando Cortes was the _____ who engineered the conquest of Mexico and destroyed the highly advanced civilization of the Aztecs.

7. The _____ was chaperoned by her duenna.

8. The plot failed; all members of the _____ were arrested.

9. The bull gored the _____ as he was going in for the kill.

10. Mexican Americans are proud of their fellow _____ Cesar Chavez for his contributions to the American labor movement.

11. Some men reveal their _____ attitude by trying to show how tough and aggressive they are.

12. The band played mainly _____ music, like cha-chas, mambos, and sambas.

2. *Words for Warfare and Seafaring*

armada (*n.*)
är-'mä-də
fleet of warships (as the mighty but ill-fated Spanish *Armada*, sent in 1588 against England by Philip II of Spain)

bravado (*n.*)
brə-'vä-dō
pretense of bravery

cargo (*n.*)
'kär-gō
goods transported by a ship, plane, etc.; freight

comradery (*n.*)
'käm-,ra-d(ə-)rē
friendship, rapport, and good will, as among fellow soldiers; camaraderie

El Dorado (*n.*)
,el-də-'rä-dō
fabulously rich land that 16th-century explorers dreamt of; place of fabulous abundance, wealth, or opportunity

embarcadero (*n.*)
em-,bär-kə-'der-ō
landing place; wharf; quay

embargo (*n.*)
im-'bär-gō
prohibition (as when one nation bars its ports to another's ships or bans weapons shipments to another)

escapade (*n.*)
'es-kə-,pād
daring or unconventional act; adventure; caper; prank

flotilla (*n.*)
flō-'ti-lə
small fleet; fleet of small vessels

galleon (*n.*)
'ga-lē-ən
large sailing ship used in war and trade

incommunicado
(*adv.* or *adj.*)
,in-kə-,myü-nə-'kä-dō
deprived of communication with others, as a prisoner held *incommunicado*

key (*n.*)
'kē
low island or reef, often of coral

squad (*n.*)
'skwäd
small military unit; team; small group formed for a joint effort

3. *Words From the "West"*

adobe (*n.*)
ə-'dō-bē
1. brick of sun-dried clay and straw
2. structure made of such bricks

arroyo (*n.*)
ə-'ròi-ō
1. water-carved, often dry, gully
2. brook; creek

bonanza (*n.*)
bə-'nan-zə
1. large and rich mine
2. source yielding an often unexpectedly rich return

bronco (*n.*)
'bräŋ-kō
wild or half-wild horse

burro (*n.*)
'bər-ō
small donkey used as a pack animal

calaboose (*n.*)
'ka-lə-,büs
jail, especially a local one

canyon (*n.*)
'kan-yən
deep narrow valley with steep walls, often with water flowing through it,
as the Colorado River in the *Grand Canyon*; gorge

hacienda (*n.*)
,(h)ä-sē-'en-də
1. large estate or ranch; plantation
2. main house on such an estate

mesa (*n.*)
'mā-sə
flat-topped rocky hill with steep sides

mustang (*n.*)
'məs-,taŋ
bronco

pueblo (*n.*)
'pwe-blō
1. Native American village of southwestern U.S.
2. communal dwelling of adobe or stone in such a village

sierra (*n.*)
sē-'er-ə
mountain range having an irregular or serrated (saw-toothed) outline

sombrero (*n.*)
səm-'brer-ō
broad-rimmed, high-crowned hat of felt or straw

stampede (*n.*)
stam-'pēd
sudden, wild, headlong rush (as of cattle or people)

EXERCISE 10.2

In each blank, insert the most appropriate word from groups 2 and 3.

1. Up the rugged slope, the patient _____ bore its cumbersome load.

2. So many prospectors labored, but so few struck a(n) _____!

3. Secure, the Hopi village sat atop a(n) _____, high above the plain.

4. That house made of _____ has lasted over two hundred years.

5. The bully's defiance was mere _____; he fled before dawn.

6. The weekend after Thanksgiving saw a _____ of shoppers to the malls.

7. By 3:00 P.M., the whole _____ of fishing vessels had returned with the day's catch.

8. The prolonged stress of battle only strengthened the platoon's _____.

9. One _____ in the action film followed another, drawing gasps and laughs.

10. _____s of heavily armed soldiers combed the coral islets for the junta's foes.

11. But these foes were nowhere to be found on the _____s.

12. Having started a brawl, the rowdy cowboys wound up in the _____.

4. Words for Food and Festivity

bodega (*n.*)
bō-'dä-gə

grocery store; wineshop

bolero (*n.*)
bə-'ler-ō

1. Spanish dance with sharp turns, stamping, and sudden pauses with one arm arched over the head; music in 3/4 time for this dance
2. loose waist-length jacket worn open at the front

cabana (*n.*)
kə-'ban-yə

cabinlike shelter at a beach or pool

cafeteria (*n.* or *adj.*)
,ka-fə-'tir-ē-ə

self-service or counter-service restaurant; offering that invites consumers to make varied choices (as an educational *cafeteria* or a *cafeteria* curriculum)

castanets (*n. pl.*)
,kas-tə-'nets

hand instruments clicked together to accompany music or dancing

fiesta (*n.*)
fē-'es-tə

saint's day celebrated with processions and dances; festival; holiday

olla podrida (*n.*)
'ä-lə-pə-'drē-də

highly seasoned meat-and-vegetable stew

patio (*n.*)
'pa-tē-,ō

paved outdoor dining or lounging area adjacent to a house; inner courtyard open to the sky

pimento (*n.*)
or **pimiento**
pə-'men-tō

thick-fleshed pepper used for stuffing olives and as a source of paprika

seviche or **ceviche**
(*n.*) sə-'vē-chā

appetizer of raw fish marinated in lime or lemon juice

siesta (*n.*)
sē-'es-tə

rest or nap, usually after the midday meal

taco (*n.*)   tortilla folded around a filling such as meat, cheese, or lettuce
ˈtä-kō

tortilla (*n.*)   disk of unleavened corn or wheat bread
tȯr-ˈtē-yə

5. Miscellaneous Words

barrio (*n.*)   Spanish-speaking neighborhood
ˈbär-ē-,ō

indigo (*n.*)   blue dye (from the *indigo* plant or chemical synthesis)
ˈin-di-,gō

mañana (*adv.* or *n.*)   tomorrow; (in) the indefinite future
mən-ˈyä-nə

mantilla (*n.*)   1. woman's light scarf worn over the head and shoulders
man-ˈtē-yə   2. short cloak or cape

olio (*n.*)   mixture; hodgepodge; medley; olla podrida
ˈō-lē-,ō

pampa (*n.*)   vast, treeless, grassy plain, especially in Argentina; prairie
ˈpam-pə

peccadillo (*n.*)   slight offense; small fault
,pe-kə-ˈdi-lō

poncho (*n.*)   1. blanketlike cloak with a slit in the middle for the head
ˈpän-chō   2. waterproofed and hooded raincoat of similar shape

temblor (*n.*)   earthquake
ˈtem-blər

 **EXERCISE 10.3**

In each blank, insert the most appropriate word from groups 4–5.

1. The dancers performed the bolero to the accompaniment of clicking
   _____.

2. The blue dye called _____ has been used for more than 3,000 years.

3. Taking a bribe is no _____, but a serious infraction of ethics.

4. Do today's work today; don't put it off to _____.

5. The _____s in Argentina are famous for their cattle, corn, and wheat.

6. The _____ stayed open to oblige evening grocery shoppers.

7. At first, the newly arrived Latino immigrants chose to live in the city's _____.

8. Shall we stay indoors, or would you prefer to sit on the _____?

9. The gaucho's _____ serves as both a blanket and a cloak.

10. My lunch had been filling, the afternoon was hot, and so I lay down for a(n) _____.

11. These _____s are made of cornmeal.

12. There were no plain olives on the shelves, only olives stuffed with _____.

13. The celebrants' singing, dancing, and dazzling costumes enlivened the _____.

Review Exercises

REVIEW 1: MEANINGS

In the space provided, write the *letter* of the word or expression in each group that has the *same meaning* as the italicized word.

___ 1. *duenna*   a. duet   b. junta   c. chaperon   d. twosome   e. fiancé

___ 2. *indigo*   a. hill   b. sugar   c. clay   d. native   e. blue

___ 3. *peccadillo*   a. pepper   b. groundhog   c. alligator   d. petty officer   e. slight offense

___ 4. *olio*   a. grease   b. mixture   c. fuel   d. page   e. noise

___ 5. *macho*   a. reckless   b. domineering   c. excessive   d. roguish   e. eminent

___ 6. *aficionado*   a. zeal   b. connoisseur   c. fan   d. trifler   e. fictional hero

___ 7. *conquistadors*   a. discoverers   b. conquests   c. explorers   d. conquerors   e. bullfighters

___ 8. *renegade*   a. infidel   b. desperado   c. rogue   d. villain   e. turncoat

___ 9. *arroyo*   a. dart   b. gully   c. mesa   d. waterfall   e. bronco

___ 10. *siesta*   a. holiday   b. sojourn   c. fiesta   d. nap   e. sierra

REVIEW 2: SENTENCE COMPLETION

In each blank, enter the *letter* of the choice that best completes the sentence.

___ 1. A section of Fifth Avenue will be closed to traffic tomorrow for a daylong
_____.

   a. siesta   *b.* bonanza   *c.* bolero   *d.* fiesta   *e.* vendetta

___ 2. To maintain anonymity, the leader of the junto employed a _____.

   a. lackey   *b.* grandee   *c.* pseudonym   *d.* poncho   *e.* peon

___ 3. _____ are Argentine cowboys who inhabit the _____.

   a. Gauchos . . pampas   *b.* Caballeros . . mesas   *c.* Desperadoes . . sierras
   d. Vaqueros . . pueblos   *e.* Picaros . . adobes

___ 4. A famous painting by Murillo depicts a smiling señorita looking down from a
window with her mantilla-clad _____ by her side.

   a. protégé   *b.* aficionado   *c.* duenna   *d.* grandee   *e.* fiancé

___ 5. Benedict Arnold was the American _____ whose plot to surrender West Point
resulted in a _____.

   a. patriot . . vendetta   *b.* renegade . . coup d'etat   *c.* grandee . . junto
   d. turncoat . . fiasco   *e.* apostate . . détente

___ 6. One cannot dine alfresco _____.

   a. on the patio   *b.* in the canyon   *c.* on the mesa   *d.* in the hacienda
   e. on the pampa

___ 7. As a rule, a _____ does not offend anyone.

   a. macho   *b.* desperado   *c.* picaro   *d.* caballero   *e.* renegade

___ 8. At the airport, we talked with some Chicanos from _____.

   a. Spain   *b.* Arizona   *c.* Quebec   *d.* Peru   *e.* Portugal

___ 9. The filling of a taco resembles but is not the same as the topping of a(n) _____.

   a. croissant   *b.* aperitif   *c.* pizza   *d.* tortilla   *e.* bonbon

___ 10. When you hear a _____, you are listening to Latino music.

   a. foxtrot   *b.* waltz   *c.* polka   *d.* rumba   *e.* lindy

REVIEW 3: BRAINTEASERS

Fill in the missing letters.

1. A friend of ours has a **c a b** __ __ __ at the beach.

2. Occasionally, a **m a t** __ __ __ __ is gored by an enraged bull.

3. Several customers in the **b o d e** __ __ were waiting to be served.

4. Her face was partly veiled by a(n) __ **a n t** __ __ __ __.

5. How many vessels were there in the __ **l o t** __ __ __ __?

6. When the guests arrived, there was no one at the __ __ __ __ **e n d** __.

7. Reckless driving must not be treated as a(n) __ __ __ __ __ **d i l l** __.

8. There were fewer than a dozen conspirators in the __ **u n t o**.

9. The blouse was pale yellow, and the slacks were deep __ __ **d i g** __.

10. Before dismounting, the __ __ **b a l l** __ __ __ removed his sombrero.

REVIEW 4: CONCISE WRITING

Express the thought of each sentence below in no more than four words.

1. Wear your loose jacket that comes up to the waist and is open at the front.

_____

2. This is an investment that will pay you very rich returns.

_____

3. I took a short nap in the middle of the day.

_____

4. Males who have an exaggerated sense of masculinity often behave in a boastful way.

_____

5. Hector was the bullfighter who was assigned to kill the bull.

_____

6. Elena respected the elderly lady who was acting as her chaperon.

_____

7. They were held without being given an opportunity to get in touch with anyone, or even to make a telephone call.

_____

8. The dancers used hand instruments that they clicked together to accompany the music.

_____

9. Some were wearing tall-crowned hats that had very wide brims.

_____

10. The group of military officers who engineered the coup d'etat and took over the government lacks experience.

_____

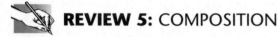

REVIEW 5: COMPOSITION

Answer in two or three sentences.

1. Suppose a security guard is discovered taking a siesta while on duty. Should the matter be treated as a peccadillo? Explain.

_____

_____

2. Why would it be wrongheaded for someone to exhibit his machismo when confronted by armed desperadoes?

_____

_____

3. Why is a fiesta usually a bonanza for local merchants? Explain.

_____

_____

4. Explain why a poncho is extremely valuable not only to a gaucho on the pampa, but to campers and hikers everywhere.

_____

_____

5. Why might the members of a junto hesitate to admit a renegade from a rival party?

_____

_____

REVIEW 6: ANALOGIES

Write the *letter* of the word-pair that best expresses a relationship similar to that existing between the capitalized word-pair.

___ 1. MATADOR : SWORD

    a. gaucho : poncho   d. desperado : loot

    b. picador : lance   e. toreador : bull

    c. torero : horse

___ 2. BONANZA : MINER

    a. legacy : heir   d. jackpot : gambler

    b. crop : farmer   e. bull's-eye : sharpshooter

    c. diploma : student

___ 3. ADOBE : PUEBLO

    a. settlement : Indian   d. seaport : flotilla

    b. cabana : beach   e. concrete : turnpike

    c. terra-cotta : clay

___ 4. OLIO : INGREDIENT

    a. concerto : instrument   d. entrée : dessert

    b. medley : tune   e. aria : opera

    c. potpourri : confusion

___ 5. SIERRA : CANYON

    a. zenith : nadir   d. grandee : hidalgo

    b. arroyo : mesa   e. monarch : retinue

    c. indigo : red

___ 6. MACHO : ASSERTIVE

    a. cognoscente : uninformed   d. renegade : loyal

    b. martinet : inflexible   e. peon : prosperous

    c. dipsomaniac : abstemious

___ 7. PONCHO : RAIN

    a. sombrero : shade   d. taco : nourishment

    b. mentor : guidance   e. parasol : sun

    c. antitoxin : immunity

11

Expanding Vocabulary Through Derivatives

Suppose you have just learned a new word—*ostentatious,* meaning "showy; done to impress others." If you know how to form derivatives, you have in reality expanded your vocabulary not just by one new word but by several words. For the new words you have learned include *ostentatious* and *unostentatious,* *ostentatiously* and *unostentatiously,* and *ostentatiousness* and *unostentatiousness.*

This chapter will help you to get the most out of each new word you learn by teaching you how to form and spell derivatives.

What is a derivative?

A derivative is a word formed by adding a prefix, a suffix, or both a prefix and a suffix, to a word or root.

PREFIX		WORD		DERIVATIVE
re *(again)*	+	apply	=	reapply *(apply again)*

PREFIX		ROOT		DERIVATIVE
e *(out)*	+	ject *(throw)*	=	eject *(throw out)*

WORD		SUFFIX		DERIVATIVE
ostentatious *(showy)*	+	ly *(manner)*	=	ostentatiously *(in a showy manner)*

ROOT		SUFFIX		DERIVATIVE
ten *(held)*	+	able *(capable of being)*	=	tenable *(capable of being held or defended)*

PREFIX		WORD		SUFFIX		DERIVATIVE
un	+	ostentatious	+	ly	=	unostentatiously
(*not*)						(*not in a showy manner*)

PREFIX		ROOT		SUFFIX		DERIVATIVE
un	+	ten	+	able	=	untenable
						(*not capable of being held or defended*)

A review of Chapters 4, 5, and 7 is an excellent way to acquire and maintain a first-rate stockpile of prefixes, roots, and suffixes, the building blocks of derivatives. Review, for example, the five exercises with which Chapter 5 opens.

See how many derivatives you can form using only the prefixes, roots, and suffixes below. Examples are ab + rupt = abrupt, cred + ible = credible, and dis + tort + ion = distortion.

PREFIXES	ROOTS	SUFFIXES
ab	cred, credit	able
ad	flex, flect	ible
con	fract	ion
de	monit	ive
dis	rupt	or, er
e, ex	strict	ory
in	ten, tent	ure
inter	tort	
re	vict	

A score of 75 words or more is excellent, 65–74 very good, 55–64 good, and 45–54 fair.

Terms used in this chapter

A **derivative** may be either a noun, an adjective, a verb, or an adverb.

A **noun** is a word naming a person, place, thing, or quality. In the following sentences, all the italicized words are nouns:

1. The dejected *motorist* very slowly drove his badly damaged *car* to the nearest *garage*.
2. *Health* is *wealth*.

An **adjective** is a word that modifies (describes) a noun or pronoun. The following words in sentence 1 above are adjectives: *dejected, his, damaged, nearest*.

A **verb** is a word that expresses action or a state of being. The verbs in the sentences above are *drove* (sentence 1) and *is* (sentence 2).

An **adverb** is a word that modifies a verb, an adjective, or another adverb. In sentence 1 above, *slowly* is an adverb because it modifies the verb "drove"; *badly* is an adverb because it modifies the adjective "damaged"; and *very* is an adverb because it modifies the adverb "slowly."

Vowels are the letters *a, e, i, o,* and *u.*

Consonants are all the other letters of the alphabet.

Forming Derivatives by Attaching Prefixes and Suffixes

1. Attaching Prefixes

Rule: Do not omit or add a letter when attaching a prefix to a word. Keep *all* the letters of the prefix and *all* the letters of the word.

PREFIX		WORD		DERIVATIVE
dis	+	similar	=	dissimilar
dis	+	organized	=	disorganized
un	+	natural	=	unnatural
un	+	acceptable	=	unacceptable
inter	+	related	=	interrelated
inter	+	action	=	interaction

 **EXERCISE 11.1**

In column III, write the required derivatives. Be sure to spell them correctly.

I. PREFIX		II. WORD		III. DERIVATIVE
1. hypo	+	active	=	_____
2. in	+	opportune	=	_____
3. dis	+	service	=	_____
4. extra	+	ordinary	=	_____
5. dys	+	function	=	_____
6. re	+	entry	=	_____
7. mis	+	shaped	=	_____
8. pre	+	monition	=	_____
9. semi	+	annually	=	_____
10. de	+	emphasis	=	_____

11. mis   +   understood   =   _____

12. re   +   election   =   _____

13. dis   +   embark   =   _____

14. pre   +   eminent   =   _____

15. mis   +   statement   =   _____

16. sub   +   basement   =   _____

17. retro   +   actively   =   _____

18. sub   +   ordinate   =   _____

19. un   +   neighborly   =   _____

20. pre   +   arrange   =   _____

21. in   +   numerable   =   _____

22. re   +   unify   =   _____

23. inter   +   relationship   =   _____

24. un   +   equal   =   _____

25. mis   +   step   =   _____

2. Attaching the Prefix UN or IN

You can give a negative meaning to a word by attaching the prefix UN or IN. Examples:

PREFIX		WORD		DERIVATIVE
un (*not*)	+	remunerative (*gainful*)	=	unremunerative (*not gainful*)
in (*not*)	+	tangible (*capable of being touched*)	=	intangible (*not capable of being touched*)

If you are not sure whether a word takes UN or IN, consult the dictionary. Learn the different forms of IN:

1. Before *l*, IN changes to IL, as in *illegal* and *illiterate*.
2. Before *b, m,* or *p,* IN changes to IM, as in *imbalance, immature,* and *improper.*
3. Before *r,* IN changes to IR, as in *irrational* and *irresistible.*

Three less frequent negative prefixes are DIS, as in *disagreeable*; NON, as in *nonstandard*; and A, as in *atypical.*

EXERCISE 11.2

Form the negative of the word in column II by writing *in, il, im,* or *ir* in column I. Then, complete the new word in column III. The first line has been done for you as a sample.

I. NEGATIVE PREFIX		II. WORD		III. NEGATIVE WORD
1. _*in*_	+	considerate	=	*inconsiderate*
2. _____	+	moral	=	_____
3. _____	+	legibly	=	_____
4. _____	+	redeemable	=	_____
5. _____	+	decisive	=	_____
6. _____	+	patience	=	_____
7. _____	+	regularity	=	_____
8. _____	+	mobility	=	_____
9. _____	+	convenience	=	_____
10. _____	+	practical	=	_____
11. _____	+	eligible	=	_____
12. _____	+	responsibly	=	_____
13. _____	+	mortal	=	_____
14. _____	+	possible	=	_____
15. _____	+	accuracy	=	_____
16. _____	+	logical	=	_____
17. _____	+	revocable	=	_____
18. _____	+	perfection	=	_____
19. _____	+	completely	=	_____
20. _____	+	limitable	=	_____

3. Attaching Suffixes: The Usual Rule

The Usual Rule: When attaching a suffix to a word, do not omit or add a letter. Keep *all* the letters of the word and *all* the letters of the suffix.

WORD		SUFFIX		DERIVATIVE
accidental	+	ly	=	accidentally
drunken	+	ness	=	drunkenness
banjo	+	ist	=	banjoist
ski	+	ing	=	skiing

Sometimes, as you will be seeing, the usual rule does not apply. Exceptions to the usual rule may occur when, for example, the word ends in *y* (as in *heavy*) or in silent *e* (as in *use*).

 EXERCISE 11.3

In column III, write the required derivatives. Be sure to spell them correctly.

I. WORD		II. SUFFIX		III. DERIVATIVE
1. soul	+	less	=	_____
2. ego	+	ism	=	_____
3. evil	+	ly	=	_____
4. solo	+	ist	=	_____
5. echo	+	ing	=	_____
6. barren	+	ness	=	_____
7. convivial	+	ly	=	_____
8. tail	+	less	=	_____
9. Hindu	+	ism	=	_____
10. hero	+	ic	=	_____

4. *Attaching Suffixes to Words Ending in* Y

If the suffix is *ing,* follow the usual rule to form derivatives: just add the *ing* to all the letters of the word ending in *y.*

WORD		SUFFIX		DERIVATIVE
betray	+	ing	=	betraying
hurry	+	ing	=	hurrying
falsify	+	ing	=	falsifying

Also, the usual rule applies to other suffixes with words such as *betray* (ending in a vowel plus *y*).

betray	+	al, er	=	betrayal, betrayer
convey	+	ed, ance	=	conveyed, conveyance
joy	+	ful, ous	=	joyful, joyous

(Exceptions: adding *ly* to *day* gives *daily.* Adding *ed* to *lay, pay,* and *say* gives *laid, paid,* and *said.* And adding *al* to *colloquy* gives *colloquial.*)

However, the usual rule does not apply if a consonant precedes the *y* and if the suffix is not *ing.* Instead, words such as *hurry* (ending in a consonant plus *y*) change the *y* to *i* before adding a suffix.

hurry	+	ed	=	hurried
spicy	+	est	=	spiciest
heavy	+	ness	=	heaviness
greedy	+	ly	=	greedily

(Exceptions: shyly, shyness, dryness, babyish, jellylike.)

Nor does the usual rule apply if the suffix is *ic.* Drop the *y* before adding *ic.*

history	+	ic	=	historic
geography	+	ic	=	geographic
irony	+	ic	=	ironic
lethargy	+	ic	=	lethargic

 **EXERCISE 11.4**

In column III, write the required derivatives. Be sure to spell them correctly.

I. WORD		II. SUFFIX		III. DERIVATIVE
1. pacify	+	ing	=	_____
2. musty	+	ness	=	_____
3. arbitrary	+	ly	=	_____
4. controversy	+	al	=	_____
5. pray	+	ed	=	_____

6. calumny	+	ous	=	_____
7. accompany	+	ment	=	_____
8. vilify	+	ed	=	_____
9. earthy	+	est	=	_____
10. pay	+	less	=	_____
11. worry	+	some	=	_____
12. flay	+	ed	=	_____
13. colloquy	+	al	=	_____
14. vivify	+	ing	=	_____
15. pudgy	+	est	=	_____
16. cursory	+	ly	=	_____
17. paltry	+	ness	=	_____
18. coy	+	ly	=	_____
19. burly	+	er	=	_____
20. ignominy	+	ous	=	_____
21. bloody	+	ly	=	_____
22. mercy	+	less	=	_____
23. refractory	+	ly	=	_____
24. sully	+	ing	=	_____
25. photography	+	ic	=	_____

EXERCISE 11.5

Insert in each line the four missing derivatives. The first line has been completed as a sample.

I. ADJECTIVE	II. ADJECTIVE ENDING IN *ER*	III. ADJECTIVE ENDING IN *EST*	IV. ADVERB	V. NOUN
1. quiet	*quieter*	*quietest*	*quietly*	*quietness*
2. _____	quicker	_____	_____	_____
3. _____	_____	happiest	_____	_____
4. _____	_____	_____	hastily	_____
5. _____	_____	_____	_____	dizziness

6. foxy	_____	_____	_____
7. _____	craftier	_____	_____
8. _____	_____	prettiest	_____
9. _____	_____	_____	readily
10. _____	_____	_____	_____ unsteadiness

5. *Attaching Suffixes to Words Ending in Silent* E

The usual rule applies for words ending in silent *e* when they add a suffix starting with a consonant.

WORD		SUFFIX		DERIVATIVE
excite	+	ment	=	excitement
care	+	ful, less	=	careful, careless
fierce	+	ly, some	=	fiercely, fiercesome
complete	+	ness	=	completeness

(Exceptions: argument, awful, duly, truly, wholly, ninth. The derivative *acknowledgment* has the alternate form *acknowledgement*; *judgment* has the alternative *judgement*; and *abridgment* has the alternative *abridgement*.)

Also, the usual rule applies for words ending in *ce* or *ge* when they add a suffix starting with *a* or *o*.

notice	+	able	=	noticeable
advantage	+	ous	=	advantageous

Similarly formed are *acreage, mileage, singeing, canoeing, hoeing,* and *shoeing*. However, you drop the silent *e* before a suffix starting with a vowel.

desire	+	able	=	desirable
use	+	age	=	usage
produce	+	er	=	producer

 **EXERCISE 11.6**

In column III, write the required derivatives. Be sure to spell them correctly.

I. WORD		II. SUFFIX		III. DERIVATIVE
1. prosecute	+	or	=	_____
2. eulogize	+	ing	=	_____
3. induce	+	ment	=	_____
4. mature	+	ity	=	_____
5. blithe	+	ly	=	_____

6. contaminate	+	ion	=	_____
7. revive	+	al	=	_____
8. judge	+	ment	=	_____
9. avarice	+	ious	=	_____
10. remorse	+	ful	=	_____
11. convalesce	+	ent	=	_____
12. rationalize	+	ed	=	_____
13. cursive	+	ly	=	_____
14. versatile	+	ity	=	_____
15. consecutive	+	ly	=	_____
16. expedite	+	er	=	_____
17. dispute	+	able	=	_____
18. undulate	+	ion	=	_____
19. courage	+	ous	=	_____
20. nine	+	ty	=	_____
21. belittle	+	ing	=	_____
22. acre	+	age	=	_____
23. abridge	+	ment	=	_____
24. service	+	able	=	_____
25. naive	+	ly	=	_____

6. *Attaching the Suffix* LY

You can change an adjective into an adverb by adding the suffix LY.

ADJECTIVE		SUFFIX		ADVERB
brave	+	ly	=	bravely
calm	+	ly	=	calmly

However, if an adjective ends in *ic,* add *al* before attaching the suffix LY.

heroic	+	al	+	ly	=	heroically
specific	+	al	+	ly	=	specifically
euphemistic	+	al	+	ly	=	euphemistically

Note that the adjective *public* has alternative adverbial forms: *publicly* and *publically.* Also note that most adjectives ending in *ic* have an alternative adjectival form ending in *ical.* One example is *philosophic* and *philosophical.* Another is *historic* and *historical.*

 **EXERCISE 11.7**

Change the following adjectives to adverbs:

ADJECTIVE   ADVERB

1. fraternal   _____

2. diabolic   _____

3. solemn   _____

4. scientific   _____

5. fallacious   _____

6. nostalgic   _____

7. grave   _____

8. public   _____

9. partial   _____

10. hermetic   _____

 **EXERCISE 11.8**

For each noun in column I, write an adjective ending in *ic* in column II, and an adverb in column III. The first line has been completed as a sample.

I. NOUN	II. ADJECTIVE	III. ADVERB
1. biology	*biologic*	*biologically*
2. geology	_____	_____
3. hero	_____	_____
4. sociology	_____	_____
5. idealist	_____	_____
6. patriot	_____	_____
7. philanthropy	_____	_____
8. geometry	_____	_____
9. economy	_____	_____
10. biography	_____	_____
11. egoist	_____	_____
12. psychology	_____	_____

13. meteorology   _____   _____

14. microbiology   _____   _____

15. socialist   _____   _____

16. technology   _____   _____

17. realist   _____   _____

18. despot   _____   _____

19. autobiography   _____   _____

20. physiology   _____   _____

7. Attaching Suffixes to Monosyllables Ending in a Consonant

Examples of monosyllables (words of one syllable) ending in a consonant are *dash, diet,* and *dub.*

A word such as *dash* (a monosyllable ending in *two* consonants) follows the usual rule to form derivatives with suffixes: just add the letters of the suffix to the letters of the words.

WORD		SUFFIX		DERIVATIVE
dash	+	ed, ing	=	dashed, dashing
halt	+	ed, ing	=	halted, halting
ask	+	ed, ing	=	asked, asking

Also, a word such as *diet* (a monosyllable ending in *two vowels* plus a consonant) follows the usual rule.

diet	+	ed, ing, er, ary	=	dieted, dieting, dieter, dietary
sail	+	ed, ing, or	=	sailed, sailing, sailor
kneel	+	ed, ing	=	kneeled, kneeling

However, a word such as *dub* (a monosyllable ending in *just one vowel* plus a consonant) *DOUBLES* the consonant if the suffix starts with a vowel.

dub	+	ing, ed	=	dubbing, dubbed
run	+	ing, er	=	running, runner
stop	+	ed, age	=	stopped, stoppage
wet	+	er, est	=	wetter, wettest

(The *t* is NOT doubled in *wetness*, as the suffix does NOT start with a vowel!)

8. *Attaching Suffixes to Polysyllables Ending in a Consonant*

Examples of polysyllables (words of two or more syllables) ending in a consonant are *deduct, detain,* and *defer.*

A word such as *deduct* (a polysyllable ending in *two* consonants) follows the usual rule to form derivatives with suffixes: just add the letters of the suffix to the letters of the word.

WORD		SUFFIX		DERIVATIVE
deduct	+	ed, ing, ible	=	deducted, deducting, deductible
condemn	+	ed, ing, able	=	condemned, condemning, condemnable
conduct	+	ed, ing, or	=	conducted, conducting, conductor

Also, a word such as *detain* (a polysyllable ending in *two vowels* plus a consonant) follows the usual rule.

detain	+	ed, ee, ment	=	detained, detainee, detainment
recoil	+	ed, ing	=	recoiled, recoiling
appeal	+	ed, ing	=	appealed, appealing
contain	+	ed, ing, er	=	contained, containing, container

In addition, a word such as *defer* (a polysyllable ending in *just one vowel* plus a consonant) follows the usual rule if, in the *derivative,* the *fer* is *not* stressed.

For example, in *defer* just by itself, the *fer* is stressed: *deFER.* But the derivative *deference* does *not* stress the *fer: DEFerence.* Thus, *defer* follows the usual rule in forming *deference.*

The derivatives *reference, inference, offered, offering,* and *offerer* are formed the same way, as the following table shows. So, too, are the derivatives of *credit* and *limit* in this table. These derivatives do *not* stress the *it* (the last syllable of *credit* and *limit*), which plays the role of *fer.*

deFER	+	ence	=	DEFerence
reFER	+	ence	=	REFerence
inFER	+	ence	=	INference
OFfer	+	ed, ing, er	=	OFfered, OFfering, OFferer
CREDit	+	ed, ing, or	=	CREDited, CREDiting, CREDitor
LIMit	+	ed, ing, less	=	LIMited, LIMiting, LIMitless

However, some derivatives of *defer*—and of other polysyllables ending in *just one vowel* plus a consonant—DOUBLE this consonant. DOUBLING occurs if the suffix starts with a vowel and if, in the *derivative,* the *fer* (the original word's last syllable) *is* stressed.

For example, in pronouncing *defer* just by itself, you of course stress the *fer* (the last syllable): *deFER.* If you now add a suffix that starts with a vowel, say *al,* the derivative *deferral* results. *Deferral* doubles the *r* because, in pronouncing this derivative, you stress *defer*'s last syllable: *deFERral.* (The *r* is NOT doubled in *deFERment,* as the suffix does NOT start with a vowel!)

deFER	+	ed, ing, al	=	deFERred, deFERring, deFERral
reFER	+	ed, ing	=	reFERred, reFERring
transMIT	+	ed, ing, er	=	transMITted, transMITting, transMITter
readMIT	+	ed, ing, ance	=	readMITted, readMITting, readMITtance

(Exceptions:

exCEL	+	ence, ent	=	EXcellence, EXcellent.)

In sum, the derivatives in Sections 7 and 8 follow the usual rule, but sometimes double a consonant before the suffix. To firm up your grasp of these two sections, take a moment now to review the guidelines for spelling the following derivatives of *dub* and *defer*.

dubbing	dubbed			
deferring	deferral	deferred	deferment	deference

 **EXERCISE 11.9**

In column III, write the required derivatives. Be sure to spell them correctly.

I. WORD		II. SUFFIX		III. DERIVATIVE
1. dispel	+	ing	=	_____
2. occur	+	ence	=	_____
3. accredit	+	ed	=	_____
4. acquit	+	al	=	_____
5. differ	+	ed	=	_____
6. beget	+	ing	=	_____
7. slip	+	ed	=	_____
8. hot	+	est	=	_____
9. suffer	+	ing	=	_____
10. regret	+	able	=	_____
11. confer	+	ence	=	_____
12. excel	+	ing	=	_____
13. gallop	+	ing	=	_____
14. stoop	+	ing	=	_____
15. defer	+	al	=	_____
16. excel	+	ent	=	_____
17. propel	+	er	=	_____
18. inject	+	ed	=	_____

19. commit	+	ee	=	_____
20. libel	+	ous	=	_____
21. fat	+	er	=	_____
22. equip	+	ing	=	_____
23. permit	+	ed	=	_____
24. repel	+	ent	=	_____

 EXERCISE 11.10

For each word at the left, complete the four derivatives indicated.

1. concur	_____ing	_____ed	_____ent	_____ence
2. defer	_____ing	_____ed	_____able	_____ence
3. retain	_____ing	_____ed	_____able	_____er
4. rebel	_____ing	_____ed	_____ious	_____ion
5. prefer	_____ing	_____ed	_____able	_____ence
6. ship	_____ing	_____ed	_____er	_____ment
7. differ	_____ing	_____ed	_____ent	_____ence
8. control	_____ing	_____ed	_____able	_____er
9. commit	_____ing	_____ed	_____ee	_____ment
10. excel	_____ing	_____ed	_____ent	_____ence

9. Troublesome Suffixes

Words ending in such troublesome suffixes as (1) *able* or *ible*, (2) *er* or *or*, and (3) *ant* or *ent* have to be studied individually. Develop the habit of consulting the dictionary when in doubt about which suffix is right.

(1) Adding *able* or *ible*. Study the following adjectives.

ABLE	IBLE
demonstrable	credible
impregnable	fallible
indisputable	flexible
memorable	illegible
navigable	incontrovertible
returnable	invincible

serviceable	plausible
tenable	reprehensible
unmanageable	resistible

Note: Adjectives ending in *able* become nouns ending in *ability*. Adjectives ending in *ible* become nouns ending in *ibility*.

ADJECTIVE	NOUN	ADJECTIVE	NOUN
impregnable	impregnability	flexible	flexibility
venerable	venerability	invincible	invincibility

(2) Adding *er* or *or*. Study the following nouns.

ER	OR
consumer	aggressor
defender	censor
foreigner	contributor
mariner	creditor
observer	debtor
philosopher	governor
producer	originator
reporter	possessor
subscriber	progenitor
sympathizer	speculator

Note: Verbs ending in *ate* usually become nouns ending in *or,* rather than *er.*

VERB	NOUN
demonstrate	demonstrator
liberate	liberator

(Exception: debate, debater.)

(3) Adding *ant* or *ent*. Study the following adjectives.

ANT	ENT
brilliant	complacent
buoyant	decent
flamboyant	eloquent
flippant	eminent
fragrant	iridescent
malignant	obsolescent
nonchalant	pertinent
poignant	potent
relevant	recurrent
vacant	repellent

Note: Adjectives ending in *ant* become nouns ending in *ance* or *ancy*. Adjectives ending in *ent* become nouns ending in *ence* or *ency*.

ADJECTIVE	NOUN	ADJECTIVE	NOUN
nonchalant	nonchalance	eloquent	eloquence
vacant	vacancy	decent	decency
brilliant	brilliance, brilliancy	complacent	complacence, complacency

EXERCISE 11.11

Fill in the missing letter.

1. IRRESIST ___ BLE

2. MALIGN ___ NCY

3. EXCELL ___ NCE

4. DEBT ___ R

5. OMNIPOT ___ NT

6. INCRED ___ BLE

7. CONSUM ___ R

8. LEG ___ BILITY

9. UNNAVIG ___ BLE

10. SPECULAT ___ R

11. FLEX ___ BILITY

12. VAC ___ NCY

13. INFLEX ___ BLE

14. OBSOLESC ___ NCE

15. SERVICE ___ BILITY

16. SUBSCRIB ___ R

17. IMPERTIN ___ NCE

18. DISPUT ___ BLE

19. POIGN ___ NCY

20. IRRELEV ___ NT

EXERCISE 11.12

For each noun, write the corresponding adjective. The first adjective has been filled in as a sample.

NOUN	ADJECTIVE
1. infrequency	*infrequent*
2. resistance	
3. visibility	

4. urgency   _____

5. dependability   _____

6. defiance   _____

7. negligence   _____

8. constancy   _____

9. unpredictability   _____

10. stringency   _____

11. self-reliance   _____

12. comprehensibility   _____

13. convalescence   _____

14. contingency   _____

15. diffidence   _____

16. preeminence   _____

17. hesitancy   _____

18. intangibility   _____

19. incompetence   _____

20. adolescence   _____

Review Exercises

 **REVIEW 1**

Insert in each line the two missing derivatives. The first line has been completed as a sample.

I. VERB	II. NOUN ENDING IN *ER* OR *OR*	III. NOUN ENDING IN *ION*
1. create	*creator*	*creation*
2. _____	_____	production
3. _____	elector	_____
4. possess	_____	_____
5. _____	_____	subscription
6. _____	promoter	_____
7. indicate	_____	_____

8. _____   _____   contribution

9. _____   liberator

10. violate   _____   _____

 **REVIEW 2**

Insert in each line the two missing derivatives. The first line has been completed as a sample.

I. NOUN	II. ADJECTIVE	III. ADVERB
1. apathy	*apathetic*	*apathetically*
2. _____	vivid	_____
3. _____	_____	monotonously
4. fraternity	_____	_____
5. _____	hypersensitive	_____
6. _____	_____	lethargically
7. maladroitness	_____	_____
8. _____	weary	_____
9. _____	_____	controversially
10. euphemism	_____	_____
11. _____	pathetic	_____
12. _____	_____	eloquently
13. naiveté	_____	_____
14. _____	peripheral	_____
15. _____	_____	sheepishly
16. quarrelsomeness	_____	_____
17. _____	hypothetical	_____
18. _____	_____	avariciously
19. homogeneity	_____	_____
20. _____	heterogeneous	_____

 **REVIEW 3**

Insert in each set the five missing derivatives. The first set has been completed as a sample.

ADJECTIVE AND OPPOSITE	ADVERB AND OPPOSITE	NOUN AND OPPOSITE
1. moral	*morally*	*morality*
immoral	*immorally*	*immorality*
2. _____	_____	_____
intemperate	_____	_____
3. _____	comprehensibly	_____
_____	_____	_____
4. _____	_____	_____
_____	dissimilarly	_____
5. _____	_____	fallibility
_____	_____	_____
6. _____	_____	_____
_____	_____	unostentatiousness
7. flexible	_____	_____
_____	_____	_____
8. _____	_____	_____
abnormal	_____	_____
9. _____	plausibly	_____
_____	_____	_____
10. _____	_____	_____
_____	incontrovertibly	_____
11. _____	_____	pertinence
_____	_____	_____
12. _____	_____	_____
_____	_____	untenability

13. rational   _____   _____

_____   _____   _____

14. _____   _____   _____

incredible   _____   _____

15. _____   mortally   _____

_____   _____   _____

16. _____   _____   _____

_____   unconventionally   _____

17. _____   _____   retentiveness

_____   _____   _____

18. _____   _____   _____

_____   _____   irrelevance

Vocabulary Questions on Pre-College Tests

Your study of Chapters 2–11 has earned you an enhanced stock of words and a good deal of experience in determining the meanings of words, not only from their contexts but also from their components (prefixes, roots, and suffixes). You will find these two assets valuable for success in college and in your profession. Also—as the rest of Chapter 12 suggests—you will find the same two assets helpful on examinations that many colleges use for admission, placement, and scholarship decisions. Examples of such examinations are the SAT I and ACT Assessment.*

To give you an overview of the ways pre-college examinations currently test vocabulary, here is a brief look at three common types of vocabulary questions.

■ Type 1: The Analogy Question (SAT I)
■ Type 2: The Sentence-Completion Question (SAT I)
■ Type 3: The *As-Used-In* Question (SAT I and ACT Reading Test)

---

*Intensive-study guides devoted exclusively to pre-college tests include the following Amsco publications: *Amsco's Preparing for the SAT I Reasoning Test—Verbal*, Henry I. Christ and *Amsco's Preparing for the ACT: English & Reading*, Robert D. Postman. Web sites for the SAT I and ACT Assessment are www.collegeboard.com and www.act.org. Both the College Board and the American College Testing Program distribute free booklets that include a complete sample of their respective examinations.

1. The Analogy Question (SAT I)

The first type of vocabulary question asks you how two words are related. Thus, in an Analogy Question on the SAT I (as it now stands), you are given one capitalized word-pair followed by five lowercase word-pairs, choices (A)-(E). To show that you understand how the words in the capitalized pair are related, you are to choose the lowercase pair whose words are related the same way. An example follows.

VORACIOUS : APPETITE
(A) illiterate : health
(B) euphoric : ennui
(C) flimsiness : disrepair
(D) keyboard : piano
(E) gullible : mind

You proceed as in "Analogies" Exercises 3.7 and 3.14 (Chapter 3, pages 56 and 68). Let the first capitalized word, VORACIOUS, be X, and the second word, APPETITE, be Y. You can then express the VORACIOUS : APPETITE relationship as "X describes a person's Y."

Next, check if this relationship for the capitalized word-pair holds for any of the lowercase word-pairs, choices (A), (B), (C), (D), and (E). Here's how you might analyze each lowercase word-pair.

(A) illiterate : health

In word-pair (A), *illiterate* is X, and *health* is Y. X does NOT describe a person's Y. Because the relationship for the capitalized pair does NOT also hold for the lowercase pair in choice (A), you rule (A) out. Note that "X describes a person's Y" would hold if choice (A) were instead *excellent : health*.

(B) euphoric : ennui

In word-pair (B), *euphoric* is X, and *ennui* is Y. X does NOT describe a person's Y. Rather, the relationship is that "X describes a feeling contrary to Y." So, you rule out choice (B). Note that "X describes a person's Y" would hold if choice (B) were instead *euphoric : mood*.

(C) flimsiness : disrepair

In word-pair (C), *flimsiness* is X, and *disrepair* is Y. X does NOT describe a person's Y. The relationship is "X causes Y." (Or "Y results from X.") So, you rule out choice (C).

(D) keyboard : piano

In word-pair (D), *keyboard* is X, and *piano* is Y. X does NOT describe a person's Y. The relationship is "X is a part of Y." (Or "Y contains X.") So, you rule out choice (D).

(E) gullible : mind

In word-pair (E), *gullible* is X, and *mind* is Y. "X describes a person's Y" holds BOTH for the capitalized pair AND for the lowercase pair of choice (E), making (E) your answer.

As you might expect, the above Analogy Question, and the two other types of questions also to be described, incorporate college-level vocabulary, which underscores the value of the enhanced word stock you have been acquiring. For example, in the above question, *euphoria* and *ennui* are studied in Chapters 4 and 8. Also, *gullible* and *voracious* are studied in Chapters 2 and 5. Further, the Latin prefixes *il* and *dis* of *illiterate* and *disrepair* are studied in Chapter 5.

Review the explanatory text at the start of "Analogies" Exercises 3.7 and 3.14. Then, hone your skills on these sets of questions.

Chapter	Review or Exercise	Starting on Page	Number of Type 1 Items
3	7	56	5
3	21	79	5
3	35	102	5
6	6	213	10
9	R6	270	10
10	R6	283	7

Also relevant are the following "Analogies" Exercises or Reviews: 3.14 (p. 68), 3.28 (p. 91), R7 (p. 122), R14 (p. 142), R9 (p. 176), R18 (p. 199), 7.4 (p. 225), and R11 (p. 255). Then try **Practice Test I: Analogies**, pp. 309–310.

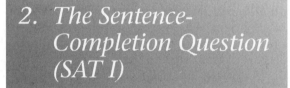

2. The Sentence-Completion Question (SAT I)

The second type of vocabulary question asks you how to fill in a text's blanks. Thus, in a Sentence-Completion Question on the SAT I, you are given a sentence with one or more blanks. Each blank stands for an omitted word (or set of words). You are also given five choices of ways to fill in the blanks. An example follows.

Violence—one way the oppressed react to their oppressors—is impractical, argues Dr. King, because it is self-defeating: its _____ of "bitterness in the survivors and brutality in the destroyers" helps make "brotherhood impossible," its "legacy" to future generations is "meaningless chaos," and its aftermath clutters history with "the wreckage of nations."
(A) retribution
(B) remission
(C) residue
(D) retinue
(E) repertoire

Let X be the word that best fills this blank. (Think of X as if it were one of those many "new words" whose meanings you derived from context clues in Chapter 2.) Here, words similar in meaning to X provide clues to it.

The words *legacy*, *aftermath*, and *clutters* are such clues. They suggest that X means something passed on, something left behind, or something remaining. Choice (C), *residue* (studied in Chapter 2) has this meaning.

Here is an example of the type of question that asks you to choose a set of words to complete the sentence correctly:

As video games become more and more _____, the players become more and more _____ in their search for new challenges.
(A) sophisticated . . discriminating
(B) garish . . alert
(C) metallic . . vigorous
(D) alike . . embarrassed
(E) timely . . defiant

Let X and Y be the two words that will best complete this sentence. Remember that *both* words in your choice must fit. For instance, the players may become more alert (B) or vigorous (C) in their search, but the pair words "garish" and "metallic" don't fit. It is doubtful that the players are either "defiant" or "embarrassed." This leaves choice (A), which makes sense in the context of the sentence.

For additional practice with these types of vocabulary questions, begin by reviewing the four Pretests of Chapter 2 ("Contexts with Contrasting Words," pp. 5–7; "Contexts with Similar Words," pp. 15–17; "Common-sense Contexts," pp. 24–26; and "Mixed Contexts," pp. 33–35.

Then, go on to tackle some of VCB's abundant sets of questions that ask you to complete sentences. Here are a few suggestions.

Chapter	Review or Exercise	Starting on Page	Number of Type 2 Items
2	26	43	5
3	5	54	10
3	11	66	5
3	37	104	5
4	R3	119	10
5	R3	171	10
6	2	210	10
7	5	226	10
8	R2	241	12
9	R2	267	10
10	R2	280	10

When you have finished the reviews and feel you are ready to test yourself, take **Practice Test II: Sentence Completion**, found on pp. 311–312.

3. The As-Used-In Question (SAT I and ACT Reading Test)

The third type of vocabulary question asks you how a context uses a word (or set of words). Thus, in "Critical Reading" on the SAT I and in the "Reading Test" on the ACT Assessment, you are given a context of many sentences; commonly, they fill a half column to two columns on a two-column page. This multi-sentence context is the basis for about ten reading-comprehension questions, each with four or five choices.

One or more of these questions specifically focuses on vocabulary: what is the meaning of a word (or a set of words) *as it is used in* the context? You answer this question by matching this meaning with the meaning of one of the choices.

An example follows (based on a brief text taken from George Orwell's *Animal Farm*).

1 Rumours of a wonderful farm, where
2 the human beings had been turned out
3 and the animals managed their own
4 affairs, continued to circulate in vague
5 and distorted forms, and throughout
6 that year a wave of rebelliousness ran
7 through the countryside. Bulls which
8 had always been tractable suddenly
9 turned savage, sheep broke down fences
10 and devoured the clover, cows kicked
11 the pail over, hunters refused their
12 fences and shot their riders on to the
13 other side.

As used in line 8, of this passage, *tractable* most nearly means:
(A) easily controlled
(B) aggressive
(C) abrupt
(D) unruly

Let X be *tractable*, and infer its meaning as in Chapter 2's Pretest 1, pp. 5–7, "Contexts With Contrasting Words."

One context clue is the word *savage*. It contrasts with *tractable* because the bulls *suddenly turned savage*, which suggests that they had previously been the opposite of *savage*. Of the four choices, (A), *easily controlled*, comes closest to being the opposite of *savage* and so is the closest match to *tractable*. On the other hand, choices (B) and (D), *aggressive* and *unruly*, are **similar** in meaning to *savage*. Choice (C), *abrupt*, refers not so much to *savage* but to the rapid change in the bulls' conduct, which changed *suddenly*.

Another context clue is *rebelliousness* (line 6). It states the theme for the next sentence: how bulls, sheep, cows, and hunters rebelled, how they abruptly turned from serving humans to defying humans. Again, choice (A), *easily controlled*, is consistent with—matches—the behavior of the bulls before their revolt.

Here are two more challenges based on Orwell's passage.

Suppose that choice (B) is now *flexible* (instead of *aggressive*). Would choice (A) still be better than choice (B)? (Suggestion: make sure to check your dictionary's definitions of *tractable* and *flexible*.)

Second, try your hand at inferring the meaning of another word in the above passage. (Suggestion: review Chapter 2's Pretest 3, "Commonsense Contexts," pp. 24–26, and check your dictionary's definition of *hunter*.)

As used in line 11 of Orwell's passage, *hunters* most nearly means:

(A) persons who hunt
(B) dogs trained for hunting
(C) horses trained for hunting
(D) predatory fauna

Pretests 2, 3 and 4 in Chapter 2 will give you some practice determining meanings from context. In addition, review exercises 2.27, 3.38, 4.16, and 5.20.

When you have finished reviewing and feel you are ready to test yourself, take **Practice Test III: As Used In** on pp. 313–315.

Practice Test I: Analogies

The following questions are taken from *Amsco's Preparing for the SAT I* by Henry I. Christ (Amsco, 2002).

Directions: Write the letter for the word pair that best completes each analogy. Remember to think about the relationship between the two UPPERCASE words. Choose the answer that comes closest to expressing the same relationship.

____ 1. STRAIGHTFORWARD : LIAR ::

    (A) brilliant : genius

    (B) dreary : onlooker

    (C) popular : outcast

    (D) generous : friend

    (E) sympathetic : artisan

____ 2. IMMEDIATELY : DELAY ::

    (A) voluntarily : motive

    (B) urgently : aid

    (C) continuously : effort

    (D) flawlessly : error

    (E) accidentally : injury

____ 3. STRUT : OSTENTATIOUS ::

    (A) vacillate : modest

    (B) cringe : servile

    (C) flinch : indolent

    (D) waver : arrogant

    (E) sputter : fastidious

____ 4. ADORN : EXAGGERATE ::

    (A) empower : diminish

    (B) replenish : reaffirm

    (C) furbish : absorb

    (D) soak : saturate

    (E) crochet : create

____ 5. HUB : WHEEL ::

    (A) diameter : circle

    (B) apex : triangle

    (C) eye : hurricane

    (D) clasp : tie

    (E) top : desk

____ 6. WINCE : PAIN ::

    (A) forget : confidence

    (B) tremble : fright

    (C) grovel : embarrassment

    (D) glower : anguish

    (E) growl : delight

____ 7. VALUABLES : SAFE ::

    (A) jewelry : gemstone

    (B) water : droplet

    (C) dessert : dish

    (D) corn : granary

    (E) fish : ocean

____ 8. RACKET : TENNIS ::

    (A) puck : hockey

    (B) rifle : duck

    (C) hammer : nail

    (D) ball : soccer

    (E) bat : baseball

____ 9. RIPPLE : TIDAL WAVE ::

    (A) breeze : hurricane

    (B) blizzard : avalanche

    (C) valley : earthquake

    (D) puddle : downpour

    (E) rock : waterfall

___ **10.** MILL : PENNY ::

(A) silver : quarter

(B) currency : nickel

(C) dime : dollar

(D) check : cash

(E) wallet : money

___ **11.** TALK : WHISPER ::

(A) discover : deteriorate

(B) fly : tour

(C) listen : disagree

(D) walk : amble

(E) jump : marvel

___ **12.** WEAVE : CLOTH ::

(A) destroy : barricade

(B) write : narrative

(C) call : messenger

(D) droop : trees

(E) reduce : statue

___ **13.** ELECT : INAUGURATION ::

(A) attempt : oblivion

(B) grow : uncertainty

(C) drill : hole

(D) climb : tree

(E) success : study

___ **14.** MAGICIAN : DELUDES ::

(A) potentate : obeys

(B) swimmer : relaxes

(C) comedian : entertains

(D) welder : rivets

(E) acrobat : complains

___ **15.** DEPOSED : RULER ::

(A) checkmated : chess player

(B) watchdog : bark

(C) employee : discharged

(D) manuscript : writer

(E) surgeon : operates

Practice Test II: Sentence Completion

The following questions are taken from *Amsco's Preparing for the SAT I* by Henry I. Christ (Amsco, 2002).

Directions: Choose the letter of the word or set of words that best completes each sentence.

____ 1. The ex-champion's muscles became _____ from lack of exercise.

(A) delicate

(B) flabby

(C) flimsy

(D) limp

(E) loose

____ 2. The characters in this novel are _____ and bear no intentional resemblance to actual people.

(A) fabulous

(B) mythical

(C) legendary

(D) imagined

(E) fictitious

____ 3. The owner was unreasonable because he expected nothing short of _____ in his employees.

(A) merit

(B) excellence

(C) virtue

(D) quality

(E) perfection

____ 4. Some wrinkle-free fabrics are made of _____ fibers.

(A) fake

(B) phony

(C) unreal

(D) synthetic

(E) counterfeit

____ 5. Homeowners must _____ their property from theft.

(A) barricade

(B) militarize

(C) arm

(D) protect

(E) isolate

____ 6. Yvonne's _____ athletic ability almost guarantees her success as a tennis player.

(A) insufficient

(B) inbred

(C) internal

(D) ingrained

(E) indispensable

____ 7. Andy Warhol, commenting upon the _____ nature of fame, once said that everyone can be a celebrity for fifteen minutes.

(A) indomitable

(B) repetitive

(C) dormant

(D) fanatical

(E) transient

___ 8. In an Agatha Christie mystery, Miss Marple early on suspected the identity of the murderer, but her proof was _____.

(A) invulnerable

(B) inconclusive

(C) fallacious

(D) uninspiring

(E) unintelligible

___ 9. Harold is able to hold two divergent points of view at the same time without realizing their _____.

(A) incomprehensibility

(B) spontaneity

(C) variability

(D) incompatibility

(E) symmetricality

___ 10. Thor Heyerdahl, on the *Ra* papyrus boat, discovered floating _____ of oil in the mid-Atlantic, pointing to the continuing _____ of the seas.

(A) cans . . commerce

(B) mounds . . beautification

(C) globs . . pollution

(D) glimpses . . mining

(E) tankers . . revival

___ 11. Settlers from the Northeast sometimes find it difficult to _____ themselves to the low humidity and _____ beauty of the American Southwest.

(A) transport . . luxurious

(B) invite . . unexpected

(C) adjust . . dank

(D) will . . contrary

(E) acclimate . . austere

___ 12. Mike McElroy, eminent scientist and _____ professor of chemistry at Harvard, has _____ interests that carry him from the atmosphere of planets to the origins of life.

(A) dapper . . planetary

(B) prestigious . . wide-ranging

(C) retiring . . enjoyable

(D) emaciated . . biased

(E) susceptible . . meager

___ 13. Charles made a _____ bid to mend the broken relationship, but Laura _____ refused to open his letter.

(A) hopeless . . cheerfully

(B) tentative . . disdainfully

(C) lighthearted . . resentfully

(D) fanatical . . casually

(E) pointless . . modestly

___ 14. A Washington group teaches children how to _____ with handicapped children by working with puppets that show various kinds of physical _____.

(A) converse . . activities

(B) compete . . variations

(C) walk . . characteristics

(D) win . . aids

(E) interact . . disability

___ 15. Nature films on television frequently inject a powerful plea for regulations limiting the _____ of natural areas and the inevitable _____ of wildlife.

(A) closure . . hunting

(B) opening . . improvement

(C) depiction . . expansion

(D) exploitation . . destruction

(E) mapping . . census

Practice Test III: As Used In

The following vocabulary questions are based on passages found in *Amsco's Preparing for the ACT English and Reading* by Robert D. Postman (Amsco, 1999).

___ 1. Across the United States, the teaching of multiculturalism became an educational priority in the 1990s.

As used in this sentence, *priority* means

(A) preference

(B) advantage

(C) main concern

(D) principle

(E) problem

___ 2. Schools were encouraged to teach appreciation for the diversity of American society and to foster respect for the beliefs and practices of all cultures.

As used in this sentence, *diversity* means

(A) competition

(B) economy

(C) creativity

(D) differences

(E) uniformity

___ 3. The President introduced to Congress a $172.5 million proposal to strengthen the U.S. Border Patrol and reduce visa fraud and false asylum claims.

As used in this sentence, *asylum* means

(A) mental institution

(B) political refuge

(C) insurance

(D) inheritance

(E) insanity

___ 4. The IRCA offered amnesty and eventual citizenship to an estimated 3.7 million illegal aliens.

As used in this sentence, *amnesty* means

(A) language lessons

(B) cash awards

(C) citizenship classes

(D) official pardon

(E) transportation

___ 5. Some environmentalists have urged an immediate halt to immigration to preserve the ecosystem and the quality of life.

As used in this sentence, *ecosystem* means

(A) ecological network

(B) economy

(C) improvement

(D) patriotism

(E) employment

6. Although many Americans have regarded the new immigrants as poor, uneducated, and unskilled, the majority have proven to be enterprising.

   As used in this sentence, *enterprising* means

   (A) meek

   (B) wealthy

   (C) ambitious

   (D) infuriating

   (E) enjoyable

7. Baroque music flourished in Italy, and Italian musicians had enormous influence elsewhere in Europe.

   As used in this sentence, *flourished* means

   (A) thrived

   (B) declined

   (C) grew

   (D) influenced

   (E) performed

8. Born in Germany, Handel studied in Italy and settled permanently in England after his patron, the ruler of Hanover, had become King George I.

   In this sentence, *patron* means

   (A) boss

   (B) customer

   (C) minister

   (D) benefactor

   (E) frequenter

9. If you could move faster than light, outpacing your shadow, your time would move backward.

   In this sentence, *outpacing* means

   (A) defeating

   (B) overtaking

   (C) eliminating

   (D) outmaneuvering

   (E) enlarging

10. Along with Carl Rogers, the other guiding spirit of the humanist movement, Maslow, believed that all members of society should be given the chance to realize their full potential as human beings.

    As used in this sentence, a *humanist* is one who

    (A) believes in human ideals and possibilities

    (B) believes that a sense of humor is essential to well-being

    (C) believes people should have more humility

    (D) believes people should not have to work

    (E) believes people should be kinder to animals

11. Even if he does manage to unite his layers, there will still be a number of hurdles to get over before a robot with artificial skin can become as adept as a human.

    In this sentence, *adept* means

    (A) strong

    (B) large

    (C) skillful

    (D) successful

    (E) useful

Read the passage below. Then answer
Questions 12–15.

Frankenstein (1818) and *Wuthering Heights*
(1847) are not usually seen as related
works, except insofar as both are famous
nineteenth-century literary puzzles, with
Mary Shelley's plaintive speculation about
where she got so "hideous an idea" (for the
monster in Frankenstein), finding its coun-
terpart in the position of Heathcliff's creator
as a sort of mystery woman of literature.
Still, if both Emily Bronte and Shelley wrote
enigmatic, curiously unprecedented novels,
their works are puzzling in different ways:
Shelley's is an enigmatic fantasy of meta-
physical horror, Bronte's an enigmatic
Romantic and "masculine" text in which
the fates of subordinate female characters
seem entirely dependent upon the actions
of ostensibly male heroes or anti-heroes . . .
—From *Madwoman in the Attic,*
    by Sandra Gilbert and Susan Gubar

___ 12. In this passage, *speculation* means

    (A) bet

    (B) supposition

    (C) gamble

    (D) conjecture

    (E) gossip

___ 13. In this passage, *enigmatic* means

    (A) fanatical

    (B) straightforward

    (C) puzzling

    (D) understandable

    (E) creative

___ 14. In this passage, *unprecedented* means

    (A) unpublished

    (B) run-of-the-mill

    (C) unpredictable

    (D) new

    (E) incomprehensible

___ 15. In this passage, *subordinate* means

    (A) abnormal

    (B) minor

    (C) stupid

    (D) providential

    (E) subservient

Answers for Chapter 12 Practice Tests

Practice Test I: **Analogies**	**Practice Test II:** **Sentence Completion**	**Practice Test III:** **As Used In**
1. C	1. B	1. C
2. D	2. E	2. D
3. B	3. E	3. B
4. D	4. D	4. D
5. C	5. D	5. A
6. B	6. D	6. C
7. D	7. E	7. A
8. E	8. B	8. D
9. A	9. D	9. B
10. C	10. C	10. A
11. D	11. E	11. C
12. B	12. B	12. D
13. C	13. B	13. C
14. C	14. E	14. D
15. A	15. D	15. E

Dictionary of Words Taught in This Text

This dictionary lists most of the words taught in *Vocabulary for the College-Bound Student*. The focus is on those words offering some degree of difficulty. Definitions are often condensed and are followed by page numbers on which the words appear.

Use this dictionary as a tool of reference and review. It is a convenient means of restudying the meanings of words that you may have missed in the exercises. It is also a useful device for a general review before an important vocabulary test. Bear in mind, however, that you will get a fuller understanding of these words from the explanations and exercises in the foregoing chapters.

abase: humiliate; degrade; lower   72
abatement: lessening; remission   190
abhor: utterly detest; loathe; hate   26
abhorrent: loathsome; repugnant   26
abiogenesis: spontaneous generation   124
abject: deserving contempt; wretched   71, 187
aboard: on a ship, train, bus, etc.; on   216
abominable: odious; abhorrent   26
abridge: shorten; abbreviate   202
abrupt: broken off; steep; sudden   154, 183, 259
abstemious: temperate; abstinent   83
abstinent: sparing in eating and drinking   83
absurd: preposterous; ridiculous   63, 94
abysmal: profound; immeasurably great   71
abyss: bottomless, immeasurably deep space   71

a cappella: without musical accompaniment   259
access: entrance   183
acclaim: welcome with approval; applaud   61
acclivity: upward slope   69
accredited: officially authorized or recognized   167
acme: highest point; summit; pinnacle   69
acquit: exculpate; pronounce not guilty; conduct oneself   35
acrid: pungent; sharp in smell or taste   74
acrophobia: fear of being at a great height   107
adagio: slow; in an easy, graceful manner   257
adaptable: versatile   189
adherent: follower   234
adieu: good-bye; farewell   237
adjacent: lying near or next to; bordering   86
adjoining: adjacent; bordering   86
admonish: warn of a fault; rebuke; reprove   26, 166
admonition: counseling against a fault or error   26, 166
admonitory: conveying a gentle reproof   166
adobe: brick of sun-dried clay and straw   275
adolescent: growing from childhood to adulthood   80
adolescent: teenager   80
Adonis: very handsome young man   203
adulation: excessive praise   51
advert: turn attention; refer   188
aegis: shield; protection; sponsorship   203
affidavit: sworn written statement   169
affirmation: oath   203
aficionado: fan; devotee   272

afoul: in a state of entanglement   216
afoul of: into conflict or collision with   216
aggressive: disposed to attack; assertive   183
agoraphobia: fear of open spaces   107
a la carte: dish by dish   246
alacrity: cheerful willingness; readiness   69
a la mode: according to fashion   246
alfresco: in the open air; outdoor   265
allegro: quick; brisk; lively   257
allopathy: ant. homeopathy   135
aloof: withdrawn   216
alto: highest male or lowest female voice   256
altruism: unselfish concern for others   97
amazon: tall, strong, bold woman   203
ambience: surroundings; atmosphere   248
ambrosia: food of the gods   203
ambrosial: extremely delicious   27
ameliorate: become better; improve; enhance   8
amenable: tractable   9
amiss: wrong; imperfect; faulty   216
amoral: without a sense of moral responsibility   114
amorphous: having no form; shapeless; unorganized   95, 114, 136
amphibious: able to live on land and in water   124
analogy: likeness in some respects; comparison   84
analysis: anatomy   125
anarchy: absence of rule; disorder; confusion   114, 133
anatomy: structure of organisms or science that deals with it; dissection   125
andante: moderately slow, but flowing   257
anemia: abnormal lack of red blood cells   114
anent: about; concerning; in respect to   220
anesthesia: loss of sensation, as from ether   114
anesthetic: drug that produces anesthesia   114
Anglophile: supporter of the English   109
Anglophobe: one who dislikes the English   108
Anglophobia: dislike of the English   107
anguish: extreme pain   50
anhydrous: destitute of (without) water   114
anomalous: not normal; abnormal   114
anomaly: deviation from the common rule   114
anon: soon; presently   220
anonymous: nameless; of unknown or unnamed origin   115
anoxia: state of being without oxygen   115
antediluvian: antiquated; before the Flood   80
anteroom: foyer; vestibule   249

anthropology: science dealing with humankind   122
anthropomorphic: given human characteristics   136
antibiotic: germ-killing substance   124
anticlimax: decline into triviality; comedown   71
antidote: remedy for a poison or evil   59
antipasto: appetizer; hors d'oeuvres   265
antipathy: dislike; aversion   69, 135
antipodes: diametrically opposed global points   127
anxious: apprehensive; fearful   186
apathy: lack of feeling or interest; indifference   135
apéritif: alcoholic drink taken as an appetizer   246
apex: farthest point from the base; vertex   71
aphelion: orbit's farthest point from the sun   137
apiary: place where bees are kept   58
aplomb: self-possession; poise   236
apnea: temporary cessation of breathing   115
apogee: orbit's farthest point from earth   70, 134, 137
apostate: renegade; one who has left the faith   273
appellation: name   203
appendectomy: surgical removal of the appendix   125
apprehend: take into custody; understand   186
apprehensive: anxious; quick to grasp   186
appropriate: take for oneself   202
approximate: nearly correct   86
apropos: appropriate; relevant; pertinent   248
apropos: by the way; incidentally   248
aqueduct: channel to lead water from afar   179
arbiter: person having power to decide a dispute   92
arbitrary: proceeding from a whim; despotic   92
arbitrate: act as an arbiter   92
arbitrator: judge   92
archaic: old-fashioned   80
aria: melody for a single operatic voice   260
aristocracy: elite; class thought superior   209
armada: fleet of warships   275
aroma: pleasant odor; bouquet   74
aromatic: sweet-scented; fragrant   74
arpeggio: rapid playing of individual chordal tones   259
arrogant: haughty; overweening   97
arroyo: water-carved, often dry, gully   275
arthropod: invertebrate with jointed legs; insect   127

ascetic: self-denying; austere 48
aseptic: free from disease-causing microbes 115
asinine: like an ass; stupid; silly 224
assertive: acting and speaking boldly 183
assuage: pacify; soothe 202
astringent: substance that shrinks tissues 59, 157
astringent: causing contraction; stern; severe 59, 157
asunder: apart 216
asymmetrical: not balanced in arrangement 95
asymptomatic: showing no symptoms of disease 115
atheism: godlessness 115
atlas: book of maps 204
atom: smallest particle of an element 125
atomizer: device to convert a liquid to a spray 126
atrophy: lack of growth, as from from disease 115, 130
attaché: member of the diplomatic staff 234
attenuate: make thin; weaken 50
atypical: unlike the typical 115
au courant: well-informed; up-to-date 232
audiophile: high-fidelity enthusiast 109
au revoir: good-bye; till we meet again 237
auriferous: bearing or yielding gold 192
auroral: resembling dawn; rosy; radiant 204
auspices: aegis; sponsorship; patronage 203
austere: stern 157
austere: ascetic; shunning pleasures 48
autarchy: rule by an absolute sovereign 133
autobiography: a person's life story written by that person 124
avant-garde: experimentalists; innovators 244
avarice: greed 203
averse: disinclined; loath 69
aversion: strong dislike; antipathy 69, 135
avert: avoid; prevent 188
aviary: place where birds are kept 58
avoirdupois: weight; heaviness 248
axiom: self-evident truth; maxim 92
axiomatic: self-evident 92

bacchanalian: wild with drunkenness 204
bacchic: bacchanalian 204
bactericide: substance that kills bacteria 155
bacteriology: science dealing with bacteria 122
badger: nag; annoy 58
baffle: bewilder 17
bagatelle: trifle 248
banter: playful teasing 62

baritone: male voice between bass and tenor 256
barrio: Spanish-speaking neighborhood 278
bas-relief: sculpture whose figures project slightly from background 244
bass: lowest male voice; basso 256
basso: lowest male voice 256
bathos: sudden decline in style; triteness; anticlimax 71
baton: conductor's rod for directing a band 244
bearish: rough; depressing stocks 224
beget: bring into existence; procreate 201
begrime: cover with grime; make dirty 217
behest: command; order 220
beholden: bound in gratitude; indebted 220
behoove: be necessary for; be proper for 220
belittle: disparage; make seem little 217
benediction: blessing 203
benighted: unenlightened; ignorant 217
benign: not dangerous; gentle; kindly 59
beset: attack on all sides; surround 217
besmirch: defile; tarnish 86
bête noire: dreaded object; bugbear 239
betimes: early 220
bias: partiality; prejudice; predilection 92
bibliophile: lover of books 109
bibliophobe: one who strongly dislikes books 109
bigoted: narrow-minded; intolerant 92
bigotry: bigoted behavior; intolerance 92
billet-doux: love letter 238
biochemistry: chemical processes in organisms 124
biocidal: destructive to life 124
biocide: substance that destroys organisms 155
biodegradable: decomposable by microorganisms 124
biogenesis: life developing from preexisting life 124
biography: story of a person's life written by another person 124
biology: science dealing with living organisms 122, 124
biometrics: statistical analysis of biologic data 125
biometry: biometrics 125
biopsy: diagnostic examination of living tissue 125
biota: plants and animals living in a region 125
biped: two-footed animal 184
blandishment: mild flattery; enticement 51
blasé: tired of pleasures; bored 232
bliss: perfect happiness 46
blithe: merry; joyous; heedless 47

bloodthirsty: eager for violence; sanguinary 225

bluster: bully; hector; intimidate 205

boa constrictor: snake that crushes its prey 157

bodega: small grocery store 277

bolero: Spanish dance; waist-length jacket 277

bombastic: using pompous language; grandiloquent 191

bona fide: made in good faith; genuine 169

bonanza: source yielding a rich return 276

bonbon: piece of candy 246

bon mot: clever saying; witticism 238

bouffant: full; puffed out 247

bouquet: pleasant odor 74

bourgeois: middle class; lacking culture 232

boutique: small, fashionable clothing shop 247

bovine: cowlike; oxlike; sluggish 224

bow: forward part of a ship; prow 84

bowdlerize: remove objectionable material from a book; expurgate 85

bravado: pretense of bravery 275

bravo (brava): a shout applauding excellence; well done 265

bravura: display of daring or brilliancy 260

brazen: shameless; impudent; made of brass or bronze 97

breach: gap; violation; rupture 71, 203

brine: salty water; ocean 84

brisk: lively 257

brochure: pamphlet 238

bronco: wild horse; mustang 276

buckaroo: vaquero 274

buffo: male singer playing a comic operatic role 263

bugbear: object of dread; bête noire 239

bullish: obstinate; boosting stocks 224

buoy: keep afloat; raise the spirits of 47

buoyant: cheerful; able to float 47

burly: strongly and heavily built; husky 50

burro: small donkey used as a pack animal 276

buxom: plump and attractive 50

caballero: gentleman; cavalier; horseman 272

cabana: cabin-like shelter at a beach 277

cafeteria: self- or counter-service restaurant 277

cajole: wheedle; coax 51

cajolery: persuasion by flattery; coaxing 51

calaboose: jail, especially a local one 276

callow: young and inexperienced; unfledged 80

calumnious: slanderous; defamatory 61

calumny: false and malicious accusation 61

camaraderie: friendship; good will; comradery 275

cameo: gem cut in relief; brief role 261

campanile: bell tower 261

canard: false rumor; absurd story; hoax 238

canine: doglike; pointed tooth 224

cantata: vocal and instrumental work 260

canto: chief division of a long poem 261

canyon: deep narrow valley with steep walls 276

capitulate: yield; succumb 202

cardiology: science dealing with the heart 122

cargo: freight; goods transported 275

caricature: description emphasizing peculiarities 62

carnivore: flesh-eating animal 158

carnivorous: flesh-eating 158

carousal: drunken revelry; drinking party 83

carrion: decaying flesh of a carcass 85

carte blanche: freedom to do as one sees fit 239

Cassandra: prophet of doom; pessimist 204

castanets: hand instruments clicked together 277

caudillo: military dictator 272

cause célèbre: famous case in law 239

celestial: of the heavens 70

censure: adverse criticism 157, 191

centipede: "hundred-legged" creature 184

chagrin: embarrassment; mortification 48

changeling: infant exchanged for another 219

chargé d'affaires: substitute ambassador 234

charlatan: mountebank; quack 264

chasm: deep breach; wide gap or rift 71

chef d'oeuvre: chief work; masterpiece 244

chemise: loose-fitting, sacklike dress 247

cherub: angel in the form of a baby or child 50

cherubic: chubby and innocent-looking 50

Chianti: dry, red Italian wine 265

chiaroscuro: painter's use of light and shade 262

chic: stylish 232

Chicano: American of Mexican descent 272

chimerical: fantastic; unreal; absurd 204

chiropodist: specialist in the care of the feet 127

chutzpah: effrontery; nerve 35

cinema: movies; motion picture industry 17

cinematography: art of making movies 17

circuitous: tortuous; tricky 160

circumlocution: roundabout speaking 191

circumlocutory: periphrastic; roundabout 137

clairvoyant: unusually perceptive; able to perceive things beyond the senses   233

clamorous: noisy; vociferous   192

claustrophobia: fear of confined spaces   107

cliché: trite or worn-out expression   238

climactic: put in order of increasing force   70

clique: small and exclusive set of persons   235, 273

cogitate: think; deliberate; ponder   92, 202

cognoscente: expert; connoisseur   263

coiffure: style of arranging the hair   247

coincide: concur; agree; happen together   182

collected: unruffled; unflustered   37

colloquial: conversational; informal   191

colloquy: conversation; conference   191

coloratura: ornamented musical passages   257

colossal: prodigious; huge   36

commendable: praiseworthy   61

commitment: consignment; pledge   190

complacent: too pleased with oneself; smug   47

complaisant: willing to please; obliging   233

complex: complicated; intricate   35

complimentary: expressing esteem; favorable   61

composure: calmness; sangfroid; equanimity   237

comprehensible: understandable   186

comprehensive: extensive; including much   186

compunction: regret; misgiving   48

computerphobe: one who fears computers   108

comradery: friendship; rapport; good will   275

concave: curved inward, creating a hollow space   95

concentric: having a common center   128

concerto: long musical composition   260

concierge: doorkeeper; janitor   234

concise: expressing much in a few words; terse   182

concord: harmony   8

concur: agree; happen together; coincide   182

concurrent: occurring at the same time   182

condescend: bow; stoop   201

conducive: tending to lead to; contributive   179

conduct: lead; guide; escort   179

confidant(e): one to whom secrets are entrusted   169

confident: having faith in oneself; self-reliant   169

confidential: communicated in trust; secret   169

confine: imprison; shut up   27

confinement: imprisonment   27

conflagration: fire   203

confrere: colleague; co-worker; comrade   234

congratulate: express joy at another's success   176

coniferous: bearing cones   192

conjectural: hypothetical; assumed; supposed   130

conjecture: speculate; supposition; guess   94, 187

connoisseur: expert; critical judge   234

conquistador: conqueror   272

consanguinuity: blood relationship   72

consecrate: bless   201

consecutive: following in order; successive   181

consequence: result; importance   181

conserve: keep from waste, loss, or decay; save   8

consign: hand over; transfer; commit   35

consignee: person to whom something is shipped   35

consommé: clear soup; broth   246

constrict: bind; draw together; shrink   157

consume: eat; devour   202

consummate: perfect; superb   70

contact: touching; meeting; connection   185

contaminate: make impure; defile; pollute   85

contemporary: of the same period   80

contemporary: one living at same time as another   80

contend: strive in opposition   182

contiguous: touching; adjoining; in contact   86, 185

contingent: dependent; accidental   185

contort: twist out of shape   160

contortionist: one who twists into odd postures   160

contour: outline of a figure   95

contralto: alto; lowest female voice   256

contrariwise: on the contrary   218

contretemps: embarrassing situation; inopportune occurrence   239

contrite: showing regret for wrongdoing   48

contrition: repentance; regret for wrongdoing   48

controversy: dispute; quarrel   188

convalesce: recover health; recuperate   59

convalescent: person recovering from sickness   59

conventional: orthodox; generally accepted   93

convert: transform   188

convex: rounded like the exterior of a circle   95

convict: prove guilty; person serving a sentence 161

conviction: being judged guilty; strong belief 161

convince: persuade conclusively by argument 161

convivial: fond of eating with friends; jovial 47, 159

conviviality: sociability 47

corporal: bodily 178

corporation: body authorized by law 178

corps: organized body; military branch 178

corpse: dead body 178

corpulent: bulky; obese; very fat 50, 178

corpus: body of writings, laws, etc. 178

corpuscle: blood cell; minute particle 179

corpus delicti: body of the murder victim 179

corroborate: confirm 202

corrupt: changed from good to bad; vicious 154

corrupt: falsify; pervert; debase 154

corsage: small bouquet worn by a woman 247

coterie: set of acquaintances; clique 234

countermand: issue a contrary order 167

countertenor: highest male voice; alto 256

coup de grâce: decisive finishing blow 249

coup d'état: sudden overthrow of government 243

coy: pretending to be shy 96

cravat: necktie; neckband; scarf 247

credence: belief as to the truth of something 167

credentials: documents inspiring trust 168

credible: believable 168

credit: belief; faith; trust 168

credo: creed 168

credulous: too ready to believe; easily deceived 168

creed: summary of principles believed in 168

crescendo: gradually increasing in loudness 232

criminology: scientific study of crimes 122

criterion: standard; rule or test for judging 92

croissant: flaky crescent-shaped roll 246

crone: withered old woman 80

crux: most important point; essential part 92

cuisine: style of preparing food 246

cul de sac: blind alley; dead end 239

culmination: highest point; apex; peak; apogee 70, 134

culpable: reprehensible; blamable 186

cumbersome: burdensome; unwieldy 37, 218

cupola: rounded roof; dome 262

current: now in progress; flowing 182

curriculum: course of study in a school 182

curriculum vitae: résumé 238

curry favor: seek to gain favor by flattery 51

cursive: running or flowing 182

cursory: superficial 182

deadlock: impasse 240

debacle: collapse; disaster; rout 239

debonair: gracious; charming 233

debut: first introduction into society 234

debutante: young woman whose debut was recent 234

decade: period of ten years 27

decapitate: behead 201

deceased: dead; defunct 80

deceptive: misleading; fallacious 93

declivity: downward slope 71

decontaminate: rid of contamination 85

decrepit: weakened by old age 80

decrescendo: gradually decreasing in loudness 232

deduce: derive by reasoning; infer 93

deduction: subtraction; reasoning from general to particular 180

defamatory: calumnious; harming a reputation 61

defeat: vanquish; conquer 161

defective: flawed; incomplete; imperfect 185

defensible: able to be defended; tenable 94

defile: make filthy; contaminate; sully 86

deflect: turn aside 164

defunct: dead; extinct 80

degradation: worsening; humiliation 7

degrade: lower; humiliate; abase 72

dejected: depressed; downcast; discouraged 48, 187

delectable: very pleasing; delightful 47

deleterious: not beneficial; not salubrious 36

deliberate: ponder; cogitate 92, 154

demarche: maneuver; course of action involving a change 243

demise: death 190

demitasse: small cup of strong black coffee 246

demure: falsely modest or serious; grave; prim 96

denouement: solution of the plot; outcome 244

denunciation: public condemnation 184

dermatology: science dealing with the skin 122

derogatory: expressing low esteem; disparaging 61

desperado: bold, dangerous criminal 272

despicable: worthy of contempt 17

despise: loathe 17

despotic: tyrannical; autocratic; arbitrary 92

detente: relaxing of strained relations 243

detention: act of keeping back or detaining 165

deterioration: retrogression 183

detonate: explode; cause to explode 27

detriment: damage; disadvantage 8

devotee: ardent adherent; fan; aficionado 234, 272

devour: eat greedily or ravenously; destroy 158, 202

diabolic(al): wicked; fiendish 224

dichotomy: cutting or division into two 126

diffident: lacking faith in oneself; shy; timid 96, 169

digressive: rambling; tangential 185

dilemma: situation requiring a choice between two bad alternatives; predicament 93

dilettante: nonprofessional follower of an art 263

dimorphous: occurring under two distinct forms 136

diplomatic: tactful 185

dipody: verse (poetic line) of two feet; dimeter 127

dipsomania: alcoholism 83

discerning: clairvoyant 233

disconsolate: cheerless; inconsolable 48

discredit: cast doubt on; disgrace 168

discursive: going from one topic to another; rambling; digressive 182

disgruntled: in bad humor; discontented 49

disgruntlement: bad humor; dyspepsia 111

disharmony: discord; lack of harmony 8

disintegrate: break up 201

disparaging: derogatory; belittling 61

disrupt: break apart; cause disorder 154

distort: twist out of shape; misrepresent 95, 160

diva: principal female opera singer; prima donna 263

diversion: entertainment; amusement 188

divert: turn aside; amuse; entertain 188

docile: easily led; tractable 9, 180

doctrinaire: dogmatic 93

dogmatic: asserting opinion as fact; doctrinaire 93

dolce: soft; sweet 232

dolce far niente: delightful idleness 264

doldrums: calm part of the ocean; listlessness 84

doleful: causing sadness; mournful; lugubrious 49

dolorous: full of sorrow 49

domicile: home; residence 203

dour: gloomy 49

down-to-earth: earthy; realistic 72

Draconian: cruel; harsh; ironhanded 204

dregs: most worthless part; sediment 71

droll: odd and laughter-provoking 62

dross: waste; refuse 85

duckling: little duck 219

duct: channel for conducting a fluid 180

ductile: able to be drawn out; docile 180

duenna: woman chaperon; governess 273

duet: music for two voices or instruments 260

dulcinea: sweetheart; inamorata 273

dwindle: wane; decrease 220

dysentery: inflammation of the large intestine 111

dysfunction: abnormal functioning 111

dyslexia: impairment of ability to read 111

dyslogistic: disapproving; uncomplimentary 111

dyspepsia: indigestion; disgruntlement 111

dysphagia: difficulty in swallowing 111

dysphasia: speech difficulty from brain disease 111

dysphoria: sense of great unhappiness 111

dystopia: imaginary dreadful place 111

dystrophy: faulty nutrition; disorder it causes 111

earldom: realm or dignity of an earl 218

earthy: down-to-earth; realistic; coarse; low 72

ebullience: high spirits; exuberance 17

ebullient: overflowing with enthusiasm 17

echolalia: repetition of what others say 204

éclat: brilliancy of achievement 236

eclectic: chosen from various sources; selective 93

ecology: science dealing with relation of life to its environment 122

ecstasy: state of overwhelming joy; rapture 47

ecstatic: in ecstasy; enraptured 47

ectomorphic: having a light body build; occurring outside 136

ectoparasite: parasite living on the surface of its host 132

effervescent: ebullient; exuberant; lively 17

effrontery: shameless boldness; temerity 35

egoism: excessive concern for oneself; conceit 97

egress: exit; means of going out 183

eject: throw out; expel; evict 187

élan: enthusiasm; eagerness for action 236

elate: lift up with joy; exalt; extol 70

elated: in high spirits; joyful 47

El Dorado: place of fabulous wealth 275

elite: aristocracy; choice group 234

elocution: art of speaking in public 191

eloquent: speaking with force and fluency 192

Elysian: delightful; blissful; heavenly 204

324 Vocabulary for the College-Bound Student

emaciated: unnaturally thin   50
emancipate: free; liberate   202
embarcadero: landing place; wharf; quay   275
embargo: ban on shipments   275
émigré(e): refugee   234
eminence: high rank   70
eminent: standing out; notable; famous   70
emissary: person sent out on a mission   190
emit: send out; give off   190
empathy: understanding of another's feelings   135
encomium: high praise; tribute; panegyric   61
encore: additional performance   245
endocarditis: inflammation of the heart's lining   132
endocrine: secreting internally   131
endoderm: tissue lining the digestive tract   132
endogamy: marriage within the social group   131
endogenous: due to internal causes   131
endomorphic: having a heavy body build; occurring within   136
endoparasite: parasite living inside its host   132
endophyte: plant growing within another plant   132
endoskeleton: internal skeleton   131
endosmosis: osmosis inward   132
engineering: technology   123
enhance: improve   7
ennui: boredom; tedium   236
en route: on the way   249
ensemble: complete costume   247
entente: agreement between governments   243
entourage: someone's attendants; retinue   234
entrée: main dish at lunch or dinner   246
entre nous: between us; confidentially   238
entrepreneur: one assuming business risks   234
environs: districts surrounding a place; suburbs   86
envoy: diplomatic agent; messenger   234
ephemeral: fleeting; short-lived   27
epitome: microcosm   113
equanimity: sangfroid; composure; calmness   211
equine: of or like a horse   225
eristic: disputatious; argumentative   204
erupt: burst or break out   154
escapade: daring or unconventional act   275
esoteric: not readily understandable   132
esprit de corps: group spirit   179, 236
ethereal: of the heavens; delicate; intangible   70

ethnology: study of the human races   123
etiquette: code of behavior   249
eugenics: science of improving hereditary factors   112
eulogistic: expressing praise   61
eulogize: praise; extol; laud; glorify   61, 112
eupepsia: good digestion   112
euphemism: "good" word(s) substituted for "bad"   112
euphonious: pleasing in sound   112
euphoria: sense of great happiness or well-being   112
euphoria: state of being elated   47
euthanasia: so-called "advantageous death"   112
euthenics: science of improving living conditions   112
evict: expel by legal process; oust   161, 187
evince: show clearly; disclose; reveal   161
exaggerate: overstate; magnify   18
exalt: lift up, as with joy; raise in rank   70
excoriate: flay; fleece; skin; censure   202
excruciating: unbearably painful; agonizing   35
exculpate: acquit; exonerate   35
excursion: going out or forth; expedition   182
execrate: curse   201
execute: carry out; put to death   181
exhort: urge   18
exhortation: urgent recommendation   18
exocrine: secreting externally   131
exogamy: marriage outside the social group   131
exogenous: due to external causes   131
exonerate: exculpate; acquit   35
exoskeleton: hard structure outside the body   132
exosmosis: osmosis outward   132
exoteric: readily understandable   132
exotic: foreign; strikingly unusual; strange   8, 132
expectorate: spit   202
expedite: accelerate; speed up; make easy   184
expertise: expertness; know-how   18
expurgate: purify (as a book); bowdlerize   85
extinct: no longer in existence   80
extol: praise   61
extort: wrest money or promises from someone   160
extraneous: not relevant; beside the point   96
extrovert: someone whose thoughts are turned outward   188

facade: face; front; false front   249
facetious: said in jest without serious intent   62
facilitate: expedite; make easy   184

fait accompli: thing already done 239
fallacious: based on an erroneous idea; deceptive 93
fallacy: erroneous idea 93
fallible: liable to be mistaken 93
falsetto: artificially high voice 256
farcical: exciting laughter; ludicrous 63
fastidious: finicky; persnickety 18
fatal: causing death 177
fathom: plumb; get to the bottom of 72
fauna: animal life 204
faux pas: misstep; blunder 239
fawning: slavishly attentive 51
fealty: loyalty; faithfulness 169
feline: catlike; sly; stealthy 224
feminine: womanly 224
fester: form pus; rot; putrefy; rankle 59
fete: festival; to honor with a party 249
fetid: ill-smelling; malodorous 74
fiancé(e): person engaged to be married 235
fiasco: crash; ridiculous failure 264
fidelity: faithfulness to a trust; accuracy 169
fiduciary: held in trust; confidential 169
fiesta: festival; holiday 277
filament: thread 203
filet: boneless slice of meat or fish 246
filial: befitting a son or daughter 72, 223
finale: last part of a musical composition 260
finesse: skill in handling a difficulty 237
finicky: hard to please; fastidious 18
firmament: heaven 203
flamboyant: flamelike; ornate; showy; vivid 248
flex: bend 164
flexible: able to be bent; pliable; tractable 164
flexor: muscle that serves to bend a limb 164
flippant: treating serious matters lightly 63
flora: plant life 205
flotilla: small fleet; fleet of small ships 275
flotsam: wreckage floating on the sea; driftage 84
folly: lack of good sense 8
forbearance: leniency; patience 36
forebear: ancestor; progenitor 80
forefather: ancestor 73, 80
former: preceding 8
formerly: previously 8
forte: loud 232
fortissimo: very loud 232
forum: place for open discussion 205
foundling: infant deserted then found 220
foyer: lobby; vestibule; anteroom 249
fraction: fragment 162
fractious: apt to break out into a passion; cross 162
fracture: break; crack; breaking of a bone 162
fragile: easily broken; frail; delicate 162

fragment: part broken off; fraction 162
fragrant: having a pleasant odor 74
Francophile: supporter of the French 109
Francophobe: one who dislikes the French 108
fraternal: brotherly 73, 223
fratricide: killer of (or killing) one's brother 155
freeloader: parasite 58
fresco: painting on damp fresh plaster 262
frivolity: trifling gaiety; levity 63
frolic: play and run about happily; romp 47
frolicsome: full of merriment; playful 47
frugivorous: feeding on fruit 158
frustrate: baffle 17
fulsome: repulsive; offensively insincere 51, 218
fungicide: substance that kills fungi 155
fusty: stale-smelling; musty; old-fashioned 74

gala: characterized by festivity 48
gall: brazen boldness; nerve; vex 18, 35
gallant: gentleman; cavalier; caballero 272
galleon: large sailing ship 275
garrulous: loquacious; talkative 191
gastrectomy: surgery removing part of the stomach 126
gauche: lacking social grace; tactless 233
gaucho: South American cowboy 273
gaunt: excessively thin 50
gendarme: armed police officer 235
genealogy: account of one's descent; lineage 73, 123
generate: cause; bring into existence 201
genocide: deliberate extermination of a people 155
genre: kind; sort; category; style 245
gentility: good manners; upper class; gentry 73
genuflect: bend the knee 164
geocentric: measured from the earth's center 133
geodesy: mathematics of the earth's shape 133
geodetic: pertaining to geodesy 133
geography: study of the earth's surface 134
geology: science of the earth's history through rock study 123, 134
geometry: mathematics of surfaces and solids 134
geomorphic: pertaining to the shape of the earth 134
geophysics: science of forces modifying the earth 134
geopolitics: influence of geography on politics 134

geoponics: art or science of agriculture   134
georgic: agricultural; poem on farming   134
geotropism: response to earth's gravity   134
germ: microbe   113
Germanophilia: admiration of the Germans   108
Germanophobe: one who dislikes the Germans   108
Germanophobia: dislike of the Germans   108
germicide: substance that kills germs   155
gigantic: prodigious   36
glee: joy; hilarity   63
glum: gloomy; moody; dour   49
goatish: goatlike; coarse; lustful   225
gondola: boat used in Venice's canals; cabin   265
gosling: young goose   220
gourmand: glutton; lover of eating   235
gourmet: connoisseur of food and drink   235
gracious: pleasant; courteous   176
gradation: change by steps or stages   183
grade: step; stage; degree; rating   183
gradient: rate of rise or fall; slope   183
gradual: step-by-step; by small degrees   183, 154
graduate: receive a diploma or degree   183
graduated: arranged in regular steps   183
grandee: nobleman of the highest rank   273
grandiloquent: using lofty or pompous words   191
graphic: vivid; clear   159
grateful: thankful; obliged   176
gratify: give or be a source of pleasure   176
gratis: without charge or payment   176
gratitude: thankfulness   176
gratuitous: given freely; unwarranted   176
gratuity: tip; money given for a service   176
grave: deserving serious attention; weighty   96
grave: slow (the slowest tempo in music)   257
grotto: cave   265
gruesome: horrifying; repulsive   60
guerilla: fighter in an irregular unit   273
gull: deceive; cheat   27
gullible: easily deceived   27
gusto: liking; taste; hearty enjoyment   265

habeas corpus: bar to illegal imprisonment   179
hacienda: large ranch or main house on ranch   276
haggard: careworn   50
haggle: argue over a price; bargain   27
halcyon: calm; peaceful   58
hamper: interfere with; hinder; impede   36
harass: annoy   181
harlequin: clown; buffoon   63

harmony: peaceable relations; concord   8
heath: tract of wasteland   220
heavenly: ambrosial   27
hector: bully; bluster   205
herbicide: substance that kills plants   155
herbivore: plant-eating animal   158
herbivorous: dependent on plants as food   158
Herculean: requiring Hercules' strength   205
heretical: rejecting accepted beliefs; heterodox; nonconformist   93
hermetic: airtight; secret; obscure   205
heterochromatic: having different colors   128
heteroclite: deviating from the common rule   128
heterodox: opposing accepted beliefs; unorthodox   93, 128
heterogeneous: dissimilar; varied   128
heterology: lack of correspondence between parts   128
heteromorphic: exhibiting diversity of form   128, 136
heteronym: word spelled like another   128
hidalgo: member of the minor nobility   273
hierarchy: pecking order   133
hilarious: boisterously merry; very funny   63
hilarity: noisy gaiety   63, 203
hircine: goatlike, especially in smell   225
hireling: one working only for the pay   219
hoary: white or gray with age; ancient   81
hoax: canard; deception   238
hodgepodge: mixture; olio; medley   278
homeopathy: practice that treats a disease by giving tiny doses of a remedy that, in healthy persons, would cause symptoms of the disease   135
homicide: killing of one human by another   155
homocentric: having the same center; concentric   128
homochromatic: monochromatic; unicolor   128
homogeneous: similar; uniform   128
homology: similarity of structure   128
homomorphic: exhibiting similarity of form   128
homonym: word sounding like another   128
homophonic: having the same sound   128
hors d'oeuvres: foods served as appetizers   246, 265
humble: of low position; modest; unpretentious   72, 96
humiliate: lower the dignity of; degrade   72
humility: freedom from pride; humbleness   72
hydrophobia: dread of water; rabies   108

hyperacidity: excessive acidity   129
hyperactive: overactive   130
hyperbole: extravagant exaggeration of statement   130
hypercritical: overcritical   130
hyperemia: superabundance of blood   130
hyperglycemia: excess of sugar in the blood   129
hyperopia: farsightedness   130
hypersensitive: supersensitive   130
hypertension: abnormally high blood pressure   129
hyperthermia: especially high fever; hyperpyrexia   130
hyperthyroid: of thyroid gland overactivity   130
hypertrophy: enlargement of a body part   130
hypoacidity: weak acidity   129
hypochondriac: one morbidly anxious about health   59
hypodermic: injected under the skin   130
hypoglycemia: abnormally low blood sugar level   129
hypotension: low blood pressure   130
hypothermia: subnormal body temperature   130
hypothesis: supposition; assumption; conjecture   93, 130
hypothetical: supposed; conjectural; assumed   93, 130
hypothyroid: of thyroid gland underactivity   130

ignominy: shame   203
ignoramus: stupid person; nincompoop   9
ignore: disregard   9
illusion: false impression; misconception   93
imbibe: drink   202
imbroglio: complicated disagreement   264
immaculate: spotless; pure; absolutely clean   85
immerse: plunge into a liquid; dip; engross   27
immersion: state of being deeply engrossed   27
immortal: not subject to death; imperishable   177
immortality: eternal life; lasting fame   177
immunity: disease resistance; freedom; exemption   59
impasse: deadlock; stalemate   240
impede: hinder; obstruct; block   36, 184
impediment: hindrance; obstacle   9, 184
impertinent: rude; not pertinent; irrelevant   97, 165

imperturbable: unruffled; collected   37
impregnability: strength; invincibility   203
impresario: organizer; manager; promoter   263
impudent: brazen; insolent   97
imputation: false charge; insinuation   62
inadvertently: carelessly; unintentionally   188
inamorata: woman who loves or is loved   263
inamorato: man who loves or is loved   263
inane: silly; pointless; insipid; vapid   18
inanity: foolishness; shallowness   18
incense: substance burned for its aroma   74
inclination: slope; gradient   183
incognito: disguised state   265
incommunicado: deprived of communication   275
incomprehensible: not understandable   186
inconsequential: unimportant; trivial   181
incontrovertible: certain; indubitable; indisputable   93, 189
incorporate: combine so as to form one body   179
incorruptible: inflexibly honest; not bribable   155
incredible: not believable   168
incredulity: disbelief   168
incredulous: disbelieving; skeptical   168
incrustation: crust; coating   262
incur: meet with something undesirable   182
incursion: a rushing into; raid   182
indemnify: reimburse   18
indigenous: native   7
indigo: blue dye   278
indisputable: indubitable; not open to question   93
indolent: lazy; lackadaisical   9
indubitable: certain; incontrovertible   93
induce: lead on; move by persuasion   180
induct: admit as a member; initiate   180
induction: initiation; reasoning from facts   180
inebriated: drunk; intoxicated   83
infallible: incapable of error   93
infanticide: killer of (or killing) an infant   156
infantile: babyish; like a young child   81, 224
infer: derive by reasoning; deduce   93
inference: conclusion; conjecture   187
infernal: Stygian; hellish   209
infidel: one not accepting a faith; unbeliever   169
infidelity: faithlessness   169
inflection: change in the pitch of one's voice   164
inflexibility: rigidity; firmness   164
infraction: breach; violation   162, 203
ingenue: naive young woman   235

ingenuous: naive; artless   233

ingrate: ungrateful person   177

ingratiate: establish (oneself) in someone's favor   51, 177

ingratitude: ungratefulness   176

initiate: begin; originate   201

inject: force in a liquid or a remark   187

insatiable: incapable of being satisfied   158

insecticide: preparation for killing insects   156

insectivorous: dependent on insects as food   158

insomnia: inability to sleep   27

insomniac: person suffering from insomnia   27

intact: untouched; left complete   9, 185

intaglio: design cut in a surface   262

intangible: unable to be touched; ethereal   70, 185

interject: throw in between; insert   187

interlocutor: participant in a conversation   191

intermezzo: short, independent musical work   260

intermittent: coming and going   190

interpose: place between; interject   187

interrupt: break into or between; hinder; stop   155

intimidate: frighten; hector   205, 202

intolerant: narrow-minded; bigoted   92

intoxicated: drunk; inebriated   84

intractable: hard to manage; refractory   162

intricate: complicated; labyrinthine   35, 182

introvert: someone whose thoughts are turned inward   189

intrusive: pushy; meddlesome   219

invalid: having no force; void   9

invalidate: make valueless   201

invert: turn upside down   189

invertebrate: animal having no backbone   127

inveterate: deep-rooted; habitual   81

invigorate: strengthen   202

invincible: incapable of being conquered   161

involuntary: not done of one's own free will   69

iridescent: having colors like the rainbow   205

ironic(al): containing or expressing irony   63

irony: using words so that their intended meaning is opposite to their surface meaning   63

irrational: senseless; absurd; preposterous   94

irrelevant: not pertinent; inapplicable   96, 165

itinerant: peripatetic; traveling about   137

jejune: inane; juvenile; insipid   18

jetsam: goods cast overboard   84

jettison: throw (goods) overboard; discard   84

jocose: given to jesting; playfully humorous   63

jocular: jocose; done as a joke   63

jocund: merry; cheerful; lighthearted   48

jovial: jolly; merry   205

jubilation: rejoicing; exultation   48

junta: council; military rulers; junto   273

junto: clique; plotters; faction; cabal   273

juvenile: youthful; immature   81

juxtapose: put side by side or close together   86

juxtaposition: close or side-by-side position   86

key: low island or reef, often of coral   275

kith and kin: friends and relatives; kindred   73

kudos: fame or praise due to achievement   61

labyrinthine: intricate; complicated   205

lackey: servile follower; toady   51

laconic: using words sparingly; concise   205

laissez-faire: noninterference   243

lament: mourn; deplore   49

lamentable: pitiable; rueful   49

languid: lacking in vigor   159

lank: lean; ungracefully tall; lanky   51

lapse: cease being in force; become invalid   27

lapse: slip; error; interval   27

larceny: theft; peculation   203

largo: slow and dignified; stately   257

Latino (Latina): Latin American   273

latter: later; second; last   8

laudable: praiseworthy; commendable   61

laudatory: expressing praise; eulogistic   61

lax: remiss; careless   190

leeward: in the direction away from the wind   85

legato: smooth and connected   259

legerdemain: sleight of hand   237

legitimate: rightful; legal; not arbitrary   92

lento: slow   257

lesion: injury; hurt   59

lethargic: unnaturally drowsy; sluggish   205

lettre de cachet: letter ordering imprisonment   243

levity: lack of proper seriousness   63

liaison: bond; linking up; coordination   240

libel: false, defamatory written statement   62

libelous: injurious to reputation; defamatory   62

liberate: free   202

libretto: text or words of an opera   260

lighthearted: jocund; merry; cheerful 48
limber: lissom; nimble 219
lineage: genealogy; pedigree 73
lionize: treat as highly important 58
lissom(e): flexible; limber; nimble 219
lithe: slender and agile 51
loath: disinclined; averse; unwilling 69
loathe: detest 69
lobotomy: brain surgery for mental disorders 126
longevity: long life; length of life 81
loquacious: talkative; garrulous 191
Lucullan: luxurious; sumptuous 206
ludicrous: exciting laughter; farcical 63
lugubrious: doleful; mournful; dolorous 49
lupine: of or like a wolf; ravenous 225

machismo: strong sense of masculinity 273
macho: man exhibiting machismo 273
macro: computer instruction 113
macrocosm: great world; universe 113
macron: horizontal mark indicating a long vowel 113
macroscopic: visible to the naked eye 113
maestro: eminent conductor; master in an art 264
maître d'hôtel: headwaiter 235
majolica: enameled Italian pottery 262
maladroit: unskillful; clumsy 233
malaise: vague feeling of discomfort 237
malediction: curse; execration 203
malign: vilify; traduce; speak evil of 62
malignant: threatening to cause death; very evil 60
malleable: capable of being shaped by hammering; adaptable 95
malodorous: ill-smelling 74
mañana: tomorrow 278
mandate: authoritative command; a trust territory 167
mandatory: required by command; obligatory 167
maneuver: demarche; trick 243
mantilla: woman's light scarf; cloak; cape 278
marathon: long-distance footrace 206
marine: of the sea or shipping; maritime 85
mariner: sailor; seaman 85
maritime: nautical; marine 85
martial: pertaining to war; warlike 206
martinet: very strict disciplinarian 235
martyrdom: state of being a martyr 218
masculine: opposite of feminine; manly 224
mastectomy: surgical removal of a breast 126
masticate: chew 201
matador: bullfighter who is to kill the bull 273

maternal: motherly; on the mother's side 73, 223
matriarch: mother and ruler of a family or tribe 81
matriarchy: rule by the mother 133
matricide: killer of (or killing) one's mother 156
mature: full-grown; carefully thought out 81
maudlin: weakly sentimental and tearful 49
mean: low 72
meddlesome: interfering; intrusive 219
medley: mixture; olio 240, 278
meekness: lack of nerve 17
melancholy: sad 49
melange: mixture; medley; potpourri 240
memento: keepsake; reminder; souvenir 250
menace: threat 203
menagerie: place where animals are kept 58
menial: low; mean; subservient 72
mentor: wise advisor; tutor; coach 206
mercurial: quick; changeable; crafty; eloquent 206
mesa: flat-topped, steep-sided, rocky hill 276
mestizo: person of both Native American and European ancestry 273
metamorphosis: change of form 136
meteorology: science of weather 123
mettlesome: spirited 219
mezzanine: theater's intermediate story 262
mezzo-soprano: voice between contralto and soprano 257
mezzotint: engraving on copper or steel 262
microbe: microscopic life form; microorganism 113, 125
microbicide: agent that destroys microbes 113
microcosm: little world; epitome 113
microdont: having small teeth 113
microfilm: film of very small size 113
microgram: millionth of a gram 113
micrometer: millionth of a meter 113
microorganism: microscopic animal or plant 113
microscopic: invisible to the naked eye 113
microsecond: millionth of a second 113
microsurgery: surgery with microscopes 113
microvolt: millionth of a volt 113
microwatt: millionth of a watt 113
microwave: short electromagnetic wave; oven 113
milieu: environment; surroundings 249
militant: aggressive; given to fighting 183
millipede: "thousand-legged" creature 184
mirage: optical illusion 240
mirth: hilarity; merriment 63, 203
misandry: hatred of males 110
misanthrope: hater of humanity 110

misanthropy: hatred of humanity   110
misconception: erroneous belief   93
misogamy: hatred of marriage   110
misogyny: hatred of women   110
misology: hatred of argument or discussion   110
misoneism: hatred of anything new   110
missile: weapon propelled from afar   190
missive: letter; written message sent   190
moderato: in moderate time   257
modest: humble; unpretentious   96
modesty: freedom from vanity; humility   72, 96
molt: shed feathers, skin, hair, etc.   58
momentous: grave; weighty; important   96
monarchy: state ruled by a single person   116, 133
monitor: keep track of a process   166
monochromatic: of one color   116
monocle: eyeglass for one eye   116
monogamy: marriage with one mate   116
monogram: two or more letters interwoven   116
monograph: written account of a single thing   116
monolith: single stone of large size; obelisk   116
monolithic: massive and rigidly uniform   116
monolog(ue): long speech by one person   116
monomania: excessive concentration on one idea   116
monomorphic: having a single form   116, 136
monophobia: fear of being alone   108
monosyllabic: having one syllable   116
monotheism: belief that there is one God   116
monotonous: continuing in an unchanging tone   116
monument: lasting reminder, as a statue or tomb   166
morbid: having to do with disease; gruesome   60
moribund: dying; near death   177
morose: saturnine; sullen; glum   50, 208
morphology: form and structure of an organism   123, 136
mortal: human; destined to die; fatal; person   177
mortality: death rate; mortal nature   177
mortician: undertaker   177
mortification: shame; embarrassment; chagrin   48, 177
mortify: humiliate; shame; embarrass   178
mortuary: funeral home   178
mot juste: the exactly right word   238

mountebank: charlatan; boastful pretender   264
mournful: sorrowful; lugubrious; doleful   49
musicale: social event featuring music   245
mustang: bronco   276
musty: moldy; stale   74
myopia: nearsightedness   130
myrmidon: obedient, unquestioning follower   206
mythology: account or study of myths   123

nadir: lowest point   72
naive: ingenuous; simple; unsophisticated   233
narcissistic: in love with oneself   206
nautical: of the sea or shipping; marine   85
navigate: sail   202
necrology: list of recently deceased persons   123
nectar: exceptionally delicious drink   207
nemesis: punishment for or punisher of evil   207
nepotism: favoritism to relatives   73
nerve: effrontery; gall   35
nettlesome: irritating; annoying; vexing   36
neurology: study of the nervous system   123
noblesse oblige: conduct befitting high rank   237
noisome: offensive to smell; harmful   74, 219
nom de plume: pen name; pseudonym   238
nonage: legal minority; period before maturity   81
nonagenarian: person 90–99 years old   81
nonbiodegradable: not biodegradable   124
noncarcinogenic: not cancer producing   9
nonchalant: without concern; indifferent   233
nonpareil: paragon   235
non sequitur: illogical statement   181
nostalgia: homesickness; yearning for the past   49
notwithstanding: despite   217
nouveaux riches: persons newly rich   235
nowise: in no way; not at all   218
noxious: harmful; noisome   74
nugatory: trifling; invalid; worthless; useless   96
nuptials: wedding   203
nutriment: food   203

obelisk: monolith   116
obese: extremely overweight; corpulent; portly   50
obesity: excessive body weight; corpulence   50
obituary: necrology   123
object: protest; disapprove   187
obligatory: required   167

oblivion: state of being unknown; forgetfulness 36
oblivious: forgetful; unmindful; unwitting 36
obloquy: censure; public reproach 191
obscure: relatively unknown; hermetic 205
obsequious: excessively willing to serve 51
obsolescent: going out of use; becoming obsolete 82
obsolete: no longer in use; out-of-date 82
obverse: front of a coin, medal, etc. 189
Occident: West 18
occidental: western 18
octogenarian: person 80–89 years old 81
odious: abhorrent; abominable 26
odoriferous: having an odor 74, 192
odorous: having an odor, usually fragrant 74
odyssey: long series of wanderings 207
offal: waste parts of a butchered animal; refuse 85
officialdom: officials collectively 218
olfactory: pertaining to the sense of smell 74
oligarchy: rule by the powerful few 133
olio: mixture; medley; olla podrida 278
olla podrida: meat-and-vegetable stew; olio 277
Olympian (Olympic): majestic; godlike 207
omnibus: bus; book containing a variety of works 163
omnibus: covering many things at once 163
omnifarious: of all varieties, forms, or kinds 163
omnific: all-creating 163
omnipotent: unlimited in power; almighty 163
omnipresent: present everywhere; ubiquitous 163
omniscient: knowing everything 163
omnivore: person or animal that eats everything 158
omnivorous: avidly taking in or eating everything 158, 163
opera: play mostly sung 260
opinionated: unduly attached to one's own opinion 93
oppress: persecute 181
optional: not compulsory; discretionary 167
oratorio: music for voice and orchestra 260
ornate: elaborate; flamboyant 248
ornithology: study of birds 58
orthodox: conforming to accepted doctrines 93
ostentatious: done to impress others; showy 97
osteopath: practitioner of osteopathy 135
osteopathy: treatment by manipulation of bones 135

oust: expel 161
overweening: thinking too highly of oneself 89
ovine: of or like a sheep 225

pacify: calm; assuage; soothe 202
paean: song or hymn of praise or joy 207
paleontology: science of life in the remote past 123
palette: artist's board for mixing colors 245
palladium: safeguard; protection 207
paltry: practically worthless 96
pampa: treeless, grassy plain; prairie 278
panegyric: eulogy; tribute 61
panic: sudden, overpowering terror 207
paradox: seemingly contradictory statement 94
paradoxical: seemingly contradictory 94
paragon: one of unequalled excellence 210
paramount: chief; supreme; above others 96
parasite: one living on others; freeloader 58
parasol: umbrella to protect from the sun 249
par excellence: above all others of the same sort 249
parody: humorous imitation 63
parrot: repeat mechanically, like a parrot 58
parsimonious: stingy; miserly; tightfisted 9
partiality: bias; predilection 92
parvenu(e): upstart 235
passé: old-fashioned; behind the times 249
pasta: paste or dough, as in macaroni 265
paternal: fatherly; on the father's side 73, 223
pathetic: arousing pity 49, 135
pathogenic: causing disease 135
pathological: due to disease 135
pathology: study of disease; something abnormal 123
pathos: quality that arouses pity 49, 135
patina: green film on bronze or copper 262
patio: outdoor dining or lounging area 277
patriarch: father and ruler of a family or tribe 82
patriarchy: rule by the father 133
patricide: killer of (or killing) one's father 156
peaceable: not quarrelsome; not fractious 162
peccadillo: slight offense; small fault 278
peculate: steal 202
pedal: lever acted on by the foot 184
pedestal: foot of a column or statue 184
pedestrian: commonplace; unimaginative 184
pedestrian: person traveling on foot 184
pedigree: genealogy 73
penitent: feeling regret for wrongdoing 48
pensive: thoughtful in a sad way 49
peon: unskilled worker; landless laborer 273
perfidious: false to a trust; treacherous 169

perfidy: violation of a trust; treachery   169

pericardium: membranous sac enclosing the heart   137

perigee: orbiting body's nearest point to earth   134, 137

perihelion: orbit's nearest point to the sun   137

perimeter: outer boundary of a figure   137

periodontics: dentistry of bone and gum diseases   137

peripatetic: traveling about; itinerant   137

peripheral: on the periphery (outside boundary)   137

peripheral: equipment attachable to a computer   137

periphery: outside boundary   137

periphrastic: roundabout; circumlocutory   137

periscope: submariner's device to view surface   137

peristalsis: wavelike intestinal contractions   138

peristyle: columns around a building or court   138

peritoneum: membrane lining the abdominal cavity   138

peritonitis: inflammation of the peritoneum   138

persecute: oppress; harass; annoy   181

persistence: tenacity; perseverance   165

persnickety: fastidious; finicky   18

pert: bold; saucy; impertinent; lively; spirited   89

pertinacious: adhering firmly to an opinion   165

pertinent: relevant   96, 165

perusal: reading; study   18

peruse: read   18

perverse: corrupt; wrongheaded   189

pervert: corrupt; give a wrong meaning to   154, 189

pesticide: substance that kills rats and insects   156

pestiferous: pestilential; infected with disease; evil   192

pestilential: pestiferous; deadly   60, 192

petrology: scientific study of rocks   123

petty: paltry; trifling   96

philanthropist: lover of mankind   108,   110

philanthropy: love of mankind   108,   110

philatelist: stamp collector   109

philately: collection and study of stamps   109

philharmonic: pertaining to a symphony orchestra   109

philhellenism: support of the Greeks   109

philippic: bitter denunciation; tirade   207

philogyny: love of women   109

philology: study (love) of language   109

philosopher: lover of wisdom   109

phlebotomy: opening a vein to draw off blood   126

phobia: fear; dread; aversion   108

photophobia: aversion to light   108

physiology: study of the functions of life forms   123

pianissimo: very soft   232

piano: soft   232

piazza: town square; open market; veranda   265

picador: bullfighter who lances the bull   273

picaro: (picaresque, *adj.*) rogue; wanderer   273

piddling: paltry; trifling   96

pièce de résistance: main dish; showpiece   246

pimento: thick-fleshed pepper   277

pince nez: eyeglasses clipped to the nose   249

pinnacle: highest point; acme; summit   69

piscine: of or like a fish   225

pizza: pie of flattened dough   265

pizzicato: plucking, not bowing, the strings   259

plaudit: applause; enthusiastic praise   61

plausible: apparently trustworthy   94

pliable: flexible; not rigid   164

pliant: easily bent; malleable; adaptable   95

plight: unfortunate state; predicament   49

plumb: get to the bottom of; fathom   72

plutocratic: influential due to wealth   207

podiatrist: chiropodist   127

podium: dais; low wall serving as a foundation   127

poignant: painfully touching; piercing   49

politico: politician   264

pollute: contaminate; make unclean   85

Pollyanna: irrepressible optimist   204

polyarchy: rule by many   116

polychromatic: multicolored; variegated   116

polygamy: marriage to several mates   117

polyglot: person who speaks several languages   117

polyglot: speaking several languages   117

polygon: closed plane figure having many angles   117

polymorphic: having various forms   117

polyphonic: having many sounds or voices   117, 128

polysyllabic: having many syllables   117

polytechnic: dealing with many applied sciences   117

polytheism: belief in a plurality of gods   117

poncho: blanketlike cloak; hooded raincoat   278

ponder: think about; cogitate; deliberate   92

porcine: of or like a pig 225
portfolio: briefcase; collection of work ???
portico: roof supported by columns 262
portly: obese; corpulent 50
posthumous: published or occurring after death 82
postlapsarian: after the fall of mankind 82
potpourri: mélange; medley; mixture 214
precipice: cliff 70
precipitous: steep as a precipice; hasty 70
précis: brief summary 238
precursor: forerunner; predecessor 182
predecessor: precursor; forerunner 182
predicament: unfortunate state; plight; dilemma 49, 93
predilection: partiality; inclination; bias 92
preeminent: standing out above others; superior 70
prehensile: adapted for seizing 186
prejudice: bias; partiality 92
prelapsarian: before the fall of mankind 82
premier: prime minister 243
premiere: first performance 249
premonition: forewarning; intuitive anticipation 166
premonitory: conveying a forewarning 166
preposterous: senseless; absurd; irrational 94
prestissimo: at a very rapid pace 258
presto: quick 258
presumptuous: overweening; taking liberties 97
pretentious: done to impress others; ostentatious 97
prevaricate: lie 202
prima donna: diva; vain person 264
primeval: pertaining to the world's first ages 82
primitive: primeval 82
primordial: existing at the very beginning 82
pristine: in original state; uncorrupted 82
probe: investigation 28
prober: investigator 28
procreate: beget 201
procrustean: cruelly enforcing conformity 207
prodigious: enormous; gigantic; colossal 36
prodigy: extraordinarily able person; wonder 36
profound: very deep; deeply felt 72
progenitor: forefather; ancestor 73
progeny: offspring; children; descendants 73
progress: going from worse to better 183
progressive: going to something better 183
project: thrust or throw forward 187
projectile: object to be shot forward 187
proliferous: producing new growth rapidly 192

propinquity: kinship; proximity; nearness of place 87
prosecute: follow to the end; sue 181
prostrate: lie face down 201
protean: readily assuming different forms 207
protégé(e): one under another's protection 235
prow: forward part of a ship; bow 84
proximity: nearness of place; propinquity 87
pseudopod: temporary extension of the protoplasm 127
psychology: science of the mind 123
psychopathic: mentally diseased; insane 135
puberty: physical beginning of adulthood 82
pudgy: short and plump; chubby 50
pueblo: Native American village of southwestern U.S. 276
puerile: foolish for adults to say or do 82, 224
pungent: sharp in smell or taste; biting; acrid 74
purge: cleanse; purify; rid of undesired element 85
putrefy: rot; fester 59
putrid: stinking from decay; corrupt 74
Pyrrhic: gained at too great a cost 207

qualm: misgiving; regret; remorse; scruple 48
queue: line of waiting persons or vehicles 249

raconteur: one who excels in storytelling 235
raillery: good-natured ridicule; banter 62
raison d'être: reason for existing 249
rancid: unpleasant to smell or taste 74
rank: offensive; rancid; extreme 75
rankle: fester 59
rapport: harmonious relationship 237
rapprochement: state of cordial relations 244
rapture: state of overwhelming joy; ecstasy 47
rash: precipitous; hasty 70
ratiocinate: reason 202
rational: able to think clearly; based on reason 94
rationalize: devise excuses for one's actions 94
ravine: deep, narrow gorge worn by running water 72
raze: demolish 9
reactionary: resisting change 183
realistic: earthy; down-to-earth 72
rebuff: snub; insult; slight 28
recuperate: recover health; convalesce 59
recur: happen again 182
reek: emit a strong, disagreeable smell 75
reflect: bend back light, as from a mirror; think 94, 164

reflex: involuntary response to a stimulus 164
refract: bend light from its path, as by a prism 162
refractory: intractable; hard to manage 162
regicide: killing (or killer) of a king 156
regime: system of government or rule 244
regimen: set of rules to improve health 60
regressive: disposed to move backward 183
reimburse: indemnify; repay 18
reinvigorate: give new vigor to; rejuvenate 36
reject: refuse to take; discard 187
rejuvenate: make young again; reinvigorate 36
relevant: bearing upon the matter at hand 96
reluctant: disinclined; averse 69
remand: send back; recommit, as to prison 167
remiss: negligent; careless; lax 190
remission: period of lessening (as of symptoms) 190
remit: send money due; forgive 190
remorse: regret for wrongdoing 48
render: deliver; give 28
rendering: presentation; interpretation 28
rendezvous: prearranged meeting place; appointment 250
renegade: traitor; turncoat; deserter 273
repartee: witty reply 238
repast: meal 28
repentant: contrite; penitent; remorseful 48
repertoire: collection; stock 245
replenish: refill 28
reprehend: reprimand; rebuke; censure; find fault with 186
reprehensible: culpable; blamable 186
reproof: admonition; rebuke 166
reprove: admonish; rebuke; disapprove 166
repugnance: strong dislike; antipathy 69
repulsive: offensive; disgusting 51
reserved: reticent 9
residual: remaining after a part is used 36
residue: remainder; rest 36
restrict: keep within limits; confine 157
restriction: stricture 157
résumé: summary; curriculum vitae 238
retentive: able to retain or remember; tenacious 165
reticent: inclined to be silent; reserved 9
retinue: attendants of a distinguished person 165
retire: withdraw from active duty; go to bed 10
retort: reply sharply; quick or witty reply 10, 160

retrograde: going backward; becoming worse 183
retrogression: going from better to worse 183
retrogressive: regressive 183
revere: venerate; worship 202
reverse: back of a coin, medal, etc. 189
revert: go back; return 189
revive: bring back to life; restore 159
rialto: marketplace; theater district 262
rift: crack; opening 71
rigor mortis: body's stiffness after death 178
riposte: retort; repartee; return thrust 238
rogue: picaro; tricky, deceitful fellow 273
rotund: rounded out; plump; full-toned 95
rotunda: round building; large round room 262
rout: defeat; debacle 214
rueful: pitiable; lamentable 49
rupture: break; breaking; hostility; breach 155, 203
Russophobe: one who dislikes the Russians 108

salubrious: salutary; curative; healthful 36, 60
salutary: beneficial; healthful; salubrious 36
salvo: simultaneous discharge of shots 266
sangfroid: equanimity; coolness of mind 237
sanguinary: bloodthirsty; bloody 225
sanguine: ruddy; confident 225
sarcasm: sneering language intended to hurt 63
sarcastic: expressing sarcasm 63
sardonic: bitterly sarcastic; mocking; sneering 64
satire: work exposing abuses to ridicule 64
satiric(al): expressing satire 64
saturnine: gloomy; morose 208
savoir faire: knowing just what to do 237
scavenger: one that removes refuse or decay 58
scent: get a suspicion of 75
scent: smell; perfume 75
scherzo: playful part of a musical work 261
scintillate: sparkle; twinkle 202
score: twenty 28
scruple: compunction; regret; misgiving 48
scrupulous: not remiss; careful 190
scrutinize: examine very closely; inspect; vet 36
scrutiny: examination; inspection; review 36
scuffle: struggle; wrestle; grapple 19
sebaceous: greasy; secreting sebum (fatty matter) 60
sedate: staid; of settled, quiet disposition 96
seduction: enticement; act of leading astray 180

selective: eclectic   93

senile: showing the weakness of age   83

señor: gentleman; Mr.; Sir   273

señora: lady; Mrs.; Madam   274

señorita: young lady; girl; Miss   274

septuagenarian: person 70–79 years old   81

sequel: something that follows; outcome   181

sequence: succession; orderly series   181

sequential: arranged in a sequence; serial   181

serpentine: sinuous; winding; tortuous; twisting   95

serrated: saw-toothed   276

servile: subservient; menial   72

seviche (ceviche): appetizer of raw fish   277

sforzando: accented; stressed   232

shard: fragment   203

sibling: brother or sister   73, 220

sierra: serrated mountain range   276

siesta: nap, usually after the midday meal   277

silhouette: outline; shadow   250

simpatico (simpatica): likable; congenial   264

simultaneous: occurring at the same time; concurrent   182

Sinophile: supporter of the Chinese   109

sinuous: bending in and out; serpentine   95

siren: dangerous, attractive woman   208

skeptical: incredulous; disbelieving   168

slander: false, defamatory spoken statement   62, 180

slanderous: calumnious; maliciously accusing   61

slatternly: untidy; slovenly   86

sloven: person habitually untidy   86

snub: insult; rebuff   28

sober: not drunk; temperate; serious   84

sobriety: temperance; abstinence   84

sobriquet: nickname   250

sociology: study of human society   123

solo: music for one voice or instrument   261

solon: legislator; wise lawgiver   208

sombrero: broad-brimmed, high-crowned hat   276

somniferous: inducing sleep   192

sonata: music for one or two instruments   261

sophistry: clever but deceptive reasoning   94

soprano: highest voice in women and boys   257

sordid: filthy; vile   86

sororicide: killer (or killing) of one's sister   156

sot: drunkard; drunken fool   84

sotto voce: in an undertone; privately   266

soup du jour: soup of the day   246

souvenir: keepsake; reminder; memento   250

Spartan: like Sparta's disciplined people   208

specious: apparently, but not really, reasonable   94

speculate: reflect; take risk for profit   94

spirited: pert; lively; vivacious   97

spurn: reject   18

squad: small military unit; team   275

squalid: filthy from neglect; degraded   86

squalor: filth; degradation; sordidness   86

staccato: disconnected (notes)   259

staid: sedate; of settled, quiet disposition   96

stalemate: impasse; deadlock   214

stampede: sudden, wild, headlong rush   276

starboard: ship's right-hand side looking forward   85

starveling: one thin from lack of food   219

stentorian: very loud   208

stern: back part of a ship   84

stevedore: one who loads or unloads ships   274

stigma: mark of disgrace   62

stigmatize: brand with a mark of disgrace   62

stipend: fixed pay for services   19

stricture: criticism; censure; restriction   157

stringent: strict; rigid; severe   157

stripling: lad   220

stucco: plaster for covering exterior walls   262

Stygian: dark; gloomy; infernal   209

subject: expose; make liable   187

sublimate: redirect one's energies; purify   71

sublime: uplifting; exalted; elevated; noble   71

subservient: menial; servile   72

subversion: sabotage; undermining   10

subvert: undermine   10

succession: sequence; order   181

successive: consecutive   181

succumb: yield; capitulate   202

suckling: child or animal that is nursed   219

suicide: act of killing oneself; one who does so   156

sullen: resentfully silent; glum; morose   50

sully: soil; besmirch; defile   86

sultry: sweltering; torrid   37

summit: highest point; acme; pinnacle   69

sumptuous: luxurious; Lucullan   206

superannuated: retired on a pension; very old   83

supersede: force out of use; displace; supplant   36

supersensitive: excessively sensitive   130

supplant: replace; supersede   36

supposition: guess; conjecture   130, 187

supreme: above others; chief; paramount   96

surveillance: close watch   19

survive: outlive; remain alive after   159

suture: stitch   28

svelte: slender; lithe   51

sweltering: oppressively hot; sultry; torrid   37

sycophant: parasitic flatterer; truckler 51

symbiosis: cooperation of two unlike life forms 125

symmetrical: balanced in arrangement 95

symmetry: balance; harmony 95

sympathy: sharing of feeling; compassion 135

table d'hôte: fixed-price, complete meal 247

taco: tortilla folded around a filling 278

tact: sense of what is appropriate; savoir faire 185, 211

tactful: showing tact; diplomatic 185

tactile: pertaining to touch; touchable 185

tangent: touching at only one point 185

tangential: merely touching; digressive 185

tangible: touchable 185

tantalize: tease 185

tarnish: sully; soil 86

taurine: of or like a bull 224

technology: applied science; engineering 123

tedium: boredom 211

teetotaler: abstainer from intoxicating drink 84

telepathy: transference of thoughts to another 135

temblor: earthquake 278

temerity: insolence; effrontery; nerve 35

tempera: painting using colors mixed with egg yolk 262

temperate: moderate, as in eating and drinking 84

tenable: capable of being maintained or defended 94

tenacious: inclined to hold fast 165

tenacity: firmness in holding fast; persistence 165

tenancy: period a tenant holds real estate 165

tenet: principle generally held to be true 165

tenor: voice between baritone and alto 256

tenure: period for which a position is held 165

tepid: lukewarm 19

tepidly: unenthusiastically; lukewarmly 19

terpsichorean: pertaining to dancing 209

terra-cotta: hard clay; reddish-brown 262

terse: laconic; concise; free of unnecessary words 205

tête à tête: private conversation 238

theology: study of religion and religious ideas 123

theory: hypothesis supported by much evidence 93, 130

therapeutic: curative 60

thespian: pertaining to the drama 209

throes: pangs; anguish 50

titanic: of enormous strength or size 209

tome: one of several volumes; scholarly book 126

tonsillectomy: surgical removal of the tonsils 126

toreador: bullfighter 274

torero: bullfighter 274

torrid: sweltering 37

torsion: act of or stress due to twisting 160

torso: human trunk 262

tortilla: disk of unleavened bread 278

tortuous: winding; serpentine; tricky 160

torture: inflict severe pain upon 160

toupee: wig; hairpiece to cover baldness 248

tour de force: feat 250

toxic: poisonous 60

tracheotomy: surgical cutting into the windpipe 126

tractability: obedience 10

tractable: easily led; docile 10, 164

traduce: malign; slander; vilify; calumniate 62, 180

tranquillity: harmony 8

transgress: step beyond the limits 183

transient: emphemeral; fleeting 27

transitory: fleeting; ephemeral 27

transmit: send across or through 190

travesty: imitation that ridicules its model 64

treatise: written account 212

treacherous: perfidious 169

tremolo: rapid repetition of a tone 259

tribulation: suffering; distress 50

tribute: high praise; eulogy; panegyric 61

trio: music for three voices or instruments 261

tripod: three-legged utensil, stool, or caldron 127

truckle: submit servilely to a superior 51

turncoat: renegade; traitor; apostate 273

tutti: direction for all to perform together 261

tutti: section performed by all the musicians 261

tyrannicide: killer (or killing) of a tyrant 156

unfledged: immature; callow 80

unflustered: calm 37

unguent: ointment; salve 60

unicolor: one color; monochromatic; homochromatic 128

unintentionally: unwittingly; inadvertently 28

unipod: one-legged support 127

unmanageable: unwieldy; cumbersome 37

unrestricted: unconfined; free; open to all 157

unruffled: not upset; imperturbable; calm 37

unsavory: offensive to taste, smell, or morals 75

untenable: incapable of being held or defended   165

unwieldy: bulky; cumbersome; unmanageable   37

unwittingly: unintentionally; by accident   28

ursine: of or like a bear   224

utopia: imaginary place of ideal perfection   111

vagabond: wanderer; picaro; rogue   273

vain: conceited; worthless; empty; futile   97

vainglorious: excessively proud or boastful   97

valet: manservant   235

valid: legally or logically correct; sound   93

vanity: condition of being too vain; conceit   97

vanquish: overcome in battle; conquer; defeat   161

vapid: jejune; inane; insipid; dull   18

vaquero: herdsman; cowboy; buckaroo   274

variegated: multicolored; polychromatic   116

velocipede: child's tricycle   184

velocity: speed; celerity   203

vendetta: feud for blood revenge   265

venerable: worthy of respect   83

venerate: worship; revere   202

veracity: truthfulness   203

verity: truth   203

versatile: adaptable   189

verse: line of poetry   189

vertex: point opposite the base; apex   71

vertigo: dizziness   189

vestibule: foyer; lobby; entrance hall   249

vet: scrutinize   36

veteran: experienced person; ex-soldier   83

viaduct: road or railroad over a valley   180

vibrato: pulsating tone   259

victor: winner; conqueror; vanquisher   161

vignette: short verbal description   245

vile: sordid; hateful   86

vilification: smear; defamation   203

vilify: speak evil of; traduce; malign   62, 180

violate: transgress   183

viral: caused by a virus   60

virile: having male physical abilities   224

virtuoso: musician of great technical skill   264

virulent: extremely poisonous; very bitter   60

virus: disease-causing or corruptive agent   61

vis à vis: opposite; in relation to   250

vivace: brisk; spirited   258

vivacious: lively in temper or conduct   17, 159, 183

vivacity: liveliness of spirit   159

vivid: having the vigor and spirit of life   159

vivify: enliven; make vivid   159

vivisection: research operation on a live animal   159

vociferous: producing a loud outcry   192

vogue: fashion; accepted style   248

void: invalid   8

volition: will   69

voracious: greedy in eating; insatiable   158

vulpine: like a fox; crafty; cunning   225

wager: bet; risk   19

wane: decrease; dwindle   19, 220

warlock: sorcerer; wizard   220

warp: lengthwise threads in a loom   221

wax: grow; increase   221

wheedle: persuade by flattery   51

winsome: winning; cheerful; merry   219

withal: in addition; despite that   221

withdraw: take back; draw back; retreat   37, 217

withdrawal: removal; retreat; departure   37

withhold: hold back   217

withstand: stand up against; resist   217

witticism: bon mot; witty remark   238

womanly: feminine   224

woof: crosswise threads in a woven fabric   221

wrangle: haggle; bargain   27

wrench: twist violently   160

wretched: sunk to a low condition; abject   71, 187

writ of mandamus: court order to perform a duty   167

xenophobia: aversion to foreigners   108

yclept: named; called   221

yearling: one who is a year old   219

yore: long ago   83

zany: clown; buffoon   37

zany: mildly insane; loony; clownish   37

zenith: point directly overhead; peak; culmination   71